NEGRO CIVILIZATION
IN THE SOUTH

NEGRO CIVILIZATION IN THE SOUTH

By

Charles Edwin Robert

The Black Heritage Library Collection

BOOKS FOR LIBRARIES PRESS
FREEPORT, NEW YORK
1971

First Published 1880
Reprinted 1971

Reprinted from a copy in the
Fisk University Library Negro Collection

INTERNATIONAL STANDARD BOOK NUMBER:
0-8369-8906-6

LIBRARY OF CONGRESS CATALOG CARD NUMBER:
70-173614

PRINTED IN THE UNITED STATES OF AMERICA
BY
NEW WORLD BOOK MANUFACTURING CO., INC.
HALLANDALE, FLORIDA 33009

NEGRO CIVILIZATION

IN THE SOUTH;

EDUCATIONAL, SOCIAL AND RELIGIOUS ADVANCEMENT

OF THE

COLORED PEOPLE.

A REVIEW OF SLAVERY AS A CIVIL AND COMMERCIAL QUESTION.
THE "DIVINE SANCTION OF SLAVERY." A GLANCE
AT AFRICAN HISTORY. ETHNOLOGICAL
STATUS OF THE NEGRO, ETC.

He hath not dealt so with any nation.—PSALM CXLVII, 20.
Liberty said, Let there be light, and, like a sunrise on the sea, Athens arose.—SHELLY.

BY

CHARLES EDWIN RÔBERT,

AUTHOR OF "NASHVILLE AND HER TRADE," "EVANSVILLE, HER COMMERCE AND
MANUFACTURES," ETC., AND LATE MEMBER OF THE PRESS OF
TENNESSEE, INDIANA AND KENTUCKY.

NASHVILLE, TENN.:
PRINTED BY WHEELER BROS. FOR THE AUTHOR.
1880.

TO THE

Hon. Alexander H. Stephens

OF GEORGIA,

That Venerable Counselor and Humane and Christian Gentleman, whose Wisdom,
Moderation and Integrity endear him to the hearts of his
United Compatriots,

IN THE NAME OF

JUSTICE, LIBERTY AND CHRISTIAN CONSCIENCE,

THIS LITTLE BOOK IS

RESPECTFULLY DEDICATED,

With the earnest request that he lend his Influence toward lifting up by Education, by
Sympathy, by Humane and Religious Means that

UNHAPPY RACE OF PEOPLE,

Born in Slavery, adopted by Freedom, and now an important element of our

REPUBLICAN CITIZENSHIP.

PREFACE.

This little book is the result of prayer. It has been worked out with fear and trembling. Scarce a line in it that has not required *nerve* to write. At first I thought of making it a newspaper article, but it has grown into a volume, and this will explain whatever lack of rhetorical finish in may have. But when I had determined to publish I made solemn promise to a friend that I would adhere strictly to truth; and believe I am able conscientiously to declare, I have not departed from it.

Although it is quite well known that I am a theological student, I wish to disarm all criticism, and to repeat positively, it is not by any manner of means a *political pamphlet*, but an appeal for humane and respectful consideration of the Colored race.

If it be said, I have given a rose-colored view of the Negro, let me answer I have written of Negro *civilization* and not Negro *degradation*, that in considering men collectively, we cannot with justice think only of what is mean and base; that it is better to seek out whatever is noble in human nature and encourage rather than condemn. Let me answer, too, that I despise kid-gloved philanthropy, that I think the solemn, serious business of Jesus Christ is to practice common every-day charity, and to advance the cause of justice, and secure popular enlightenment and popular morality, is the only sure and lasting foundation for rational political and spiritual liberty. The time has come for men to have larger ideas and a wider horizon of thought. They must understand that this is the age of responsibility and of duty, that if humanity be retarded at home, it is retarded abroad, and illiberal and narrow-minded views fetter the brain, warp the conscience and impregnate the universe with pernicious influences. I therefore declare this an eminently patriotic work, and one whose truth sooner or later will find a victory sure in every living conscience.

Still, there are some of to-day who will not accept my views. They will refuse to see any good in the Negro. They will close their eyes to fact, and do like the aged savage who in his old age went back to his savage tribe and said, he had "tried civilization for forty years, and it was not worth the trouble." So, then, if at first, I felt a painful diffidence in obtruding my views on the country, I could not escape the conviction that the time had come when plain truths should be spoken in plain words. I feel that diffidence no longer. I claim the right to form opinions, and to utter thoughts. I complacently take my seat behind this *Gibraltar of Fact*, and shall rest quietly, knowing that it must be punctured by a keener weapon than can be found in all the vast arsenal of stolid bigotry and insensate rage.

CHARLES EDWIN RÔBERT.

NASHVILLE, TENN., Jan., 1880.

NEGRO CIVILIZATION

IN THE SOUTH.

TRUTH, whether admitted, or rejected, is, and remains always truth. It is independent of time; independent of individuals, or classes or parties, and, therefore, must prevail, though it excite the hatred or opposition of the ignorant, the weak or the prejudiced.

The writer of this treatise begs no pardon for employing the truth, asks no excuse from the responsibility of a self-imposed task, but regardless of the opinions of unreasonable opponents of the subject—for the sake of common humanity —for the promotion of justice and charity—for the upbuilding of intelligence and morality, desires to show the world what has been the advancement of a race of people who less than a generation since were in ignorance and bondage—in darkness and slavery. Under the will of God they have emerged into the brighter light of liberty and learning. Under the will of God they now enjoy civil and religious freedom, and, by virtue of these blessings are making brave, manly steps toward refinement of morals, mind and manners.

The educational progress of the Colored people of the South—those who have enjoyed unrestricted advantages— since the close of the late war, is truly astonishing. It is a progress which should be a source of pride, not alone to the race themselves, but highly gratifying to their friends everywhere. Philanthropists of whatever creed—statesmen of whatever party—broad-hearted, true-souled people of whatever clime, will regard these assertions with interest, and if they can be proven, will surely hail them with honest pleasure, and

cheer the Americo-African with the hearty plaudits of con-
gratulation.

And, why not? Is philanthropy bounded by State lines or
national limits? Does the brotherhood of mankind claim
no wider domain than the restricted area of narrow and
cramped commonwealths? Or, on the other hand, shall we
suffer them to go abroad for that sympathy which should
begin at home—that "love for our neighbor" that makes him
a better man for the reception—makes us better for the
giving and more Christ-like and obedient for entertaining?
What matters it that our feet are chained to our native heath
and that we choose for our pen a theme the narrow-minded
have sneered at as mean and homely? True philanthrophy
does not ask that the mystic atmosphere of the East envelop
the object of its regard, nor that the blue skies of classic
Greece bend above it, nor that the splendid pomp of ancient
Rome surround it, nor yet that the centuries of modern
Europe reveal themselves as in a magic glass. True philanthropy has love for these, but has love for all. True philanthropy worships at the shrine—in whatever quarter it may be,
where the vestal flame of joy doth burn for the struggling or
the mournful. Wherever freedom has uplifted the race,
wherever patient labor and heroic endurance have exalted a
people, wherever learning and morality have flourished, wherever the Truth of the Spirit has shone, there is a triumph of
civilization which is a rich legacy to the lover of mankind—a
golden sheaf ready to be garnered by the just husbandman
of history.

But, before proceeding further, it may be proper to state,
positively, that this is not a political document, gotten up for
campaign purposes, or the glorification of any party or sect.
The writer, although not in politics, is a Democrat and a
Southerner, with warm-hearted love and fidelity for the South
ever aglow in his bosom. The song of the patriotic Jew
finds echo in his heart: "If I forget thee, O Jerusalem, let my
right hand forget her cunning. If I do not remember thee, let
my tongue cleave to the roof of my mouth."[1] He therefore
defies unjust or biased views of his motives. But reared
among a slave-holding people it was quite natural that certain
prejudices should be instilled into his mind—prejudices which
the broad culture of experience and the solid argument of

---

[1] Psalm cxxxvii, 5, 6.

fact alone have removed. In giving expression therefore to what follows he believes them, in great measure, nothing more, nothing less, than confessions many people in the South are at this day willing to make.

Nor is it intended to open old wounds in thus referring to an institution already completely overthrown. Slavery is dead! Slavery is dead beyond the power of resurrection. "Japhetic rights to Hamitic service" both as a civil and religious question in this country was settled by the war—settled so far as the generations of the ninteenth century are concerned, and as far as the horizon of the future can be scanned—settled forever! We might as well discuss the possibility of returning in allegiance to our British mother as discuss the impossibility of re-enslavement. Or for the matter of that, we might as well attempt re-organization of all the buried empires since the world began as to think now of tearing out a single stone from the Temple of Liberty, reared by Christian civilization, and guarded by the invincible genius of the age—the Genius of Freedom!

It may be said then, that this is not the place to discuss this question, but we are bound to say at all events what is the truth, in order that we may see from what humble and discouraging conditions the Americo-African has sprung. There may be question as to its expediency, but there can be no question, no halting, no temporizing, when a matter of justice is involved, or the cause of human progress is leastways concerned. To describe a fact, without descending to the causes or rising to the consequences, will not bring forth the desired fruit. It might seem like evasion or logical inability to solve a most useful problem. We do not magnify the subject, then, when we say it is not merely sectional, or national, but cosmopolitan in importance. Collective humanity is interested in the question of the Colored man's intellectual capacity, and we propose to gratify that interest to the best of our ability, fearlessly and truthfully. Moreover, as a modern philosopher[1] has well said, "There is for every man a statement possible of that truth which he is most unwilling to receive—a statement possible, so broad and so pungent that he cannot get away from it, but must either bend to it or die of it." No man can hide his heart from Truth any more than he can hide his soul from God. The truth is more deadly to

---

[1] Ralph Waldo Emerson.

its enemies than the bullet of the ancient hunter, which superstition taught will hit its mark when first dipped in the marks-
man's blood. A man's judgment is frequently erroneous,
but the truth always testifies correctly. If one hears the truth
it will go straight home to his heart, no matter how he may
wince or how he may fight it off. Swifter and surer than
Apollo's dart, which stretched the bravest of the Grecian
chieftains dead upon the field of Troy, the truth—which is
living light, the truth—which is *the sword of God*, finds the
vulnerable part, and enters in and subdues.

SLAVERY AS A COMMERCIAL AND CIVIL QUESTION.

But on this subject of slavery there has never been full,
fair and candid discussion. If a writer espoused one side
he gained neither attention or respect from the other. And
the reason now is plain. Gen. Garfield, in a speech at the
Soldier's Reunion at Cambridge, Ohio, August 27th, 1879,
speaking of the causes of the late war, makes a candid confession, though a tardy one, "The first of these causes," says
he, "was the institution of slavery. Those who fought on
the side of that institution were not responsible for the cause.
They were born to it. We in the North were educated
against it, and under other circumstances might have been its
friends, for human nature is about the same. The institution
grew so strong that it became necessary to either destroy the
Union or destroy slavery."
Consequently, up to the beginning of the war there had
been nothing but crimination and recrimination. The North
charged the South with maintaining an institution defiant of
the laws of God and antagonistic to the rights of humanity.
The South retorted with the well-known charge that the
North first stole the slaves, sold them South, and had no right
to intermeddle. Now, if both were just charges, both were
clearly in the wrong ; and two wrongs have never made one
right. If it was wrong for New England to steal slaves, it
was wrong for the South to receive them, knowing them to
have been stolen. The receiver of stolen goods, so says the
spirit of the civil law, is *particeps criminis* with the thief; and to
be *particeps criminis* is not more virtuous, nor more respectable
than to be the thief. There is a distinction, but where is the
difference ? It matters not how much money the South paid

for the slaves—the New England slave-trader might also plead that he spent money and risked his life besides in procuring his cargoes. Under this view it was clearly a mercenary transaction on either side, and if we puncture the puff-bag of virtue that envelops some of our worthy forefathers we shall discover that neither the one, nor the other, can make 'broad his phylactery and exclaim, "Stand by thyself, come not near to me; for I am holier than thou."— Isaiah lxv, 5.

It might be well to back our statements here by a few undeniable facts from the historians, especially as we are writing history, and, grieve as much as we may over it, are not at liberty to alter historic truth.[1] We shall not, however, enter minutely into the history of American slavery in and during the Colonial period. All portions of our country participated in it. As early as 1620, the English began to introduce Negro Slavery into the Colony of Virginia,[2] a Dutch war vessel having landed twenty Negroes for sale on the banks of James river in the month of August, 1620. In 1637, the Puritans of Massachusetts are found, not only selling the Indians into servitude, but buying Negroes as slaves for their own use.[3] Rev. Dr. Belknap, of Boston, Mass., in a letter to Judge Tucker, of Williamsburg, Va., in 1795, admits the existence of Negro slavery in Massachusetts, and that the slave trade was prosecuted by merchants of Massachusetts. He says that "the slaves purchased in Africa were chiefly sold in the West Indies, or in the Southern Colonies; but when these markets were glutted, and the price low, some of them were brought hither." He says the slaves were most numerous in Massachusetts about 1745, and amounted to about 1 to 40 whites ; and probably numbered about 4000 or 5000.[4]

Mr. Samuel G. Drake, in his history of Boston, says that "many Irish people had been sent to New England," and sold as "slaves or servants." Also, that "many of the Scotch people had been sent before this in the same way.

---

[1] We are indebted for some most valuable points on this subject from an article on "The Union, the Constitution and Slavery," which first appeared in the American Quarterly Church Review, (Protestant Episcopal,) and was afterwards printed in pamphlet form—January, 1864—a time when it required courage to print the bald and naked truth.

[2] See Anderson's History of the Colonial Church, vol. i, pp. 85–9.

[3] See Fell's History of Salem, p. 167.

[4] Mass. His. Collections, vol. iv, pp. 191–211.

Some of them had been taken prisoners, at the sanguinary battle of Dunbar. There arrived in one ship, the 'John and Sara,' John Greene, master, early in the summer of 1652, about 272 persons. Captain Greene hád orders to deliver them to Thomas Kemble, of Charlestown, who was to sell them, and with the proceeds, to take freight for the West Indies." [1]

In 1790, when the Constitution had been adopted by the thirteen States, slavery existed in every one of the Northern States, except Massachusetts, where the institution was abolished in 1788. At that time New Hampshire had 158 slaves; Rhode Island, 952; Connecticut, 2759; New York, 21,324; New Jersey, 11,423; Pennsylvania, 3737; and in the entire country, there were 682,633 slaves. [2] It has been a popular argument in the South—a sort of traditional acquiescence as it were, to say that slavery had ceased to be profitable at the North; the climate was too cold, the slaves were a drug, and the institution thus died out. But there is another side to this question. Dr. Baldwin, of Nashville, one of the ablest defenders of the late slave system, said in his celebrated book, "Dominion; or, the Unity and Trinity of the Human Race," (published in 1858): "Not a century ago, the black race, as slaves, was common in New England and in the Middle States; but now only a few are found there. Climatic law, affecting both the negro and the master, has carried the slave irresistibly southward. The law of philanthropy operated with far less power in this removal than the law of interest. Philanthropy for the negro is of a more modern origin. When the Northern slave was sold to planters in a more congenial country, then philanthropy arose like Minerva, and credited its zeal to piety, rather than to Southern warmth. The southward tendency of the negro race is still witnessed in the slave States. Virginia, Maryland, Delaware, Kentucky and Tennessee, are constantly transferring negroes to warmer regions, because of greater profits from their labor, and there is no returning stream of emigration." [3] Now, this is a very unfortunate predicament in which Dr. Baldwin has left us Southerners. It either forces us to withdraw the charge against the North, or else to confess, with him, that

---

[1] History and Antiquities of Boston, 1855, p. 342.
[2] Curtis's History of the Constitution, vol. ii, p. 55.
[3] See Baldwin's Dominion, p. 202.

the "law of interest" and not the "law of philanthropy" governed our actions also. We therefore, leave the question where it is, and retrace our steps to former considerations.

In 1787, when the Convention of Delegates from the thirteen States came together to form the Constitution, a variety of conflicting interests occupied the attention of the Convention. Among these were the basis of representation and taxation, and the rights and privileges of Trade and Commerce. "Ten States, embracing four-fifths of the American people, earnestly desired the immediate abolition of the African Slave Trade, and only three, viz., the two Carolinas and Georgia, desired its continuance. These three States, lying in the extreme southern part of the Union, under a hot climate, and embracing an immense, fertile, uncultivated territory, which could be cultivated, as their people said, only by negroes, were unwilling to be deprived of the power to import laborers from Africa, and expressed their determination not to join the new league, if the power to prohibit the slave trade should be conferred on the General Government. To gratify these States, in the first draft of the Constitution, an article was inserted expressly *withholding from Congress forever* the power to abolish the slave trade. When this article came up for discussion in the Convention, delegates from New England manifested their willingness to allow the article to stand as a part of the Constitution, if the Carolinas and Georgia insisted; but Virginia and other Middle States would not consent. Governor Randolph even went so far as to say, that he would sooner risk the Union than consent to insert in the Constitution an article depriving Congress of the power to abolish the slave trade. The result of the debate was, that the article was referred to a large committee, consisting of one member from each State in the Confederacy, to devise, if possible, some compromise, some plan, that would satisfy the Carolinas and Georgia on one side, and the determined Anti-Slave-Trade feeling of Virginia and the Middle States on the other. This committee reported as a compromise an article investing Congress with power to abolish the foreign slave trade *after the year* 1800; thus allowing the Carolinas and Georgia twelve years to import negro laborers from Africa, and allowing the other ten States, under the general power of Congress to regulate commerce, to abolish the traffic after that period. The Carolinas and Georgia would, doubtless, have been satisfied with twelve years, if they could have obtained no more; but, when the article was under discussion, with this limitation, Mr. Pinckney, of South Carolina, moved, as an amendment, that 1800 be struck out and 1808 inserted; thus allowing twenty years instead of twelve for the continuance of the trade. *This motion was seconded by a member from Massachusetts, and* when the vote was taken, *every New England State present*—Massachusetts, Connecticut and New Hampshire—with the Carolinas, Georgia and Maryland, *voted for the amendment*, while Virginia, Pennsylvania, New Jersey and Delaware stood firm for 1800. New York and Rhode Island were not present.[1]

Such was the bargain then made between the North and the South on the extension of the slave trade. In proof of this, we could quote at length from Mr. Madison's Report of the Debates in the Federal Convention for forming the Constitution. The extracts, however, would be too long, but would well repay perusal by those who wish to be thoroughly posted on this subject, and are indispensable to a right understanding of a portion of the National Constitution. But in order that our readers may know there were patriotic members of that Convention who deprecated slavery, and did all in their power to put a stop to it, and who, although not identified with the original abolitionists[2]—first in the cause of freedom, we might quote from the speeches of Mr. Dickinson, of Delaware, Mr. Langdon, of New Hampshire, Mr. L. Martin, of Maryland, and Col. Mason, of Virginia—who, not less patriotic than humane, represented the spirit of the Conservatives who stood then, as they have almost always stood—mediators and peacemakers between fanatics of the two extreme sections. In the Convention, August 21, 1787, Mr. Martin, among other pointed objections, insisted that slavery was "inconsistent with the principles of the Revolution, and dishonorable to the American character to have such a feature in the Constitution." Mr. Pinckney, of South Carolina said, "If slavery be wrong, it is justified by the example of all the world. He cited the case of Greece, Rome, and other an-

---

[1] Curtis's History of the Constitution, vol. ii.

[2] The Nashville *American* in its report of the Jonesboro, Tenn., Centennial Celebration, held in September, 1879, states the interesting fact that the first abolition paper published in the United States was Elihu Embree's, Jonesboro "*Genius of Universal Emancipation*," and that its successor was published by a Quaker named Lundy, at Greeneville, Tenn.

cient states; the sanction given by France, England, Holland, and other modern states. In all ages, one half of mankind have been slaves." But before expressing opinion, let us put a case and ask a question:—If a man is a murderer or a thief, does it bind his son in moral obligation, or indifferent acceptance, or for individual, temporary, or eternal advantage to become also a murderer and a thief? This is asked independent of the right or the wrong of slavery. But we will go farther and say, we have no patience with, nay, indeed, no respect for those who seek to justify by policy what is reprobated by morality. Mr. Pinckney was evidently afflicted with moral strabismus. It will not pass muster. If slavery be wrong—the example of the whole world does not justify it—*what is wrong can never be justified!* It is chiefly, however, to the speech of Col. Mason we wish now to refer:

" This infernal traffic," said he, "originated in the avarice of British merchants. The British Government constantly checked the attempts of Virginia to put a stop to it. The present question concerns not the importing States alone, but the whole Union. The evil of having slaves was experienced during the late war. Had slaves been treated as they might have been by the enemy, they would have proved dangerous instruments in their hands. But their folly dealt by the slaves as it did by the Tories. He mentioned the dangerous insurrections of the slaves in Greece and Sicily; and the instructions given by Cromwell to the Commissioners sent to Virginia, to arm the servants and slaves, in case other means of obtaining its submission should fail. Maryland and Virginia, he said, had already prohibited the importation of slaves expressly. North Carolina had done the same, in substance. All this would be in vain, if South Carolina and Georgia be at liberty to import. The Western people are already calling out for slaves for their new lands; and will fill that country with slaves, if they can be got through South Carolina and Georgia. Slavery discourages arts and manufactures. The poor despise labor when performed by slaves. They prevent the immigration of whites, who really enrich and strengthen a country. They produce the most pernicious effects on manners. Every master of slaves is born a petty tyrant. They bring the judgment of Heaven on a country. As nations cannot be rewarded or punished in the next world, they must be in this. By an inevitable chain of causes and effects, *Providence punishes national sins by national calamities.* He lamented that some of our Eastern brethren had, from a lust of gain, embarked in this nefarious traffic. As to the States being in possession of the right to import, this was the case with many other rights, now to be properly given up. He held it essential, in every point of view, that the General Government should have power to prevent the increase of slavery."[1]

This, then, is the record. If it is a true statement—and appealing to history for confirmation, and, therefore, defying

---

[1] Madison Papers, vol. iii, pp. 1388–97.

denial, we affirm its truth—it stands without mincing words
or equivocating terms, not merely shameful and disgraceful,
but barbarous in its enormity. "We are apt at this day,"
says a recent writer, "to look upon the past as a day of
demi-gods, when the earth was well salted with virtue."
Too true. It would be well, therefore, to observe whether
the salt hath lost it savor. Well to see whether trickery and
corruption abound only to-day—whether the government inherited no sin and the country only recently started headlong
to ruin. Perhaps, it will teach us to pipe a cheerfuller key,
for it is high time to have done with abusing our own immoral
times—immoral enough, and high time we resolve to be
better by looking at the better side of things and doing
better, because the past has no doubt been desperately
wicked, and is not to be excused on that account. History,
then, is the accusing conscience of nations. It is the book
of deeds wherein is written national sins. No nation under
the sun—no nation since the dawn of time, can exhibit a
single page of virgin purity. And it is because the history
of nations is but the history of men, and it is because men
have ever been corrupt in heart since the Fall of Adam, and
the lie of the Serpent blistered the conscience of mortality
and fain would have robbed the human race of its salvation.
But thank God error and sin and wickedness all lie behind
us. We cannot undo the deeds, but we can profit by the
experience. We cannot cover up the trail, but we can step
braver and bolder and grander under the guidance of Christian Progress. Under the leadership of that bright and
executive Genius our course is ever onward, ever upward.
Invincible Christian Progress! It is the great leveler. It
throws down mountains—raises valleys—threads labyrinths
and traverses ravines ; with more than herculean power it
smites every obstacle—prostrates every barrier. With the
omnipotence and redemptive attributes of our God it lifts up
the human soul to immortality of blessedness—and goes on
from victory to victory, until by its conquests it reaches the
summit of human attainments, whence it waves the banner
of triumph, and shouts back to the listening stars, "this is
God's highway to excellence."

So, then, we dare affirm, the nation to-day is farther from
ruin than it was a century ago, and the men are as honest
and the women are as pure. Nay, we go farther, and say,
with the curse of slavery removed we are one—two—even

ten centuries in advance of Colonial glory. We do not forget the heroism of the past, nor undervalue the grandeur and the lustre of "the far off times." No loftier work for humanity and civilization was ever done by mortal men than that which was performed by the choice and master spirits who conquered this land from savagery, and rescued it from ignorance by devoted valor; who made it illustrious by stainless swords; who consecrated it in rich blood and soul-felt tears, and transmitted it to us a home and a heritage to be nurtured, guarded, perpetuated—Heaven grant forever! Their work, in part, was a noble one, and with all their disadvantages they made a good job of their undertaking, and dying—left behind a legacy of good repute, which has enriched not their land alone, but all the world as well, with its unmatched and imperishable splendor.   And yet, we know that those "dear sons of memory, great heirs of fame," had a full share of the frailties of common life. They were not so engrossed with the great problem of civil liberty that they could not sample the beverages of the period, and chance their loose change on the spots and pictures of the gaming deck. Some of the best of them were not even averse to horse-racing and cock-fighting—while they settled personal grievances "by the book of arithmetic" and according to the *code duello.*   It is, however, a death-stab to our pride to think them conniving at what civilized nations of to-day call "piracy."

Yet how like a prophet's warning resounding across the century—that century of Freedom hitherto a misnomer—how like a prophet's warning comes the voice of that grand old Virginian patriot and humanitarian—"*Providence punishes national sins by national calamities!*"   Let a thousand battle-fields, with their eight hundred thousand brave young sleepers bring home to us the reality.   Let the widowhood and the orphanage of the nation attest.   Let the ruined homesteads —the desolated fields—the wasted treasure—the broken hearts testify.   Let the woe unspeakable for sorrow—too sad to dwell upon—too deep with the bitterest anguish to utter—let these be remembered, and the truth will sink down into our hearts and find lodgment there—*Slavery was wrong! Slavery was wrong!*

We do not underrate the courage of our adversaries, nor that of our compatriots.   "Each fought for what he thought was right."   But oh, how often in the world's his-

2

tory has Patriotism been but another name for licensed murder; and, Honor—"a blood-stained god, at whose red altar sit war and homicide." Tearful pity might have deplored the black man's service to the nation, but tearful pity did not free him. It was the sword of battle that struck the manacles from his limbs and knighted him—the captive—a citizen and a freeman on the field of strife. And now from the black man's heart and from the humane white man's heart "hope shouts over the cloud whose waters are to revive Sahara, and make the desert blossom as the rose."

Battle and tyranny—slaughter and tears—poverty and want—pestilence and famine have come upon the South in terrible and swift succession. But if these were the chastisements of Heaven and the coercives to action and fidelity, to manly effort and heroic patience—if this was Heaven's wise plan for the purification and ennoblement of the South—who shall say aught against it? Have we not seen Nebuchadnezzar and Cyrus, Alexander and Cæsar, the chosen drivers of the car of progress as it thunders along the track of the centuries—out of darkness into light—out of the regions where the brain was fettered into the noonlight where the soul expands. There is wisdom in the axiomatic truth—"whatever is, is right," or rather, "Let God be true and every man a liar." The Negro is here—and we may make the most of it. He did not come *willingly*—and we may make the most of that. And besides, *since he is here, as a Christian people, we are bound to make the most of him.*

All this on one hand. Now turn to the other, and see the chastisement of Heaven as plainly demonstrated. But first let us be sure we are right, and to make that assurance doubly sure, let us quote from a Northern historian. Mr. Arnold, ex-Congressman from Illinois, in his "History of Abraham Lincoln, and the Overthrow of Slavery," says, "An immense property interest invested in the production of cotton, owning lands and negroes, was organized in the South, and soon there arose in sympathy to some extent with it, a powerful cotton manufacturing interest at the North, and these two were interwoven into the web of the slave power."[1] Yet in order to be still more correct, let us supplement this statement by some astonishing data from De Bow's Review:

---

[1] See Arnold, p. 30.

"In 1850, the exports from the United States were $134,900,233, of which only $34,903,221 were from the North and West. The cotton, rice, tobacco, naval stores, sugar and hemp, amounted to $238,691,990. Three-fourths of the exports: or 75 per cent. were from the Southern States in Northern vessels. Again, 75 per cent. of American shipping was owned in the North; and official reports showed 2,700,000 tons engaged in foreign trade, which yielded to the owners $64,800,000 per annum; and of this sum, $48,600,000 was earned by Northern ship-owners in carrying slave products. The coasting transportation of Southern products gave $7,000,000 more to Northern men. The ships built in the North in 1850 cost $7,016,-094, while those in the South cost only $300,000. Massachusetts alone had $35,000,000 invested in the cotton business. The South exchanged with the North (1850) $52,950,520 of her products. Or, to aggregate some of the facts:

The Northern shipping was worth,	$111,665,960
Capital invested in commercial houses,	81,000,000
In cotton factories,	105,000,000
In machine-making incident to factories.	2,000,000
In railroads dependent on factory prosperity,	30,000,000
Total,	$329,665,960

All of this vast amount of capital in the North depended on slave labor."[1]

And so, the New Englander grew rich and built him large barns. He waxed fat in luxury and lolled in his easy chair. But, the sins of the fathers overstepping the second and third generations, strikes the fourth as unerringly as the dart of death. Let us retrospect the past few years. When the tide of battle rolled back from the South—when Moloch had sated his hungry maw, and Nemesis turned pale over her sweep of destruction, did *results* find the Northern people *satisfied?* Did the Angel of Peace fold her wings and find dwelling-place in the hearts of our victorious countrymen? History says, "No." The aristocracy overthrown at the South was succeeded by a dangerous aristocracy at the North. Bonded wealth began to enslave the poor white man—soul and brain and body. Capital sowed its seed in the blood of the soldier and gathered its harvest fructified under the rain-storm of tears and sweat of the artisan and and productive civilian. Pride of power—lust of conquest—the covenant of monopoly—vaulted wealth and vaulting ambition, joined hands—formed league—and while clamoring, *Down with the old Despotism*—whispered, in cold, calculating breath—*Up with the New!* Ah, it was the same old sound that issued from Versailles and rang through the streets of Paris in the days of bloody revolution. It was but the muta-

---

[1] See fully on these points De Bow's Review, vol. ii.

tion of power and the dangerous re-establishment of falsely assumed " divine right." *"Le roi est mort, vive le roi !"* can never be the accepted motto in republican America.

The harbinger of the brewing storm came when in one wild and remorseless moment the demon of fire held high carnival among the proud edifices of Boston and Chicago. But alas! and alas! that it should be true, when men enter contest under the banners of vanity and join the greedy, grasping and trampling chase after gold, their triumph is always dearly obtained. There is majesty in moral sentiment, and there is immortal grandeur in moral deed. The world had stood off with throbbing heart and undisguised rapture, and watched the kingly sweep of the Northern conqueror in his work for humanity. But as unfortunately, the Northern man is very like other men, and as unfortunately pride that comes with the accession of power is one of those failings men most unwillingly part with, the empire of wealthy vanity is the most difficult to subvert : man appears to be unable to arrive at truth and justice, until he has expended his strength in traveling through the different paths of error. So the work went on. Every interest in the land shrunk and withered under the touch of the bondholders corrupt and corrupting sway. First the elegancies of life had to be given up, next the luxuries, then the conveniences, and, finally, what we call the necessities. The manufacturing arts did not merely languish, but many absolutely ceased to exist. The Pennsylvanian iron districts grew as lonely as the sea—the Eastern cotton mills were as quiet as the grave. "Ichabod!" was written on their sign posts. And the political economist bowed his head and wept, for the sword had indeed departed from Judah!

You say this is not true? Then, answer, why was it that for nearly ten years Northern industry stood idle beside the mine, the loom, the lathe, the plow, the forge? Why did the tradesman bemoan his deserted counters, and the landlord his tenantless houses? Whence came those two millions of starving, pitiful outcasts who gloomed in their garrets, or wandered along the roadways of America? The panic came! It was a blast that struck commerce when every sail was spread, and ended its work with the wreck of the bold and the reef of the timid. And then, a dull, dead calm followed. Not the attrition of storm and tempest, but more like "the insidious dry-rot of utter stagnation." It makes us tremble to think of it, but it does seem God has avenged the black

man's wrongs—avenged them—who says unjustly?—for is
He not Jehovah, and to Him doth not vengeance belong?

Of course there are those who will deny the entire correct-
ness of this view. But to all such let us put the questions,
Whence came the panic and bankruptcy and ruin to thousands but as the result of *debt?* Whence came debt—that
grinding master more inexorable than Shylock, and whose
thralldom is slavery of body, mind and soul—debt, National
and State—debt, municipal and individual—legitimate offspring of illegitimate strife—until it has piled up a huge
pyramid, its crushing weight resting on the tender shoulders
of the people? Whence all this debt of *twenty hundred
millions of dollars*, but as the result of war, which was the
result of the enslavement of the African? Some will say
that this was but the natural outcome of the personal extra-
vagance of the people—the ruinous policy of living beyond
individual incomes, and to great extent the influence of corrupt
or vacillating legislation. That venerable Southern statesman, the Hon. Alex. H. Stephens, in a late interview said,
"The real cause of the panic in 1873 was the demonetization
of silver in Europe. Germany took the lead, the Latin States
followed, and it was brought about without the people's understanding or knowing anything about it, and it was followed
up in 1873 in this country, about six months before the panic."
A late Southern journal explains it in this way; "In 1873,
the panic which occurred was merely a symptom of a general
and inevitable decline. The entire business of the country
was involved in the mad rush and pitched upon a high key.
The break occurred in the Stock Exchange because there
was the wildest, maddest overreaching, and the most reckless gambling, but it extended from these to involve every
interest in the country, because the disease pervaded the
entire system. It was a constitutional malady, and not a
local affection. The country was like a thoroughly unsound
man, whose whole system is out of gear, so that any slight
injury or ordinarily inconsequential malady, brings out the
wide-spread unsoundness."[1] Still, while all this is quite true,
it does not exactly answer our questions. The panic was but
incidental to, and a part of the multiplied evils tramping
on the heels of war—the war, as we firmly believe, Heaven's
judgment on the United States for the enforced enslavement

---

[1] Nashville *American*, Nov. 23, 1879.

of the African.   That this is true we cannot get over the
idea, however much it may be denied.   That this is true
there are enough precedents in the ruins of history to rivet
the fact in our hearts.   Slavery has never prospered a nation.
Rome tried it when, by military exploitation, she made the
world her vassals, but the inhumanity and the crime were
their own speedy and proper avengers.   Spain attempted it,
when she neglected the useful arts at home, and sought to
dominate the nations through the force of her Western Colonies ; but from that moment her prestige declined—her
rich argosies of tropic wealth, her treasure-laden galleons
departed from the sea, and decay has been written across
the face of her once glorious kingdom.[1]   Portugal tried it ;
Holland and Greece and other nations—the result has always
been the same.   One of the most absurd laws in Athens,
was the prohibiting the exercise of the fine arts to any but
free-born men.   As if any man ought to have been considered unworthy to exercise any powers of mind, by any law of
any creatures who, like himself, were obliged to eat and
sleep to keep up existence, if the Almighty God had not
thought him unworthy of his gifts !   On this delightful principle, what would have become of the Fables of Æsop, or
the Comedies of Terence ? both of whom were slaves.   Or
what would have become of the Odes of Horace ? who was
the son of a slave.   No, indeed !   A man may be a servant
and serve with honor.   But God never intended that one
man made in His image should "crook the pregnant hinges
of the knee" as a life-long slave to another cast in the same
mould—whether potentate or priest, whether monarch or
master.   "Thou shalt have no other gods before me" stands
first in the Decalogue.[2]   Genuflection to mortal is the first
step towards idolatry, as it is among the first requirements
in that blind obeisance of blighted souls—conjured and cursed
by the wizard-craft of Rome.

But the axe was now laid to the root of the tree.   The
hoary-crowned outgrowth of Wrong and Injustice must come
down—must give way—must make room—before the sturdy
blows wielded by the pioneers of advancing civilization.   Oh,

---

[1] At last Spain has been aroused to a sense of her enormity.   Even while we have
been engaged on this work the Spanish Cortes has determined to abolish slavery in Cuba
and other Spanish dependencies.   Thus, after nearly four hundred years of servitude,
Christian civilization has reached those unhappy souls.   These are signs of the better
times.
[2] See Moses in Exodus xx, 3.

how it assails our pride in a tender—nay, in a vital spot, to admit these things. And yet it proves the patent fact, that the nature of man is the same to-day that it always was. In every age men have more or less followed the trail of the previous generation. They have kept close column at half distance with conventional forms. They have hugged the darling treasure of tradition to their souls, and done this or that simply forsooth, because our purblind forefathers did it. But not so with this and with succeeding generations. We would be but dull pupils of that hard and exacting master— Experience—to adopt their errors as our own. The scales have fallen from our eyes, and we must be equal to the emergency in this new era of responsibility. The river of destiny must sweep on—proceeding from the fountains of purity—it must sweep on and ever until it reaches the illimitable sea of God's completeness. And though the mere practical philosopher may deny God's interference in these matters, and though he may attribute this grand and mighty revolution, this astonishing renovation of the social fabric to the force of public opinion—the progress of knowledge—the softening of manners—the power of numbers—still we shall see anon

> "Earthly power doth then show likest God's
> When mercy seasons justice."

And we shall see anon there certainly was a higher Power above and beyond all of these shaping and directing the destinies of this country.

In the South the general impression prevailed that the "abolition idea" was of spontaneous outburst and confined in the North to a few choice and rampant fanatics, who charged about with firebrands in hand and hungry to devour somebody. The name of "Abolitionist" was held to be the sum total of human baseness, just as in the South, strange to say, the business of "nigger trader" was regarded as the lowest round of contemptibility. Abolition literature was excluded from the Southern States—abolition oratory was never heard —practically, there was no freedom of the press, nor freedom of speech—those inestimable boons have come to us of late— came to us, we may say, when the Negro was declared a free man. Our people, as a general thing, were ignorant of the fact that Anti-slavery claimed the support and enlisted the talents of the best speakers and writers of the other section.

Briefly, then, let us look into these points. The Quakers, we believe, were first in the field. The Abolition Society of Pennsylvania was formed in 1774, and enlarged in 1787, and Dr. Benj. Franklin was made president; Dr. Rush and other distinguished men were members. In 1777, Vermont formed her Constitution, which prohibited slavery. It is said, that soon after the revolutionary war, a suit was brought before a Vermont judge involving the title to a negro. The plaintiff produced a regular bill of sale of the negro to himself, and rested the case; the judge then inquired, " How did the man you bought of acquire title?" A regular bill of sale to him was produced. "But," said the judge, "how did this man acquire title?" "Mr. Attorney," continued the judge, addressing the counsellor for the plaintiff, "nothing will be regarded as evidence of title to a *man* by this Court, but a bill of sale from Almighty God. Unless you can procure that your case will be dismissed."

In 1770, movements were made against slavery in Massachusetts, and in 1780 it was *judicially* settled that slavery could not exist under the Constitution which declared "all men are born free and equal."[1] In New Hampshire slavery was abolished by the declaration of rights in 1784. Rhode Island, provided by law that all persons born in that State after March, 1784, should be free. Pennsylvania, in 1780, passed a law for gradual emancipation; Connecticut in 1784; New York in 1799; New Jersey in 1804. Thus, the movement went on gaining in strength slowly but surely—like the progress of durable fame or the growth of an easterly storm. It enlisted under its banners such men as John Jay, Hamilton, the Adams' family, Webster and others. The North began to educate her people into hatred of slavery by newspapers and books and lectures and speeches. Then arose that class of extremists who knew no compromise. Wm. Lloyd Garrison, who declared the Constitution "a covenant with death—a league with hell"; Channing, Theodore Parker, Thurlow Weed, Wendell Phillips, the Beechers, and, last but not least, Horace Greeley—Democratic candidate for President in 1872.

---

[1] Humboldt says : " In 1769, forty-six years before the declaration of the Congress of Vienna, and thirty-eight years before the abolition of the slave trade, decreed in London and at Washington, the Chamber of Representatives of Massachusetts had declared itself against 'the unnatural and unwarrantable custom of enslaving mankind.' " —Equi. Reg., vol. iii, p. 276. See also Walsh's Appeal to the United States, 1819, p. 312.

The Border Slave States soon began to declare in favor of emancipation, though the wisdom of their leaders preferred a *gradual* system. Arnold, the biographer of Mr. Lincoln, who has said many hard things about the South and but few in its favor, makes a confession which strikes us as conspicuous on account of its oddity. He says, "It ought to be stated in vindication of the early statesmen of Virginia, that they appreciated the injustice and wrong of slavery, and that as early as 1772, the Legislature of that Commonwealth addressed the King of Great Britain, exposing the inhumanity of slavery, and expressing the conviction that it was opposed to the security and happiness of the people, and would, in time, endanger their existence. The king, in reply, answered, that 'upon pain of his highest displeasure the importation of slaves should not be in any respect obstructed.'"[1] The distinguished statesmen of the Border States — Washington, Jefferson and Madison began early to favor emancipation, although they were slaveholders. Jefferson, the author of the Constitution, and frequently referred to as the "Father of the Democratic Party," made an unsuccessful move in the Virginia Legislature for abolishment. Randolph manumitted his slaves—three hundred in number—and provided a fund for the purchase of a tract of land for them. Henry Clay and many others were on the side of emancipation. In a speech on African Colonization, delivered in the House of Representatives at Washington, January 20, 1827, Mr. Clay said:

"If I could be instrumental in eradicating this deepest stain (slavery) from the character of our country, and removing all cause of reproach on account of it, by foreign nations; if I could only be instrumental in ridding of this foul blot that revered State that gave me birth, or that not less beloved State which kindly adopted me as her son ; I would not exchange the proud satisfaction which I should enjoy, for the honor of all the triumphs ever decreed to the most successful conqueror.

.   .   .   .

"We are reproached with doing mischief by the agitation of this question. . . . If they repress all tendencies towards liberty and ultimate emancipation, they must do more than put down the benevolent efforts of this society. They must go back to the era of our liberty and independence, and muzzle the cannon which thunders its annual joyous return. They must revive the slave trade, with all its train of atrocities. They must suppress the workings of British philanthropy, seeking to ameliorate the condition of the unfortunate West Indian slaves. They must arrest the career of South American deliverance from thraldom. They must blow out the moral lights

---

[1] See Arnold's History of Lincoln, p. 27.

around us, and extinguish that greatest torch of all which America presents to a benighted world—pointing the way to their rights, their liberties, and their happiness.   And when they have achieved all these purposes, their work will be yet incomplete.   They must penetrate the human soul, and eradicate the light of reason and the love of liberty.   Then, and not till then, when universal darkness and despair prevail, can you perpetuate slavery, and repress all sympathies, and all humane and benevolent efforts among freemen, in behalf of the unhappy portion of our race doomed to bondage." [1]

It is curious, then, to turn to the North for a sentiment seemingly at variance with this.   Hon. R. W. Thompson, (now United States Secretary of the Navy,) said in a speech at Terre Haute, Indiana, August 11, 1855 :

"These men (the Northern Abolitionists) charge upon the South what they call the sin and curse of slavery, and claim that it is the high destiny and duty of the *North* to wipe off the foul blot from our national escutcheon. Now, although I might with great propriety, as one of the sons of the South —proud of my ancestry and incapable of forgetting the home of my youth— enter upon her defense, yet I will not, because she does not need it.   To borrow the language of Mr. Webster: 'There she is—behold her and judge for yourselves.   There is her history: the world knows it by heart.   The past at least is secure.'   But I will say to my New England friends who often tauntingly charge the South alone with the responsibility for this blot upon our institutions, that *their* ancestors and not *mine* fixed it there.   At every stage of the controversy in the Convention, *New England favored the continuance* of the slave trade, while my native State of Virginia opposed it with all the power of her great men who were there.   Had New England voted with Virginia, the twenty years of slave importation would have been cut off, and there then, in all probability, would, by this time, have been very few, if any, slaves in the United States." [2]

Still the evils of the institution were well known to the Pro-slavery advocates, for their writers and speakers were men of ability.   The opposition of the North—of England—and of civilized Europe, to the slave system was pronounced and positive.[3]   The barbarous enormity as practiced by other

---

[1] See Life and Speeches of Henry Clay: Leary & Getz, Philadelphia, 1859, vol. i, pp. 281–283.   Also, Colton's Life of Henry Clay, vol. i, p. 189.

[2] Terre Haute Express print, August, 1855.

[3] We have said elsewhere that the Quakers were the first to oppose slavery and the slavery trade in the United States, this may be repeated, with the additional remark that from the beginning of their existence as a body they led in the cause in England, but neither their influence nor their numbers were large.   In the eighteenth century a sentiment of hostility to the system of slavery was shared by many literary men, philosophers and statesmen of England, who labored with zeal for its suppression.   The famous decision by Lord Mansfield in the case of "Somerset," given in 1772, gave an impetus to the cause.   This decision was that the master of a slave could not by force compel him to go out of the kingdom, though it is stated that seventy years before Chief Justice Holt ruled that "as soon as a negro comes into England he is free; one may be a villein in England, but not a slave"—and later: "In England there is no such thing as a slave, and a human being never was considered a chattel to be sold for

slave-holding nations was confessed, though we speak the truth in saying that in the United States inhumanity was the exception and not the rule. In the South there were thousands of masters who were kind-hearted, considerate, Christian gentlemen. And what is more, only, about one man in twenty in the South was a slaveholder. Still the system was pregnant with wrong. The blended blood of Japheth and Ham toiled in the cotton fields or performed the menial services of the slave—here and there, for some inhuman and sinning father. But let us pass over this dark page. Our people are very sensitive of rebuke. This step may gain the writer enemies in the South. Our friends all live here—this is our land, our birthplace. We love every mountain and valley, in its domain. We love every dale, every dell, every brook, every river. We love the genial air that` gently sweeps over its fair sunny face, every flower that blossoms on its lovely bosom. And it is because we love the South we would see her just and noble and right. Some old men of the South may not brook this recital of the past. They may say it is untimely rash, unkind—they *cannot* say it is untruthful. And besides what does that matter when a man feels he *must* do a work, that he cannot avoid a task. "Let a man *do* his work," says Carlyle, "the fruit of it is the care of Another than he." This is encouraging, and strengthens us to go forward. Slavery then brought other evils. It made our people imperious and hypercritical. It made them proud and

---

a price." In 1785, Sharp, Clarkson and Wilberforce began their Anti-slavery labors, and later on (1790 to 1823) Pitt, Fox and Buxton joined them. The agitation, like a troubled sea, surged to and fro, until finally, in 1843, Great Britain emancipated more than 12,000,000 slaves in her East Indian possessions. France had been as much committed to negro slavery as England, but moved sooner for its abolition. The National Assembly, May 15, 1791, virtually granted equal political privileges to all free men, without regard to color, and this led to those struggles in St. Domingo which put an end to slavery there. Napoleon I succeeded in restoring slavery in most of the French colonies, but failed in Hayti. In 1815, during the Hundred Days, he issued an order for the immediate abolition of the slave trade, which the government of Louis XVIII re-enacted, and the French slave trade ceased in 1819. The Congress of Vienna, composed of representatives of eight "Japhetic" nations, met in 1815, and denounced the slave trade. After much discussion in the reign of Louis Phillipe, slavery in the French colonies was abolished by the Provisional Government in 1848, without indemnity to the masters. Sweden abolished slavery in 1846-7. Denmark in 1848, and Holland in 1860. Spain agreed in 1814 to abolish the slave trade in 1820. The Netherlands abolished it in 1818, and Brazil in 1826, but the Brazilians continued to prosecute it notwithstanding. In 1820 the United States passed a law declaring the slave trade to be piracy, but no conviction was obtained under this statute until November, 1861, when Nathaniel Gordon, master of a vessel called the Erie, was convicted at New York. Since the Vienna Congress the slave trade has been practically outlawed by all civilized nations, while the British Government expends at present $700,000 per year for its suppression.—[See fully on these points Appleton's New American Cyclopædia, p. 707.]

self-consequential. It alienated them from the rest of the nation and built up sectional ambition and jealousy. It brought them factitious, cheating, transitory wealth—wealth which in the end impoverished us because it put our faculties asleep. And when a man begins to turn his whole attention to the accumulation of wealth it is only the sign of his ultimate degradation, or when a nation is bent upon abundant possessions it is but the signal of her decline.

But there will arise a class of captious disputants who will dig up the exploded system of Hobbes and assert that the *primum mobile* of all human actions is selfish interest. They will say the Negro is free—now let him go. He has worked for us, now let him shift for himself. And there will arise another class of philosophers of the Jeremy Bentham sect, who love to prate about the utilitarianism of the age; who are perfectly charmed with the conceit that they are practical men—men of hard common sense—men with no nonsense about them—men who have no time to regard the sentimentality of justice, virtue, morality and religion. To the four winds with their practicability! It is true that utility, interest, pleasure, personal well-being, is the rule, and the only rule for conduct to be drawn from the principle that sensation is the sole motive of volition. But nothing can be more widely separated than this rule and that of general interest. For what does the law of general interest prescribe? Let that close reasoner Jouffroy answer: "It commands the individual to act with reference, not to his own private good, but to the greatest good of society and mankind; or, in other words, it sets before him as his end, not his own peculiar interest and utility, but the sum total of human interests; the interests of all men must he labor to increase, and for their utility is he bound to exert his energies. . . . Nothing can be plainer than that this is true; for according to the first of these explanations of the rule of general utility, if I feel that the pleasure of possessing another's good is greater than the pain of sympathy in seeing him deprived of it, I have, then, a right to rob him; and, according to the second explanation, I have the same right, whenever I find it more profitable, on the whole, to violate than to respect his claims. Singular rule of general utility, indeed, that thus authorizes me to steal."[1] Such cold-blooded indifference will not do. It is

---

[1] Jouffroy's Ethics and Critical Survey of Moral Systems, vol. ii, p. 53.

about equivalent to robbing a man of all he possesses and then abusing him for possessing no more. It is about equivalent to appropriating a man's labor and then cursing him not because he demands pay, but because he refuses to labor longer under such manifestly unjust conditions. Happy for the South! happy for the world men of this class are few. "In the sweat of thy face shalt thou eat bread." This was the curse. We know of no exceptions in favor of any man. Thank Heaven there is no kingdom of God from which the obligations of labor and the rewards of labor are excluded.

In whatever light we regard it then, slavery has its dark side. If we open a volume about Africa to see how the slave trade is conducted there it horrifies us. Still the system now is conducted on a commercial basis, whereas formerly the Negroes were kidnapped. Mr. Stanley, who looked about him with the eyes of an accomplished reporter for one of the most careful journals of our times, (the New York *Herald*) has in his book a paragraph which puts the matter most tellingly: "We will suppose," says he, "for the sake of illustrating how trade with the interior is managed, that the Arab conveys by his caravan $5,000 worth of goods into the interior. At Unyanyembe the goods are worth $10,000; at Ujiji they are worth $15,000, or have trebled in price. $7.50 will purchase a slave in the markets of Ujiji, which will bring in Zanzibar, $30. Ordinary men-slaves may be purchased for $6 which would sell for $25 on the coast. We will say he purchases slaves to the full extent of his means. After deducting $1500 for expenses of carriage to Ujiji and back, viz: $3500—he would buy, at $7.50 each, four hundred and sixty-four slaves, on which he would realize $13,920 on an investment of $5,000, or nearly $9,000 net profit for a single journey from Zanzibar to Ujiji."[1]

In Dr. Baldwin's book, already quoted, we find a compilation of figures too matter-of-fact and too forcibly illustrative of the subject to refuse them admission to these pages. After admitting that "the slave trade was pronounced piracy by the agreement of Japhetic nations," he says, (pp. 384, 385,) "The slave trade may be computed from 1503 to 1825, a period of three hundred and twenty-two years. During one hundred and fifty-five years, or from 1670 to 1825, Humboldt says that nearly five million Africans were imported into the

---

[1] Life of Livingston, p. 417.

Archipelago of the West Indies; and two million, one hundred and thirty thousand into the British West Indies in the space of one hundred and six years, or from 1618 to 1786. If to this sum we add all that were imported from 1503 to 1824, the aggregate cannot be less than three millions, if not four millions.[1] Mr. Gallatin, former United States Treasurer, estimates the entire importation into our republic at three hundred thousand. The number transported to South America was probably five millions, if not more. . . . In the West Indies British inhumanity diminished the number of imported negroes from three millions to four hundred thousand; while in Australia the blacks are treated like beasts of the forest. In America, the *so-called* free blacks, though elevated above the level of native Africans and Australasians, are yet, in *average condition*, inferior to plantation slaves. Proscribed as a *natural caste* of subordinates, they are, by the force of public opinion, *natural instinct*, and law, kept at a respectful distance from Japhetic immunities. A few are suffered to exist as artisans and traders; but the greater proportion are barbers, cooks, chambermaids, washerwomen and scavengers. In some of the free States the law proscribes them with a severity equal to banishment; and where legal restriction is not imposed, social affiliation is regarded by the white population generally as grossly degrading."

Nor was there scarcely any hope of even gradual emancipa-

---

[1] We desire to add here a remark by Humboldt, which Dr. Baldwin omitted. It is this: "These revolting calculations respecting the consumption of the human species, do not include the number of unfortunate slaves who have perished in the passage, or have been thrown into the sea as damaged merchandise."—Humboldt's Equinoctial Regions, vol. iii, p. 278. However, as all figures on this point are of interest now, we add also the following from the New American Cyclopædia, p. 710, "The whole number of Africans taken for slaves is estimated at 40,000,000, or not quite 100,000 per annum since the beginning of the traffic; but for eighty years after the trade began, their exportation was very limited, and probably not 30,000 were taken by the Portuguese between 1444 and 1493. The weight of the exportation has been during the years that have elapsed since movements for the abolition of the trade were commenced, the demand for tropical products has immensely increased in the present century. Some of the slaves were sold in European countries, and it was supposed there were 15,000 in the British islands at the time of the decision of the Somerset case. African slaves were said to be "dispersed all over Europe." Spain and France took some of them, as well as England. The number of slaves imported into those British colonies which became the United States in 1776, is computed at 300,000 down to that year. At the first census, in 1790, the slaves in the United States numbered 697,897, all the States but Massachusetts (which then included Maine) having some servile inhabitants, though Vermont had but 17, and New Hampshire only 158. In 1800 their number was 893,041, slavery having ceased in Vermont, and but 8 slaves being left in New Hampshire. The census of 1810 showed 1,191,364 slaves, there being none in Massachusetts, New Hampshire, Vermont and Ohio, the last a new State, created out of territory that was a wilderness in 1776. In 1820 the slaves numbered 1,538,038; in 1830, 2,009,043; in 1840, 2,487,455; in 1850, 3,204,313; and in 1860, 3,952,801.

tion twenty years ago. On this point we shall quote again from Dr. Baldwin. He says, (p. 458): "A gradual emancipation of all the slaves in our country, and their transmission to Africa, under present (1858) values of labor, is an impossibility. To colonize the qualified free blacks and occasional emancipated ones, is as much as can be now accomplished. According to the most feasible plan of emancipating the *slaves* of our country and sending them to Liberia, under present circumstances, were all parties agreed, the cost would be not less than *twenty-seven hundred millions of dollars.*[1] This considerable difficulty closes the door of hope against freeing the country of slaves by gradual emancipation."

Was there ever so gloomy a picture? Drawn from life, on the spot, by one whose claims to honest report no one will deny, it is absolutely sickening to read. Can any one wonder that the Negro was downcast and desolate and hopeless? "Give a dog a bad name and it will stick to him through life." Put it in the minds of men that the Negroes were born to be slaves, and truth will have hard work to uproot the error. Yet this is just the error that found lodgment in the bosoms of many of the brave-hearted, noble-souled, chivalric Southern people. But was it just? was it even generous? Let every man who reads these pages answer for himself. Let him place liberty and slavery in juxtaposition—what is the conclusion? Liberty is germinant, so too is slavery. But liberty is the tender flower that must be nurtured and cultivated, while slavery is the rank, noxious weed that grows up with spontaniety. Some enemy of mankind hath sown the tares of slavery among the wheaten grains of liberty. If left alone they will overrun the world and encroach upon the rights of every man less strong than his neighbor. If they be not cut down and plucked up by the roots they can pension life upon the bleak rocks of prejudice and self-interest and grow up to choke and poison all the better impulses of the human heart and stifle the unlimited possibilities of the immortal soul. Liberty, therefore, is good—slavery is evil. Liberty is light, slavery is darkness. Liberty is the symbol and the gift of God, but slavery is the tyranny of the Evil One. Whoso loves liberty let him deny these facts if he can.

Personal freedom is the foundation-stone of the world's freedom. It is the basis on which is built civil and political,

---

[1] See fully on this point in De Bow's Review, vol. i, No. 3.

intellectual, moral and spiritual liberty.   Man—the freeman,
but little lower than the angels, is the god-like superstructure
of this noble edifice.   Personal freedom therefore, is the very
heart and core and centre of man's highest earthly existence.
Let the sword of aggression assail liberty in one quarter and
its effects are felt to the outer rim of the world's circumfer-
ence.   The history of one people or nation or race cannot be
written without touching in somewise upon the history of
some other.   Every being exists, not only for himself, but
forms necessarily a portion of a great whole, of which the
plan and the idea go infinitely beyond him, and in which he
is destined to play a part.   Thus the whole human race is
bound together by an invisible but actual bond of fellowship.
Thus the birth of a child or the death of a man affects or dis-
turbs the relation of the whole of mankind.   And this is true
in other respects.   A drop of water cannot be removed from
the ocean, a grain of sand cannot be displaced from the
desert without changing the condition, however slight the
degree, of the whole created universe.   If it were possible to
annihilate a single moment of time—to blot it out—to sever
it from the linked chain of duration, the effect of this action
would be felt throughout all future ages.   Little deeds!
There are no little deeds in life.   The performance of an
action ceases not in its operation until its influence reaches
the farther boundary line of the Hereafter, as a pebble
dropped into the ocean may send its radiating waves to pilfer
the sands from the shore and so change the contour of a continent.   Small words!   There are no small words spoken.
A single thought once fashioned may set in motion a train of
influences which only the trumpet of the archangel will arrest.   And so.   Jeopardize the liberty of one man or one
nation or one race, and the liberty of the world is endangered.
But raise the standard of freedom—advance its lines, and
though empires may crumble and armies be slain—freedom
will triumph—*for Freedom is immortal!*

Nevertheless, if a candid man will only read the record of
the efforts for and against slavery in this country during the
present century, he will conclude that the "door of hope"
had certainly been shut forever in the face of the Negro.
The Monroe Doctrine—the Missouri Compromise—the emancipation policy of the South American States—the Fugitive
Slave Law—the Kansas and Nebraska Bill—the Wilmot Pro-
viso—the annexation of Texas—the Dred Scott decision—

the conferences and consultations—measures and movements
—debates and discussions—in Congress and in Legislatures
—in Church as well as State—in camp and court—all, all,
seemed to preclude the vaguest possibility of their full emancipation. The country was kept at red-hot heat between the
incandescent fires of peril and agony. Exaggerated and
distorted delineations of the subject were made on both sides,
which seemed only to widen the breach instead of remove
the cause. Mrs. Stowe's "Uncle Tom's Cabin," justly
regarded as a fanatical and inflammatory view of the subject,
yet had more influence in overthrowing the system, perhaps,
than any other one human work. As a matter of interest in
this connection it may be stated that this celebrated book first
appeared as a serial in the Washington *National Era*, in
1851–1852; then in two volumes, in Boston, in 1852. It has
been translated six times in French, twelve times in German;
and in Italian, Spanish, Danish, Swedish, Flemish, Polish
and Magyar. It has been dramatized, and eulogized, and
quoted from, and still finds large and ready sale in this
country and in Europe. The next literary firebrand thrown
into the midst of all this combustible material, was Helper's
"Impending Crisis," which reached a sale of more than one
hundred thousand copies in the North, though strictly inter-
dicted in the South. All of this but proves that the civilized
world was being educated against the South. Still, as we
say, if a candid man will only read ex-Vice President Wilson's
book on the "Rise and Fall of Slave Power in America," he
can judge for himself how slim the chances for emancipation
seemed. We merely refer to these works, and do not wish
to discuss them, for we are studiously and honestly endeavoring to avoid what is known as the *political* sides of this
question. But they are matters of *history*, and if any objection is raised, let it be directed only towards the makers of the
history. We refuse to acknowledge this responsibility, and
only propose to be responsible for writing *fact*. Would to
God our duty were a pleasanter one. Would that we could
record only the moral, intellectual and material march and
growth of our beloved country. But we search in vain for
the pure gold. It is mixed with dross everywhere. Sickened
to the very soul we open the history of savage Africa, and
read there of the kingdom of Dahomey—a kingdom which
was begun in blood and cruelty, and which has maintained its
existence for more than two centuries in spite of the terrible

3

scenes continually enacted—scenes which would drive any
other nation to revolt—there almost under the shadow of
Christian mission stations, are still enacted the bloody dramas
of human sacrifices—human skulls are drinking cups! Hor-
rified, we fly to the annals of barbarism. The war-cry of
Tamerlane, the Tartar, as it rings through the trembling date
groves of the Orient—as it rises above the pride of "Araby
the Blest"—stirs us like a trumpet call. But there on the
plains of Bagdad we behold his monument of forty thousand
human skulls—and our soul sinks back aghast from the
sight of human slaughter. Surely, then, in Christian America
there yet remaineth a brighter and a sweeter picture. We
open again the cherished volume of our country's history—
the Apocalypse of the Republic. With the hot heart and
eager eye of the enthusiast we look for its sacred antiquities.
Art, science, literature, music, poetry—where are these thy
hallowed records? Benevolence, piety, religion — alas!
alas! how few thy monuments. And yet we know that our
country is rich in annals. Since childhood we were taught
this is "the land of the free and the home of the brave."
We know that our Union was rich in associations that make
her plains historic—her mountains, her valleys, her lakes and
rivers remarkable. We know that her name is beloved and
honored in many a clime. We know that she has furnished
to the world a galaxy of enlightened, loyal and intrepid sons
—whose deeds stand out distinct as the clear-cut stars on a
winter's evening, and rising beyond death's dark night are the
guiding stars of our national polity. To their patriotism,
their zeal, their labors, their influence, their talents, their
wealth, we must ever acknowledge paramount and permanent
obligation. For in so far as they sowed the seed the generation of to-day reaps the harvest in all of those grand conser-
vative principles of civilization, truth, virtue, learning, liberty
and good government; and to them are we largely indebted
for many of the useful laws, morals, enjoyments, comforts,
conveniences and blessings of our refined society. They
have left us a goodly heritage. It stretches over the far-
reaching fields of human glory. It is bounded only by Time.
    Boasting, then, of the great and the honored in theology,
in statesmanship, in military renown, in law, in medicine, in
judicature, in journalism, in commerce, in agriculture, are
there not countless thousands of the loved and lost—the
leathern-aproned sons of Anak, who were drawn into the

great current of human life and swept away with it, as by the suction of Fate itself? Where are the records and who is the historian of the "gloomy generations" on whose brows man—not God—had stamped the signet of servitude? These treasures of art and industry—these triumphs of architecture—but above all, these laughing fields of plenty—these leveled forests and rescued swamps—these evidences of labor dotting the land—say liberty-loving friend, do we read our history through the kaleidoscopic glass—is this Dahomey? and yonder Tamerlane's monument?—or do we read, This was the throne, and this the domain of the mighty monarch—the contented monarch— *King Cotton!*

It is unnecessary, however, to paint more vividly these life-pictures. By allowing the reader to exercise his own imagination, we possibly also escape the rough handling of the critics, though we do not in the least fear them. On the contrary, we dare assert, that a lover of liberty and of justice with his heart in the work, and courage to write what he thinks, cannot touch on this subject without writing strongly. To exaggerate or to adulterate, therefore, would lessen the force of a statement. Men who habitually swear acknowledge by the employment of profanity the weakness of their word and the necessity of a bolstering oath. But men who write the truth—though it may cut to the quick, will command attention and gain respect. We have already said that the "peculiar institution" of slavery brought with it many evils. We propose now to show that it also prevented much good to the South, and bore in its birth a germ of death which its illustrious founders had the weakness not to stifle. We propose to show that during the slave *regime* the North progressed, the South declined. Proofs of this strange contrast abound.[1]

According to the census of 1860, the Slave States had an area of 851,448 square miles, or 544,926,720 acres; the Free States, 612,697 square miles, or 392,092,080 acres. Consequently, the South had 238,851 square miles, or 152,834,640 acres more than the North. Notwithstanding, the white pop-

---

[1] These figures and those which shortly follow have been derived from the United States Census Reports, and compared with the figures given in Helper's "Impending Crisis," and in the admirably written work, "The Results of Slavery," by M. Augustin Cochin, ex-Maire and Municipal Councillor of Paris—a work which was crowned by the Institute of France, and translated by Mary L. Booth. Boston: Walker, Wise & Co., 1863, pp. 45-52

ulation of the North amounted to 18,669,061, while that of
the South was but 8,038,996, that is 10,630,065 less inhabitants; and if the colored population, slave and free, be added,
the North had in all 18,893,856 inhabitants, or 30.84 per
square mile; the South, adding slave and colored, 12,240,294,
or 14.34 per square mile; that is, 6,653,562 less inhabitants.

This is a most astonishing exhibit, when we remember that
the physical condition of the South is admitted as infinitely
superior to that of the North.   Indeed, it is the boast of the
South that her geographical advantages are peerless—her climate excellent, equable and inviting; the fertility of her soil un-
surpassed; her water-power immense; her mineral wealth inexhaustible; her timber ample for a population many times multiplied; that, in fact, it is a land that can produce everything
that can tempt the palate of man—certainly everything that is
absolutely necessary and of utility.   There were no draw-
backs in the way of soil, climate, seaboard outlets, or situation
as regards favorable commerce with other countries.   Excellent harbors thickly indent the coasts, as if human ingenuity,
guided by engineering skill, and not Providence cut them
there.   Clear, bright, deep, swift-rolling streams track and
intersect the land in every quarter.   Hard by the cotton
fields towered mountains of iron and coal, but unpolished
steel has no attractive qualities, and the sky-kissing peaks
grew old and bald in looking down upon the few scattered
scenes of manufacturing toil and thrift.   Adjoining the sugar
plantations were dense forests undisturbed by portable saw,
and beyond unclaimed marsh and swamp.   Beneath richest
meadows lay imbedded wondrous wealth—so weary of
lethargy that here and there it outcropped and sunned itself
in the idle atmosphere—just as tiny blades of grass peep out
in early spring to see if God's beautiful sunshine has come
again.   There can be no doubt, then, that the South had all
of the elements of prosperity—all of the requisites necessary
to attract population and to command success in manufactures
and productive pursuits.   This is an almost inexhaustible
subject, and we could enlarge on it *ad infinitum*, but space
forbids.   Enough to say, 1st. The South was in possession of
incalculable supplies of the raw materials used in manufactures.   2d. She commanded the natural means and agents
best fitted to produce power.   3d. Her position as respects
other countries was all that could be desired.   4th. The
nature of the soil and climate was altogether in her favor.

5th. She had ample capital if rightly used. Aside from these, and with these, what did we lack for aught that wisdom could employ or skillful labor produce? But let us draw a few comparisons. Take the barren and sterile soil of New England, it will not compare even with North Carolina in natural richness. Compare the rich district of Central New York with the blooming valley of the Shenandoah; the hills of Pennsylvania with the arable plains of Georgia; and as for the boasted prairies of Ohio, Indiana and Illinois they can only be *contrasted* with the charming Highlands of Middle Tennessee, while the wonderful Blue Grass Region of Kentucky seems to be the garden spot of creation. The State of Georgia has a combined water-power greater than the whole of New England. Kentucky, Tennessee, Alabama and Missouri each quite equal Pennsylvania in mineral resources. Kentucky alone has a superficies of coal lands greater than the coal area of Great Britain. Tennessee, in its three great Belts, or iron-producing regions—the Eastern, the Dyestone and the Western, according to geological report, has enough iron and coal to supply the world for centuries.[1] The Mississippi valley is richer than the valley of the Nile. Every State has the elements of an empire. Scarce a county that would not make a wealthy dukedom.

Why was it then our land drooped and withered in the summer sunlight of God's favor? Was it the fault of our people? We are not their Judge. The whole world acknowledges them a gifted, noble people; a people of warm strong feelings—the characteristics of noblemindedness and good citizenship. And our women—God bless our women; they have ever been remarkable in that exquisite womanliness which is rare among women, and found never, save in women of the highest and fairest organization. These are our jewels, the crowning glory of our sunny south, and springing, as it were, indigenous from the soil, are like the influence of climate which no resistance can overcome. Oh, then, this was the land where—

> " The old bright wine of valor fills
> The chalice of romance."

---

[1] Professor Safford, State Geologist of Tennessee, estimates the coal area of the State equal to a solid stratum eight feet thick, covering an area of 5100 square miles—underlying more than one-eighth of the entire surface of the State, and equal in volume to a block of coal eight feet high, fifty-one miles wide, and one hundred miles long. Reduced to bushels this would make 23,393,323,008,000 bushels, to which must be added the incalculable value of iron ore and uncut timber—enough to purchase a kingdom.

and this will account for the dauntless valor of our heroic sons who faced death on storied battle-plains "with fearless souls, like ample shields"—presented to every uplifted blade and verge enough for more.

But the land suffered from a scourge.   It was under the influence of *slavery!*

Let us see how far this affected the education of the masses in the two sections—not to condemn—not for ignoble motive, for every line we write in this comparison brings us deep and poignant regret.   In 1850, the North had 62,433 public schools, 72,621 teachers, and 2,769,901 pupils.   At the same time the South had only 18,507 schools, 19,307 teachers, and 581,861 pupils.   In the North 422,515 *white* adults could not read or write; in the South 512,882.   The whites therefore suffered from slavery as well as the blacks.   The following list will show the number of whites under twenty in each State who could neither read nor write:

Connecticut,	one in	568	Louisiana,	one in	38½
Vermont,	"	473	Maryland,	"	27
New Hampshire,	"	310	Mississippi,	"	20
Massachusetts,	"	166	Delaware,	"	18
Maine,	"	108	South Carolina,	"	17
Michigan,	"	97	Missouri,	"	16
Rhode Island,	"	67	Alabama,	"	15
New Jersey,	"	58	Kentucky,	"	13½
New York,	"	56	Georgia,	"	13
Pennsylvania,	"	50	Virginia,	"	12½
Ohio,	"	43	Arkansas,	"	11½
Indiana,	"	18	Tennessee,	"	11
Illinois,	"	17	North Carolina,	"	7

The cost of churches in the North in 1850, was estimated at $67,773,477; in the South $21.674,581.   The subscriptions for Bibles and religious tracts, the support of missionaries, and the return of free Negroes to Africa amounted, in 1855, to $1,005,743 in the North; while in the South they did not exceed $222,402.

In the North the number of journals in 1860 amounted to 2,888, issuing 735,520,708 copies annually; in the South to 1,193, issuing 192,430,840 copies per year.   At the North, there were, in 1850, 14,911 public libraries, containing 3,888,-234 volumes.   In the South, 695 public libraries with 649,577 volumes.

In 1855, $4,670,725 were collected for mail service in the North.   In the South $1,553,198.   The number of patents issued for new inventions in 1856 amounted in the North to 1,929 ; in the South to 268.

To these figures let us add those of the industrial, agricultural, financial and economical condition of the sections. " Compare" says Theodore Parker,[1] "these two systems of machinery; the North has reduced iron and fire to slavery; the South has transformed men into machines; compare the machinery of the nineteenth century *after* Jesus Christ, with the machinery of the nineteenth century *before* Jesus Christ ; calculate how far the productive power of the North prevails over the productive power of the South."

To begin, compare the custom-house receipts for 1854. In the North these amounted to $60,010,489; in the South $5,-136,930. In 1855, the banking capital of the North amounted to $230,100,340 ; of the South, $107,078,940.

Up to 1855, the North had excavated 3,682 miles of canals; and had expended $538,313,647 in the construction of 17,855 miles of railroads. The South had only 1,116 miles of canals, and 6,859 miles of railroad, at a cost of $95,252,581.

In the manufactures of the North (1850), with 780,576 workmen, and a capital of $430,240,051, the value of the products amounted to $842,586,058; while in the Southern States, with a capital of $95,029,879, and a corps of 161,733 workmen, they did not exceed $165,413,027.

Just here it is pertinent to inquire why this discrepancy in the manufacturing prosperity of the sections? And at this day of practical observation, and in the light of results, none will attempt to disguise the fact—slavery did not encourage manufactures. Nay. the slave system was opposed to manufactures, and invested the bulk of its capital in agricultural and kindred pursuits under the slave system. But in discussing this point it is well to observe that while capital and appropriate natural objects are vitally essential they are not the only requisites necessary for manufactures. The efficacy of all productive agents, however it may vary at different times and different places, depends upon a variety and due combination of circumstances *moral* as well as *physical.* Foremost among moral causes conducive and essential to prosperity are : 1. Freedom of industry and reasonable hopes of patronage. 2. General diffusion of intelligence among the people. 3. An abundant supply of the most effective laborers and of those

---

[1] Letter to the People of the United States, iii, 42, 1848.

qualified to direct labor.   4. The combination of labor.   We can only briefly examine these points.

1. Was there freedom of industry in the South? that is, did the institution of slavery—supporting an aristocracy in the heart of a republican form of government, and widening the breach year after year between the non-producing and the producing classes, foster and encourage manufacturing arts? We answer, No.   Was there that dignity belonging to labor justly accorded it in the South?   We answer, No.   What hope of reward had the manufacturer in the Southern States? The answer is—the hope was meagre—home manufactures, in general, were only patronized when sudden necessities arose—partly perhaps, on the principle that "charity begins at home," and seldom with a view of upbuilding the industrial arts in our midst.   It will be vain to interpose in defense the possible superiority of Northern material, for we have shown that the richest fields of the most valuable material are within the South.   Vain to say Northern workmanship was more skilled, more dexterous, and better finished.   We meet that objection with the incontestable assertion that increased consumption stimulates effort and the rich rewards of labor excite invention.

2. Was there general diffusion of intelligence among the people?   We merely refer to the half million illiterate adult whites in a population of six and half millions that there was not. The system of education was against the mechanic.   The lack of public schools to educate his children turned him back when he reached Mason & Dixon's "imaginary line."   There were no Boards of Immigration—no agents at the seaports to invite foreigners hither.   The institution of slavery was a wall the European just escaping from the monarchies of Europe did not care to scale.   It was to the interest of the system to keep foreigners at a distance.

The 3d and 4th points are answered already.   In the absence of the essentials enumerated there could be neither an abundant supply of laborers, nor a combination of labor. What was the result?   We will let another tell it.

"It is a well-known fact, that we are compelled to go to the North for almost every article of utility and adornment, from matches, shoe-pegs and paintings, up to cotton-mills, steamships and stationery, that we have no foreign trade, no princely merchants nor respectable artists.   The North is the Mecca of our merchants, and to it they must make two pilgrimages per annum—one in the Spring and one in the Fall. We want Bibles, brooms, buckets and books, and go to the North; we want pens, ink, paper, wafers and envelopes, and we go to the North; we want shoes, hats, handkerchiefs, umbrellas and pocket-knives, and we go to the North; we want furniture, crockery, glass-ware and pianos, and we go to the North; we want toys, primers, school-books, fashionable apparel, machinery, medicines, tombstones and a thousand other things, and we go to the North for them all. . . . . In infancy we are swaddled in Northern muslin; in childhood we are humored with Northern gew-gaws; in youth we are instructed out of Northern books; at the age of maturity we sow our 'wild oats' on Northern soil; in the decline of life we remedy our eyesight with Northern spectacles; in old age we are drugged with Northern physic; and, finally, when we die, our inanimate bodies, shrouded with Northern cambric, are stretched upon the bier, borne to the grave in a Northern carriage, entombed with a Northern spade, and memorized with a Northern slab!" [1]

Fatal facts! Humiliating contrast! Where were our politico-economists all this time? Were our leaders ignorant of the fact that the barbarism or refinement—the retrogression or progression of nations depends more on their productive wealth than on any other circumstance? No people have ever made any distinguished figure in philosophy or the fine arts, without having been at the same time distinguished for their employed riches—and their industry. Pericles and Phidias, Petrarch and Raphael, adorned the flourishing ages of Grecian and Italian commerce. Indeed, the influence of productive wealth, is in this respect, humanly speaking, almost omnipotent. It is the true criterion of civilization. It raised Venice from the bosom of the deep, and made the desert and sandy islands on which she is built, the powerful " Queen of the Adriatic;" and it rendered the unhealthy swamps of Holland the favored abodes of literature, science and art. And yet we were so blind as not to see.

We remember once reading of an English manual of etiquette intended for persons in good society, which contained a solemn warning against walking fast in the street, on the ground that it would lead people to take you for a " business man "—that is, for a man with work to do or engagements to

---

[1] Helper, p. 21, 1860.

keep.   It is not very long too, since a witness in an English
court turned savagely on the counsel who was examining him
because he asked him "what his business was," telling him
"he had no business, that he was a gentleman." And it goes
hard with a boy at the more aristocratic English public
schools to acknowledge that his father does anything to make
money, as hard as it went once with an American boy who
confessed to his fellows that his father did nothing. Now,
while it is not Christian to envy any man his good fortune, or
to deny that leisure and amusement are legitimate relaxations
of regular duties :—while we advance neither practical nor
theoretical ideas on communism, and make no attempt to justify all working-class discontent, we do say the practice of such
habits, while tolerable under the *regime* of slavery would be
weak spots under the *regime* of liberty.   It is true that the
citizens of Sparta and of some other Grecian cities, were prohibited from engaging in manufactures or commerce ; true that
Aristotle speaks in the most contemptuous terms of artisans
and merchants ; that Plato proposed banishing them entirely
from his imaginary republic, and that even Cicero, who had
"mastered all the philosophy of the ancient world, and
raised himself above many of the prejudices of his age and
country, does not scruple to affirm that there can be nothing
ingenuous in a work-shop ; that commerce, when conducted
on a small scale is mean and despicable, and when most extended barely tolerable." [1] But "my lords and gentlemen" of
this Practical Republic, while it might have done for the ancient Spartan to turn up his Grecian nose, or the ancient
Roman to turn up his Roman nose at honest labor, it will not
do for the modern American.   But let us have more figures :
    The North in 1855, exported $167,520,693, and imported
$236,847,810 ; represented by a tonage of 4,252,615 tons.
The exportations of the South amounted to $107,480,688,
its importations to $24,586,528, and its tonage to 855,517
tons.
    It is true, that the South was chiefly agricultural, and that
its products passed in a great part through the North.
Thus, for instance, New York alone represented imports
$164,776,511 ;   exports $113,731,238 ; tonnage 1,404,221 ;
manufactured products $237,597,249 ; expense of railroads
$111,882,503 ; banking capital $38,773,288.   This alone is a

---

[1] De Officiis, lib. i, cap. 42.

proof that the South suffered âll commercial and maritime activity to drift to the North, although it possessed excellent seaports and important cities.

Thus let us compare the oldest and most flourishing of the *ante-bellum* Slave States, Virginia, so favored by its great seaports, its position between the North and South, the West and the Atlantic, the richness of its soil and its mines, and the mildness of its climate—let us compare Virginia with the most prosperous of the Free States, New York:

In 1790 New York had 340,120 inhabitants; Virginia, 748,-308. In 1860 New York had 3,880,735 inhabitants; Virginia, 1,596,318. In 1791 New York exported $2,505,465; Virginia $3,130,865. In 1852 New York exported $87,484,456; Virginia $2,724,657. In 1791, the imports of New York and Virginia were equal; but in 1853 the imports of New York amounted to $178,270,999; while those of Virginia only reached $399,004.

Shall we compare two less important States—Massachusetts and North Carolina? The first has a superficies of but 7,800 square miles; the second, of 50,704 square miles. Nevertheless, the first saw its population increase from 378,-717 souls in 1790, to 1,231,066 in 1860; in the second it was 393,751 in 1790, while it was but 992,622, of which 331,059 were slaves in 1860. Both States possess excellent harbors. Boston in 1860 had become the second commercial city of the United States; Beaufort was scarcely known by name. The imports of Massachusetts in 1855 were $45,113,774, exports $28,190,925, tonnage 970,727 tons; while North Carolina's imports were $243,088, exports $433,818, and its tonnage, 60,077 tons.

In 1850, the products of the arts, manufactures, and mines of Massachusetts amounted to $151,137,145; those of North Carolina, $9,111,245. But in 1856 Massachusetts had increased the amount to $288,000,000, and valued her property at $574,342,286; while the valuation of North Carolina, including Negroes, did not exceed $226,800,472; and as the property in the city of Boston alone was estimated at $250,-000,000, we see that this city alone might have bought up the whole State of North Carolina.

But it was constantly affirmed that the North was a manufacturing region, unfitted for cultivation, and dependent to great extent on the South for subsistence. This was another very great mistake. According to the census of 1860 the total agricultural production—general products, viz: wheat, oats, corn, potatoes, rye, barley, buckwheat, beans and peas, grass-seed, linseed, garden stuff, pot herbs and fruits amounted in the North to 499,190,041 bushels, valued at $351,709,703; in the South they amounted to 481,766,889 bushels, valued at $306,927,067.

In special products, viz., hay, hemp, hops, flax, maple-sugar, tobacco, wool, butter and cheese, wax and honey, cotton, cane-sugar and rice (these three last being raised only in the South), the total amount produced in the North was 28,878,064,902 pounds, valued at $214,422,523; while at the South it amounted to 4,338,370,661 pounds, valued at $155,-233,415. Thus, it will be seen that the total balance of the value of general and special products was $99,971,744 in favor of the North.

Except in *cotton*, its principal wealth, *cane-sugar* and *rice*, which the South alone produced, and *corn, beans and peas, hemp, flax, tobacco* and *wax*, which the South produced in greater quantity, except in these products, the North had the advantage. "The South had cotton, which is the bread of machinery; the North had wheat, which is the bread of man."[1]

It may be even remarked, that the quantity of hay produced by the North was in itself alone superior to the *total* quantity of the special products of the South. Cochin's figures are as follows:

Product of hay in the Free States was, 12,690,982 tons.
Which, at $11.20, worth $142,138,998
Special products of the South,...................... 138,605,723
                                                        ——————
        Difference,................................. $3,533,275

These special products were:

Cotton, 2,445,779 bales, each 400 ℔s., at $32.00......$78,264,928
Tobacco, 185,026,906 ℔s., at 10 cents per ℔.......... 18,502,390
Rice, 215,313,497 ℔s., at 4 cents per ℔............... . 8,612,539
Hay, 1,137,784 tons, at $11.20 per ton................... 12,743,180
Hemp, 34,673 tons, at $112.00 per ton................... 3,883,376
Cane-sugar, 227,133,000 ℔s., at 7 cents per ℔......... 16,599,310
                                                        ——————
        Total...............................$138,605,723

---

[1] Cochin's Result of Slavery, p. 49.

The result was again in favor of the North, if we compare the agricultural products per acre. The North by free labor, improved implements, deep plowing, sub-soiling and manures, gathered to the acre 12 bushels of wheat, 27 of oats, 31 of corn and 125 of potatoes; while the South, with far more fertile lands, gathered to the acre 9 bushels of wheat, 17 of oats, 20 of corn and 113 of potatoes.

To this difference of products naturally corresponded an enormous difference in the revenues and capital value of lands. In the North the value of real and personal property in 1850 was $4,102,172,108, yielding a revenue of $18,725,-211. In the South the value of real and personal property amounted to $2,936,090,737;[1] revenues $8,343,715.

In 1850, the average value of land in the Northern States was $28.07; Northwestern States $11.39; Southern States $5.34; Southwestern States $6.26.

We might also compare the number and value of animals, the value of farming materials, etc., but it is enough to have demonstrated by manifold proofs: 1st. That the agricultural strength of the North under free labor was superior to the agricultural strength of the South with slave labor. 2d. That if the South had specific products—cotton most of all—these products were far from possessing the importance assigned them. 3d. That progress was manifesting itself more and more in the North; that the disproportion was decreasing from day to day in the South. 4th. That this condition was not only injurious to the slaveholding population, but injurious to the landholders who owned no slaves, and whose property was depreciated by reason of this scourge. Now landholders of this sort were numerous, for it was estimated that of the 544,926,720 acres which compose the superficies of the slave States, 173,024,000 acres were held by slaveholders; 40,000,000 by the Government, and 331,902,720 acres by non-slaveholders.

According to the census of 1850, there were in the South 347,525 slaveholders, in a total population (in the United States) of 23,047,898 inhabitants. These 347,525 slaveholders possessed some 3,200,304 slaves,[2] divided as follows:

---

[1] Cochin says, (p. 50,) "If the value of slaves, estimated at $1,600,000,000 be deducted, a difference remains of $2,766,081,371." Elsewhere, however, we cite Dr. Baldwin's valuation of the slaves in 1858 at $2,700,000,000. We leave our readers to adjust the difference, since the general results will not be materially altered.

[2] Results of Slavery, p. 110.

Owners of a single slave, ... 69,820
"   from   1 to   5.................................103,683
"   "   5 to 10.................. 80,763
"   "   10 to 20............................... 54,595
"   "   20 to 50............................... 29,733
"   "   50 to 100............................... 6,196
"   "   100 to 200............................... 1,479
"   "   200 to 300...............................   187
"   "   300 to 500...............................   56
"   "   500 to 1000..............................   9
"   over 1000...................   2

"But lastly," says Cochin, "judging by facts, we become sure that slavery destroys prosperity, whether we compare a State with itself at different epochs, or draw a parallel between two neighboring States, placed in like condition of fertility, climate and population."[1]   Here are the figures:

KENTUCKY.

	Wheat.	Rye.
Crop of 1840	4,803,152 bushels.	1,321,373 bushels.
Crop of 1850	2,142,822 bushels.	415,073 bushels.
Diminution,	2,660,330 bushels.	906,300 bushels.

TENNESSEE.

	Wheat.	Tobacco.
Crop of 1840	4,569,692 bushels.	29,550,432 ℔s.
Crop of 1850	1,619,386 bushels.	20,148,932 ℔s.
Diminution,	2,950,306 bushels.	9,401,500 ℔s.

VIRGINIA.

	Rye.	Tobacco.
Crop of 1840	1,482,799 bushels.	75,347,106 ℔s.
Crop of 1850	458,930 bushels.	56,803,227 ℔s.
Diminution,	1,023,869 bushels.	18,543,879 ℔s.

ALABAMA.[2]

	Wheat.	Rye.
Crop of 1840	838,052 bushels.	51,000 bushels.
Crop of 1850	294,044 bushels.	17,261 bushels.
Diminution,	544,008 bushels.	33,739 bushels.

But we close this portion of our work by making the

[1] Results of Slavery, p. 51.
[2] It ought to be stated in part explanation that it frequently happened the Southern planter would put his whole crop in cotton and in nothing else. And on the other hand it has been said that the Northern farmer "sold everything he could eat, and ate everything he could not sell."

following extract from M. de Tocqueville's oft-quoted book on America:

"The traveler who, embarked on the Ohio, suffers himself to be floated down the river by the current to its confluence with the Mississippi, steers, we may say, between liberty and slavery, and he has only to cast his eyes about him to judge in an instant which is more favorable to the human race.

" On the left bank of the river the population is thinly scattered; from time to time, a group of slaves are seen wandering with a careless air over the half-barren fields; the primitive forest constantly re-appears; one would say that the community was asleep; man seems inactive, and Nature alone offers the image of activity and life.

" On the right bank of the river, on the contrary, arises a confused hum proclaiming from afar the presence of manufactures; rich harvests cover the ground, elegant residences announce the taste and care of the workman; on every side, competence reveals itself, man appears wealthy and contented; —he labors."[1]

"On both banks," adds Cochin, in 1860, "the air is alike healthy, the climate temperate, the soil inexhaustible; each of them forms the boundary line of a vast State; on the left Kentucky, in which slaves are admitted; on the right, Ohio, which has rejected them from her midst. Kentucky was founded in 1775, Ohio, not till 1787; the latter has already 250,000 inhabitants more than the former."

But if we look at political influence, by an incredible contrast—the scene shifts—the South predominates. However, this is treading on dangerous ground, and before going even one step farther, we propose to quote from an authority of the very highest character. We refer to that distinguished gentleman, Hon. Alexander H. Stephens, of Georgia, who became Vice-President of the Southern Confederacy, and from whose speech delivered before the Georgia Convention on secession, January 16, 1861, we make following extract:

" What have we to gain by this proposed change in our relations to the General Government? We have always had the control of it, and can yet, if we remain in it, and are united as we have been. We have had a majority of Presidents chosen from the South, as well as the control and management of most of those from the North. We have had sixty years of Southern Presidents to their twenty-four, thus controlling the Executive department. So of the Judges of the Supreme Court—we have had eighteen from the South, and but eleven from the North; although nearly four-fifths of the judicial business has arisen in the free States, yet a majority of the Court has always been from the South. This we have required, so as to guard against any interpretation of the Constitution unfavorable to us. In like manner, we have been equally watchful to guard our interests in the legislative branch of the government. In chosing the presiding Presidents (*pro*

---

[1] De Tocqueville, Tom ii, p. 298.

tem.) of the Senate, we have had twenty-four to their eleven. Speakers of the House, we have had twenty-three and they twelve. While the majority of the Representatives, from their greater population, have always been from the North, yet we have so generally secured the Speaker, because he, to a great extent, shapes and controls the legislation of the country. Nor have we had less control in every other department of the General Government. Attorney Generals, we have had fourteen, while the North have had but five. Foreign ministers, we have had eighty-six, and they fifty-four. While three-fourths of the business which demands diplomatic agents abroad is clearly from the free States, from the greater commercial interests, yet we have had the principal embassies, so as to secure the world's markets for our cotton, tobacco and sugar, on the best possible terms. We have had a vast majority of the higher offices of both army and navy, while a larger proportion of the soldiers and sailors were drawn from the North. Equally so of clerks, auditors and comptrollers filling the Executive department, the record shows, for the last fifty years, that of the three thousand thus employed, we have had more than two-thirds of the same, while we have but one third of the white population of the Republic. Again, look at another item, and one, be assured, in which we have a great and vital interest; it is that of revenue, or means of supporting government. From official documents we learn that a fraction over three-fourths of the revenue collected for support of government has uniformly been raised from the North."

Comment on this is unnecessary, In a moment of madness the people suffered passion to prevail. Quick, sharp, suddenly, almost without warning, a frightfu calamity burst over the land. Open war, and war in all its horrors, was now begun. All the soft workings of humanity—what Shakspeare calls the "compunctious visitings of nature"—were now absorbed in the raging and insatiable thirst for battle. The death rattle of the war drum sounded! The murderous thunder of artillery—the lurid lightning of powder—the flash of cold, hungry steel—the glare of the torch—these, these, were the instruments employed by the demons of hate to drown the whir of machinery, to stifle the throbbing heart of trade—to blanche the rosy cheek of beauty and shed the rich sweet blood of brothers. O, Beneficent God of Peace! O, Compassionate God of Love!—forgive, forgive, this people. Our land, the richest and the fairest of the globe—from Sumter to Appomatox—for a thousand leagues was streaked with the graves of our kindred, shrouded with the deadly nightshade of sorrow, and silent under the dominion of terror. And yet the pen of the poet, the pencil and chisel of the artist, and even the voice of God's ministers were busied in maintaining the prestige of human havoc. But the true philanthropist was grieved to the soul by the sad spectacle of weakness and depravity manifested at almost the latest hour of human enlightenment, and the political economist, the real friend of nations, shrunk with amazement and horror from the desolated fields, the burned and bombarded cities, the shattered monuments of skill and industry, and the waste of power, genius and resources, with which the insensate fury of a few was permitted to disfigure the abode of intelligent beings.

It is true the Southern States, in the act of secession, committed a rash and thoughtless, but surely not a guilty deed. The right they exercised was inexpressibly injudicious, but it is a right that pulsates at the very core of American institutions. It was a heroic struggle for the liberties, the lives, the consciences, the affections, the immortal hopes of eight millions of Christian men, women and children—a grand and glorious struggle for that same immortal freedom for which we are now contending. Those who make their individual opinions of right the absolute touch-stone of human virtue must be without sin themselves before they can cast a stone. Otherwise they become the persecutors of men, when they should be the advocates of doctrine. Before a common Creator and Judge let every man stand or fall. "The *fact* of property in man is now a thing of the past in our country, and the most zealous supporters of the policy which has cancelled it, the most ardent advocates of human equality, ought to reflect whether they do not violate their own almost deified code when they visit still with their anathemas those who decline to confess themselves sinners above others because they owned slaves. God grant that Americans may speedily outgrow all remaining taints of tyranny which shows itself in hating a man because of his creed, and stand before the world in fact, as they do in name, a brotherhood on the matchless basis of unfettered conscience, the keystone of the structure which shelters them." Above all, now that slavery is gone, let us look to it that our government becomes a government of consent, and not a government of force, let us look to it that the spirit of American liberty be not crucified in her own temple. The Southern people are liberty-loving, they are generous, they are humane, and the one solemn regret that now lives in their heart of hearts, as expressed by their recent leaders and by the people is, that the South herself did not free the slaves.

The frightful waste of property in that war has scarcely been realized. Indeed it mounts up into figures almost beyond human comprehension. It is greater in the aggregate

4

than the combined expenditures of all the European wars since 1851, including the Crimean, the Italian of 1859, the Schleswig-Holstein, the Austro-Prussian, the Franco-Prussian and Turko-Russian wars.[1] It is said that the general expenditure of Great Britain upon war debt and warlike preparations since 1851, amounts to nearly seventy hundred millions of dollars,[2] but the cost of our late war, including the value of the slaves, will exceed this by about twenty-seven hundred millions and run up to the almost inconceivable sum of *ninety-seven hundred millions of dollars!* This sum at $100,000 per mile would build a railroad in length about four times the circumference of the globe, and could make nabobs of a company of contractors as large as the present United States army. Figures so enormous leave the human imagination helpless—but we gain some idea of what the tax upon the nation is when we say that it would be equal to about ten dollars per head for the population of the whole globe—the vast hordes—enlightened and unenlightened, civilized, barbarous and savage—ten dollars for every man, woman and child. And estimating the population of the United States at 50,000,000 is equal to one hundred and ninety-four dollars for every man, woman and child under the fair and ample folds of our starry flag. This sum has been taken from the productive capital of the country and utterly wasted in a conflict between Christian people who might have settled the dispute by calmer arbitrament. What wonder, therefore, that business lagged? What wonder that the world's work was left undone? When men tempt God they must bitterly—and

---

[1] Our figures are taken from a tract issued by the London Peace Society in 1877, and are as follows:

American civil war, the North..........................	$4,700,000,000
" " " the South..	2,300,000,000
To which we add—Value of slaves............................. ..	2,700,000,000
	$9,700,000,000

Crimean war...	$1,700,000,000	
Italian war of 1859...............................	300,000,000	
Schleswig-Holstein war............................	35,000,000	
Austrian and Prussian war in 1866............	330,000,000	
Franco-Prusian war.............................	2,500,000,000	
Other wars, expeditions, etc......................	200,000,000	
		5,065,000,000
	$5,065,000,000	
Leaving the frightful balance against us of..		$4,635,000,000

[2] The exact figures of Great Britain's expenditure are $6,528,163,995. But in the above list of wars, expeditions, etc., the allied expedition against China, the Indian mutiny, Abyssian, and Ashantee campaigns are excluded.

they always bitterly rue it. Some cruelly sarcastic wag of the North called the war, "the late unpleasantness;" another, more philosophic, in the South, termed it, "the rich man's war, but the poor man's fight." But enough is said, when we make bold to assert, that while the South rallied to a man to defend her soil, not a corporal's guard could be gathered to re-enslave the Negro.

The Southern people have complained bitterly against the manner in which the Federal armies waged the war. They think it was dishonorable in the North to raise the cry "Preservation of the Union!" while the freedom of the Negro was their real object. Judged from the Southern standpoint so it was. The fair and manly thing, they think, would have been to have unfurled the abolition flag in the outset. But "it was not on their banners, it was not in their war-cry, nor in their shouts of victory, nor is it on their monumental tablets, nor in their engrossed laws and decrees."[1] Yet what is the view from the other side? We know that there is a chivalry, courage and dignity of character at the North just as we know there is dauntless valor, and Christian conscience and a high-toned moral culture at the South. If the South loved the Constitution, so too did the North. If abolition was repugnant to the South, slavery was revolting to the North. By the letter of the Constitution, to which the sons of the North were bound by the solemnity of an oath, they had no right to touch it. Abraham Lincoln although an anti-slavery man, had sworn to obey the Constitution, and did not dare violate his oath. But when the Southern States tried to dissolve the Union—when they threw off their allegiance and refused to return to the compact of their fathers, then came the moment of action with the North. It had to be either a severed Union and a meaningless Constitution, or an invaded Constitution, a solid and indissoluble Union—and freedom for all her people.

As on the question of slavery, so too in regard to the Constitution, both North and South were blameworthy. We have heard a vast deal of "gas" and "buncombe'" and noisy harangue about that venerable document. Much of it reminds us of the speech Boyle Roche once made in the Irish Parliament: " Mr. Speaker, I would give the half of the Constitu-

---

[1] From a recent address delivered by Gen. Jno. S. Preston, of South Carolina, before the Students of the University of Virginia.

tion—nay the whole of it—to preserve the remainder."
Humbuggery is a prominent trait in the American character,
and, to-day when a man asserts his undying love for the Constitution one is tempted to inquire which half he means.   To
be more serious—we behold a certain class holding it above
the sacred faith of the Christian, and denying God admission
to its articles—while another, nay both, set it at defiance and
break it at will.   But men cannot debar the Omnipotent
Deity from interference with their affairs.   He holds the nation responsible for the sins of the politicians.   The people
must be wise therefore, in choosing.   And the rulers must be
just and forbearant, must be pious as well as patriotic—must
realize the awful solemnity of duties attached to office-holding.
Come then let us reason together.   Is there not apt illustration of our system of government in the sacred relations of
social marriage?   Marriage relations to be harmonious and
happy must be mutual—must be voluntary.   Concert of action
binding on one side must be binding on the other.   Freedom to one side to act alone is freedom to both sides.   It is
not granted to the man that he may be tolerably faithful any
more than it is allowed to the woman that she may be tolerably virtuous.   Loyalty in the strictest and severest letter of
the law—that is the fulfillment of the marriage contract.   So
too was this the contract of marriage between the States—
the solemn and holy union of sections.   "What therefore
God hath joined together, let no man put asunder!"

One word more as to Mr. Lincoln.   He had not only sworn
to *obey*, but also to *protect* the Constitution.   The stern justice
of the hour required heroic nerve.   "Honest Abe" they called
him and as "Honest Abe" history has written his epitaph.
Then could we but forecast our vision to a future and liberty-
adoring century—what would we behold?   It would be the
picture of a grand, though uncouth man of these times, in
whose rugged but manly bosom there waged fierce conflict
between the opposing forces of duty and of conscience.   We
would behold him sitting with the severity of a judge weigh-
ing—in one scale, the merits of the Constitution—in the
other, the most stupenduous question of modern ages.   The
thunders of battle without the walls of the Capitol do not move
him—but when the moment of decision comes—"with charity
to all, with malice toward none"—his heart, *his heart
alone*, turns the scale 'for Humanity's sake and honest conviction decides for Liberty!   And we would behold a halo of

peculiar glory encircling his name—like that which blazes around the martyrdom of a patriot and a philosopher—like that which surrounds the memory of Socrates and Regulus. And the verdict would be, he serves his party not alone, who serves his country most. The performance of a deed for humanity's sake does not put a jewel in the diadem of party splendor, but embellishes the historic page of one's birthland and one's times. In all the wide fields of human endeavor those deeds that shine out conspicuously bright are those which look beyond self—beyond party—to country and mankind. We lose sight of Andrew Jackson's *Democracy* when we read his stern epigrammatic sentence, "The Federal Union; it must and shall be preserved." We do not think of Henry Clay as simply an *Old Line Whig* while remembering his noble utterance, "I would rather be right than be President." And so the generous North of to-day eulogizes the valor of Robt. E. Lee and Stonewall Jackson, and so we of the South have come to respect the memory of Abraham Lincoln and to regard it as a rich heritage of the nation.

But the hour for the Negro's independence had struck; the fruit was ripe; it dropped from the tree. Things apparently incompatible and antagonistic worked in its favor. Many men fought on the Federal side who were not abolitionists, and many on the Confederate side who were not slaveholders. Surely then there must have been a stronger and a higher Hand at work shaping the destinies of this country than that of the Federal or Confederate soldier: For when we remember the glorious intrepidity—the splendid dash of the Southern troops—the heroic sacrifices of the Southern people, we believe that in almost any other cause they would have triumphed, but in this cause God seems to have turned his face aside, and Hope, that glittered like a sunlit sword, was quenched in gloom!

In the midst of the frightful carnage and fearful destruction, the Negroes stood aghast with terror. They did not fly to arms, though their own freedom was involved. They never fought until the arms were placed in their hands, and comparatively few then. As they had been the innocent cause of the terrible struggle, so they remained, with exceptions, to the close. Ah, who can tell that beyond their black skins there did not beat hearts of honor and love for "old marster" and "old mistis." And yet why should they have honored and

loved us? Was it not rather their fidelity and obedience to
God that sheathed the glittering blade, and left unlit the mid-
night torch? Many a matron throughout the South retired to
rest in dread of what might befall herself and her children
before morning. Many a master slept in peace and security.
But was it to the credit of the master that he slept, or to the
credit of the slave? " Two men went up into the temple to
pray; the one a Pharisee, and the other a publican. The
Pharisee stood, and prayed thus with himself, God, I thank
thee, that I am not as other men are, extortioners, unjust,
adulterers or even as this publican. I fast twice in the week,
I give tithes of all that I possess. And the publican, standing afar off, would not lift up so much as his eyes unto heaven,
but smote upon his breast, saying, God be merciful to me a
sinner."[1] Two men die a century apart; the one before, the
other after Jesus Christ; the one named Spartacus, the other
St. Peter. The slave Spartacus exclaims to his fellows,
" Arise, revenge yourselves!" The fisherman Peter, repeats
to the wretched the words of the Redeemer, " Blessed are
the poor for they shall be comforted." Watching their flocks
by night some Judean Shepherds saw a blazing planet
tremble and pause over Bethlehem's plains, and an angel of
the Lord descending and saying, " Fear not; for, behold, I
bring you good tidings of great joy, which shall be to all
people . . . Glory to God in the highest, and on earth
peace, good will toward men."[2] Toiling by day in the fields
of the South the slaves bent their ears to catch these "good
tidings" of gentleness and justice. To them liberty was
sweet—and the picture of hope—when they dared to hope,
was very beautiful. To them liberty was sweet, but the war
seemed like the very "blackness of darkness." Not a streak
of light in all the heavens! Huddled in the contraband
camps, the few fugitives congregated—"a homeless, friend-
less, pitiable throng, suffering from cold, hunger, sickness and
death." At home on the old plantation were their kindred
faithfully serving to the last.[3] But, oh, fellow countrymen,

---

[1] Luke xviii, 10–13.   [2] *Ibid*, xi, 10–14.

[3] We have before us a work testifying to this, and giving a Southern war-view of the
Negro's fidelity. It is entitled, " The South Vindicated," and was written by the Hon.
James Williams, late American Minister to Turkey, from the 2d American Edition,
published at Nashville, Tenn., Confederate States of America, by the Southern Methodist Episcopal Publishing House, and reprinted in London by Longman, Green & Longman, 1862. Mr. Williams says: "No people have ever had more unmistakable evidences that they were guided and directed by an overruling Providence, which smiled

no power, no prison-wall can hinder the voice of freedom from reaching the heart of the captive. Valiant hearts and strong arms, and double-shotted cannon faced the invader, but "Liberty said, Let there be light, and, like a sunrise on the sea, Athens arose."

We therefore, on behalf of the Americo-African challenge all history to produce a like instance of sublime moral courage and Christian patience under wrong and oppression. We may talk of Spartan firmness and Roman bravery—but they were freemen. We remember the bloody revolts of the slaves in Santo Domingo, in Greece and Sicily, but are struck by the happy contrast our land presents. There can be but one conclusion to the whole matter and that is this. Blessed be God, for he is just; he does not permit liberty to be wedded to servitude, and his sovereign hand in falling heavily upon the United States, did not smite liberty; but it blighted, it convulsed, it forever condemned slavery.

Then do our fellow Southerners see nothing to admire, nothing to pity in these poor unfortunates? Will they consent to keep up race prejudices and despise the Negro simply because he is a Negro? Let us appeal to the infallible oracle of equity that holds court in the conscience of every true Southerner. Let us have the answer, gentlemen. Before the war they were obedient, docile, patient, profitable servants. Some brought forth thirty, some forty, some an hundredfold on the investment. And now having enjoyed the fruits of their labors, and the fruits of the toiling generations gone before, with justice you might say—and ere long with justice you *will* say, "Well done good and faithful servants. You did not rise in revolt against us, but while we were at the front of battle, and our homes unguarded, you remained at home and made the crops and protected our wives and chil-

upon their undertaking, than have the people of the South since the commencement of their great struggle. To crown all, we have been blessed with the most bountiful crops that have ever before been garnered in recompense for the toils of the husbandman. While our free citizens have shouldered their muskets and have gone forth to fight the battles of their country, the Africans are contentedly working in the fields. Faithful and true to the interests of their masters; watching with kind solicitude over the unprotected women and children who have been left with no other defense than their fidelity afforded; rejoicing in the successes or mourning over the reverses of the Southern armies, of which they are themselves a chief element of strength by means of the products of their labor; resisting alike the promises and threats of the Yankee invaders; they have put to shame the enemies of the South, who predicted their unfaithfulness, and have taught mankind a lesson of experience in regard to the influences and nature of the institution of slavery in the Southern States, which it is to be hoped will be more instructive than the speculative theories which have hitherto formed the basis of public opinion."

dren. Such faithfulness challenges our admiration. Such
obedience merits our gratitude. Then let the wasted treasure be a sacrifice, let the blood be a libation forever between
our race and thine. We give you the cordial grasp of
friendship. Our country is thy country, and our God thy
God." [1]

And when this generous sentiment, which is growing day
by day, takes root in the hearts of our people, a pæan of joy
will ring through the land, and peace and plenty will bless our
prayers and reward our labors. But we must hasten on.
Not, however, without touching upon a subject intimately
connected with this. The North has marked the return of
the South to power with astonishment and alarm. She
has seen the South sending her bravest Confederate Generals
to Congress, and electing soldiers to offices in the various
States. She forgets that some of our best soldiers have also
been made bishops and clergymen, professional men, business
men—and men in all the walks of life. So, while there
is cause for astonishment there is none for alarm. When the
" Conquered Banner " went down in blood and tears—it fell
to wave no more, it fell to wave no more! When her heart-
broken soldiers turned their footsteps toward their ruined
homesteads, they did so as resolutely to keep their *paroles of
honor* as they had been brave and enterprising and daring to
defy. They accepted the situation—they accepted the results
of the war in good faith, and having fought the good fight
they have kept the faith. It is true there have been out-
breaks and lawlessness in certain quarters, but the par-
ticipants were not representative of the Southern people.
A nation should not be judged by the sins of her criminals—
neither should the South be held responsible for the outlawry

---

[1] The recent Southern General Conference received two fraternal delegates from the
African Methodist Episcopal Church, who, in our hearing, made a remarkable speech
each. The second speaker, Johnson, uttered one of the most beautiful extempore passages we have ever heard. Said he, in effect · " Brethren, there happened in this ante-
room just now a circumstance I shall never forget. You remember that David in the
cave of Adullam sighed for water from the well of Bethlehem, and three young men,
at the peril of their lives, brought the longed-for water, when David would not, after
all, drink, since it had been procured at the peril of life. He therefore poured out the
water as a libation before the Lord." Said the speaker, " When I entered this room I
was fevered, and, like David, longed for water. A gentleman took a goblet to serve me.
During his absence I learned that he was the Governor of Georgia. Realizing the chasm
between us, I thought of David, and taking the goblet from his hand I begged that I
might pour out the water as a libation forever between his race and mine." We never
saw a house more stricken, thrilled and melted by speech from any human orator.—
North-western Christian Advocate.

of the few. A people so rich in all the elements of Christian heroism cannot be kept down.   Heaven and earth has need and use for their talents, their genius, their wisdom, their courage and their integrity.   Divinely commissioned, they are moving forward in the high and holy privilege of redeeming their section, of adding to the brightness of her imperishable glory, and inscribing our country's fame above the *nomina clara* of all other nations.   Therefore, when the cause of the war had been removed, when the shackles of bondage fell from the limbs of the Negro, God's fiat went forth, "Thus far, no farther!"

"DIVINE SANCTION" OF SLAVERY.

It is both curious and interesting to note—now that the Negro is free, the change of sentiment that has taken place in the South as to "divine sanction" (?) of slavery.   Here and there may be found a former slaveholder who clings to the old idea, and here and there one who does not believe much in the divinity of anything, who would wish to have his slaves again, but the great majority freely express themselves to the contrary, they believe the curse has been removed, and are honestly and heartily rejoiced to see the race exalted to the station of freemen.   The many vicissitudes that have come upon the South they think are evidences of God's determination to burn this truth into their souls with the red-hot iron of affliction, and as amicability between the races is extending year by year, and as the lines are becoming adjusted to the new order of things, future peace, prosperity and happiness will be their portion.   Those who wish for the re-enslavement of the Negro are usually hard-hearted, mercenary men, who do not consider their fellow-men from any other point than their actual money value—the cent. per cent., rather than the goodness in their hearts or the unspeakable possibilities of mind and soul.   However, this is not strange.   Money is mammon.   Mammon is God's enemy and theirs, and ours.   Millions of souls now accursed have turned away from the high and holy One to fall down and worship the other.   Millions are to-day bound by the same horrible creed.   It has been so always, God forbid that it should be so forever!

But let us speak of the better class of Southerners.   It was a severe blow to them to lose their fortunes. It brought hardships and suffering upon thousands of worthy people. It smote the just with the unjust; it did not spare the widow nor the orphan. But it has proved a blessing notwithstanding. It is bringing out the true manhood and womanhood of the South. The real worthy will stand; the unworthy will fall. The patient and the true will triumph, but the vainglorious and the indolent must ever succumb. Sooner or later this struggle had to come, and it is better for us that it came when it did than to have left posterity to answer for what we might have righted. The truth is summed up in this, The hour of mankind's deliverance has struck, the cycle of bondage is completed. Force, for six thousand years triumphant, must henceforth divide empire with reason. A spirit of inquiry is abroad. Justice has indeed arisen! The enlightened world is on the side of liberty!

Our battles were world battles! The ideas we combatted for, the ideas we combatted against—are essential to liberty anywhere; and there is not an oppressed being on the globe —oppressed by any species of usurpation—that has not an interest in our affairs. We were watched by kings and queens and peasants. From lordly mansions, from poor men's cottages, eager eyes looked on. Our free institutions —free schools, cheap government, voluntary religion, open ballot-box—were for years shaking the monarchies of the old world. All eyes turned hither, for it involved the destiny of the coronet and the sceptre, it involved the freedom of peasant, serf, slave and savage. By our suffering we have not only recovered all but lost manhood, but we are living a higher and a nobler life. Above our fair flag is a fairer sky— and America to-day wears upon her brow the jewel of the world's freedom.

Nor do the Southern people expect to be remunerated for their slaves. To look for such bounty from our Government would be vainer than a dream, and besides, if they take it, they may touch *unholy gold.* All they want now is to be treated fairly. Grant this, and the future of the South will be a future of diversified industries, and busy fingers and happy homes; a land in which brain and muscle shall unite in common cause, and gather from Nature her choicest fruits and her richest treasures; a land which shall meet the increasing wants of its people by a constant improvement in the methods of production, and which shall scatter its abundance, with a lavish hand, on all who think and all who toil.

Twenty years ago, however, there were many people who believed in the "divine sanction" of slavery. The advocates of the system from a religious standpoint argued that the curse of Noah pronounced upon Canaan (Gen. ix, 25) involved alike "the general inferiority of the Hamitic race, and its specific condemnation to the lowest degree of political servility, consigning it either to national or personal bondage, or to both, 'until the times of the restitution of all things.'"[1] What wonder then, a creed so solemnly taught should have been battled for with fierceness? And yet these words, in one shape or another, have been uttered in the pulpit and the Senate; on the stump and in the forum; they have been read in books and newspapers; they have been heard in assemblies, academies and drawing-rooms. Would to Heaven, we had been quite as zealous, quite as ardent, quite as faithful in keeping all of the laws and commandments as this one involving the hopeless servitude of an unhappy race. And if this condemnation was true—does not the full emancipation of the Negroes indicate that "the times of the restitution of all things" are near at hand? It certainly seems so. The whole impulse and sweep of the age is towards Christian liberty. The Apostles of true science, of art and literature have become apostles of the Gospel, and are extending the triumphs of freedom, peace and joy in every direction. Surely, then, these are lines of blazing and living light running parallel with the deathless truths of God.

It will be interesting though to the reader of to-day to know what were the prevalent opinions twenty years ago. In 1858, Dr. Baldwin, in his remarkable book said:

"God's plan of elevating the Hamitic race to virtue, industry and economy is through the *humility of bondage*. And this being his plan, it is the only really feasible and benevolent one. To interrupt it, or attempt its removal or modification before it has run its needful and natural and appointed course, is to injure the very persons we purpose thereby to assist. It is not philanthropic to sound the trumpet of the great Sabbatic year before the antecedent and appointed years are ended. God has appointed a specific time of rest. 'Six days shalt thou labor,' is his command, 'but the seventh is the Sabbath (not of man but) of the Lord thy God; in it thou shalt not do any work.' The law of labor is as benevolent, under the present constitution of things, as that of rest will be in another."[2]

---

[1] See Baldwin's Dominion, p. 53.   [2] *Ibid*, p. 24

This is a most remarkable prophecy, so remarkable as to be overcharged somewhat with the marvelous, and so marvelous as to read now amazingly like a burlesque, though it comes to us supported by a grave authority and touches upon a subject too serious to treat with contempt. We shall, however, present a number of facts, which we have reason to believe will disabuse the minds of our people of this idea of slavery. The *first* is, that they who defended slavery by the Scriptural argument (and Dr. Baldwin was among the very ablest—perhaps the foremost Southern writer on this subject) seem to have forgotten that the slavery for which they pleaded, was the slavery of the white or red race, not of the black. Their whole defense was based on the curse pronounced upon Canaan, but it never has been and cannot be proved, that the Negroes of South and West Africa are descendants of Canaan, although it has been a 'popular opinion and was usually taken for granted. *Secondly*, It never has been and cannot be proved that the curse on Canaan did not expend itself on his generation. And *thirdly*, Whether the Negroes are descendants of Canaan or not, in five years from the time of Dr. Baldwin's prophecy the emancipation proclamation of Abraham Lincoln was issued—slavery was overthrown, and we of the United States beheld a most wonderful spectacle in the abrogation of the Noachian curse by the march of Christian civilization—the evident advent of the times of "the restitution of all things," when men should cease at once to serve the Devil and turn penitently and truly to serve their God. It cannot be denied that this was the general religious belief in the South. It cannot be explained why, then, if slavery was a divine institution it does not exist. *Results* are what we are looking at. Explain results. And, moreover, if we believe that we listened to false teachings— since the truth has dawned upon our minds, as Christians we ought to acknowledge it. Independence has never been forfeited, manhood has never been lowered, by seeking to do right, to act justly.

Now, the honest belief of no one is impugned, the upright motives of no one is denied, but it is, nevertheless the fact, that when men find in their hearts, a "Law" higher than the Law of God, they often seek to justify by such a law almost every act to which the propensities of the heart lead them. Man likes to justify what he practices. If you talk with a gambler, a thief or a drunkard, or even a murderer, nine out of ten, will show you the justification of their habits or deeds. This very act of justification causes them to follow the evil. To condemn a wrong is to abandon it, at least is a step toward abandonment. History is brimful of such instances. It was in the name of Religion that they burned "witches" at Salem.[1] It was in the name of Religion that the fiery zealot, Oliver Cromwell, perpetrated the most fearful tyrannies and atrocities;[2] in the name of Religion that a million poor Waldenses perished in France; in the name of Religion that nine hundred thousand orthodox Christians were slain in less than thirty years after the institution of the Jesuits; the Duke of Alva boasted of having put thirty-six thousand to death in the Netherlands, by the hands of the common executioner. The Inquisition destroyed by various tortures one hundred and fifty thousand Christians, within thirty years.[3] These are a few specimens, and but a few of those which history has recorded; the total amount will never be known "till the earth shall disclose her blood, and shall no more cover her slain." (Isaiah xxvi, 21). .It does seem, then, that those who sought to justify slavery—that act by which the people of a whole continent and grand division of the earth were in danger of passing *sub jugum*—under the yoke of bondage, while they considered the possible vague character of the curse pronounced upon Canaan should also have considered the words of Revelation—the warning of the Holy Ghost—given twenty-five centuries nearer our times: "If any man have an ear, let him hear. He that leadeth into captivity shall go into captivity; he that killeth with the sword must be killed with the sword."[4]

Seeing however that we have touched upon a subject that demands further elucidation, we shall endeavor to settle those points by introducing the incontestable testimony of history. Both sacred and profane writers record the fact that mankind sprung from the three sons of Noah, and that after the deluge they settled in the three old continents and have permanently inhabited their original localities—no transitions or emigrations having materially altered their continental habitations, except in America. The settlements of Japheth were principally in Europe and Western Asia. Those of Shem were in Asia and America; and those of Ham were in Africa,

---

[1] Upham's History of Witchcraft and Salem Village. vol. ii, pp. 267, 293, 301, 320.
[2] Macaulay's Miscellanies, vol. i, pp. 312, 313.
[3] Fox's Book of Martyrs.   [4] Revelations xiii, 9, 10.

Southern Asia and Australia. The islands pertaining to the several continents were occupied by races from the mainland contiguous. This general distribution was in accordance with a Divine order given in the days of Peleg, great-grandson of Shem, and as St. Paul says (in Acts xiii) God having created the world, hath created from out *one blood* every *type* of men to dwell on every face or fauna of the earth, and "hath determined the times before appointed, and the bounds of their habitation." According to Josephus "The children of Ham possessed the land from Syria and Amanus, and the mountains of Libanus, seizing upon all that was on its seacoasts, and as far as the ocean, keeping it as their own. Canaan, the fourth son of Ham, inhabited the country now called Judea, and called it from his own name, Canaan."[1] One of the sons of Canaan, Sidonious or Sidon, built a city and called it after himself, or as the Greeks called it Sidon. It was on the Levant close by Tyre, and became one of the most powerful maritime and commercial cities of ancient times. But what we wish to state just here is the fact that Ham had four sons, Cush, Mizraim, Phut and Canaan. From Cush, the Ethiopians in Africa, and many tribes in Asia inhabiting part of Arabia, were descended. Mizraim was the ancestor of the Egyptians, Cyrenians and Lybians; or (the word being plural) it may be the general name of the family or tribe whence they sprang. Phut was the ancestor of the Mauritanians. In short all Africa—Central, Southern, East and West, is supposed to have been peopled by Ham's posterity—descendants of his three eldest sons—Cush, Mizraim and Phut. We are told however that divine sanction of African slavery is based upon the curse on Canaan. What a slender thread! What an insecure foundation. The descendants of Canaan now traceable were the Canaanites, the Philistines, and as is quite certain, the Phœnecians. It has never been proved and cannot be proved that " the families of the Canaanites spread

---

[1] The precise language of Josephus was this: "Of the four sons of Ham, time has not at all hurt the name of Chus; for the Ethiopians, over whom he reigned, are even at this day, both by themselves, and by all men in Asia, called Chusites. The memory also of the Mesraites is preserved in their name; for all we who inhabit this country (of Judea) call Egypt Mestre, and the Egyptians Mestreans. Phut also was the founder of Libya, and called the inhabitants Phutites, from himself; there is also a river in the country of the Moors which bears that name; whence it is that we may see the greatest part of Grecian historiographers mention that river, and the adjoining country by the appellation of Phut; but the name,it has now, has been by change given it from one of the sons of Mestraim, who was called Lybyos . . Canaan, the fourth son of Ham, inhabited the country now called Judea, and called it from his own name Canaan."— Antiq. of Jews, vol. i, book i, chap. vi, 2.

abroad." (Gen. x: 18), went in the direction of Central and Southern Africa—from whence our Americo-African was stolen. But admitting that they did go in that direction it remains to be shown how the curse affected one portion of Canaan's descendants and not the other, and that it is possible some of the descendants of Cush, Mizraim and Phut may also have been enslaved.

It makes a great deal of difference as to how a man reads his Bible. If it be said that the Negroes ought to have been enslaved because Noah's curse was a prediction, then polygamy and war are justified, for they are predicted (Deut. xxviii, 30, 68, 43, Jeremiah, Joel, etc). And does the punishment of the wicked by predicting that they will be enslaved, grant amnesty to those who will enslave them? In that case, we had best not condemn the Jews—they are absolved for having crucified Jesus Christ, for it had been foretold.

But the fact is, Ham, Noah, and Canaan had nothing to do with this country, any more than Alexander, Cæsar and Napoleon. And besides, can we conceive that God would condemn to perpetual and compulsory slavery a race whose enormity—distort it as we may—does not approach that of another dispersed though free, whose crime was that of crucifying His Beloved and only Begotten Son?

Nor will it do to interpret or to pretend to interpret that all the sayings in the Bible were figurative, and should be understood to mean only the moral enfranchisement of souls, not the real emancipation of individuals. For while the practice of slavery can warp and stifle the conscience of a Christian, it is powerless to force the impenetrable entrenchment—the citadel of Liberty—that shields a heart that believes in God.

There was therefore no authority for altering the text and reading as some did, "Cursed be Ham the father of Canaan." It does not become us either to alter the Scriptures, or to act unjustly to our fellowman. Coleridge says, and truly, "To dogmatize a crime, that is, to teach it as a doctrine, is itself a crime." On questions of mere doctrine, however, there may be many and diverse interpretations, and each honest from their standpoint. But the historic facts of the Bible are fundamental truths — stable and everlasting. The early history of the world is related in but few words— the Bible alone contains it. Every word therefore must be of importance and seriousness. Having investigated this subject, as we believe, most thoroughly, we fail to find justification of African slavery in the Bible. Perhaps, however, some one more learned than the writer can explain fully—without shadow of doubt, the justice, the truth—even the plausibility of the "Canaan theory." We invite them to do so, nay, we challenge them to prove it. And if it cannot be done, it should be acknowledged, for this is the doctrine some of our theologians taught. *" Fiat justitia ruat cœlum !"*

It is true, that the devoted nations which God destroyed before Israel, were descended from Canaan ; and so, as we say, were the Phœnecians and the Carthageneans, who were at length subjugated with dreadful destruction by the Greeks and the Romans. But we demand proof that the descendants of Ham have always in all ages since the curse been the "servant of servants."[1] Another thing, can any one be *the slave of another slave?* Mede declares that "there never has been a son of Ham, who has shaken a sceptre over the head of Japheth. Shem hath subdued Japheth, and Japheth subdued Shem ; but Ham never subdued either. It is false, for the Egyptians, who were descendants of Mizraim, the son of Ham, subdued Israel, the offspring of Shem. False, for Nimrod, the son of Cush, the son of Ham, subjugated and tyrannized over the descendants of Shem, when " went forth Asshur, and builded Nineveh." (Gen. x, 11.) False, for Hamilcar conquered Spain, and Hannibal gained memorable victories over the Romans, though afterwards defeated by Scipio Africanus. It is true, on the other hand, that Africa for many ages has lain under the dominion of the Romans and then of the Saracens, and later of the Turks. It is true, that most of the inhabitants live in wickedness, ignorance, barbarity, slavery and misery ; true, that many hundreds of these poor Negroes every year are bought and sold, like beasts in the market ; and conveyed from one quarter of the world, to do the work of beasts in another. But this in no measure vindicates the covetous and barbarous oppression of those, who thus enrich themselves with the products of African sweat and blood. God never commanded *us* to enslave

---

[1] Josephus says on this point, "And when Noah was made sensible of what had been done he prayed for prosperity to his other sons, but for Ham, he did not curse him by reason of his nearness in blood, but cursed his posterity. And when the rest of them escaped that curse God inflicted it on the children of Canaan." (See Antiquities of the Jews, vol. i, book i, chap. vi, sec. 2.) But this is the record of Josephus, not of the Bible.

Negroes, as He did Israel to extirpate the Canaanites; and, therefore, He will, as He has always done, severely punish this cruel injustice.

What is slavery? " The condition of absolute bondage, in which one person is the unconditional property or chattel of another, and obliged to labor for his benefit, without his own consent having been obtained."[1] Well, then, it is not an exclusive nor a "specific condemnation." Other nations, other families than the Hamitic people have been subdued—politically and personally—but where is the "divine sanction" for *it?* Slavery has existed in some form in all nations, and still exists in many countries without respect to color, race or country. At what time it originated we have no means of ascertaining. Joseph was sold by his brethren to the Midianite merchantmen, but slaves were held in Egypt long before that time. Kidnapping was a common mode of obtaining slaves for commerce, and it was extensively followed by the *Phœnicians*, as much as 3000 years ago. Slavery first appears in China about thirteen centuries B. C. It existed among the Assyrians, the Babylonians and the Persians. The Jews had some form of slavery from the time of Abraham, with whom their historical existence commences. But in turn they were enslaved by the Egyptians, though their servitude, it is said, was of a political, not a personal nature. Slavery meets us in the annals of Greece—was firmly established in the Hellenic heroic age, and runs back to the legendary period. Prof. Carl Muller, the eminent German philologist and archæologist, whose authority in everything that relates to Greece is very high, thinks that the *helots*, or slaves " were *an aboriginal race*, which was subdued at a very early period, and which immediately passed over as slaves to the Doric conqueror."[2] In Italy, slavery prevailed even more extensively than in Greece. Blair speaks of "slaves being acquired at Rome in the reign of Romulus himself." "From that time the number and importance of the slaves of the Romans are abundantly attested, by authorities of all descriptions, and of every period, down to the fall of the Western Empire."[3] The Roman slaves were obtained by war and by trade, through the operation of law, and by

---

[1] Appleton's Cyclopædia—Slavery—p. 696.
[2] Tuffnell's Translation of Muller's Hellenic Races and Cities.
[3] Blair's Rome, p. 45.

5

birth.   Most of the captives taken at the conquest of Carthage, and who had surrendered, were sold into slavery.
But Corinth, one of the richest and most luxurious cities of
Greece, was destroyed at the same time with Carthage, and
the Corinthians were all sold into slavery.   The wars in
Spain, Illyria, Syria and Macedonia, furnished Rome with
large numbers of slaves.   The conquests of Sylla, Lucullus
and Pompey in Greece and the East, actually flooded the slave
markets, so that in the camp of Lucullus, men were sold for a
sum about equalling sixty-two cents of our money.   Cicero sold
about 10,000 of the inhabitants of Pindenissus.   The Gallic
wars of Julius Cæsar furnished almost a half million of
slaves.   Fifty slaves were a large number for a wealthy
Athenian to own, but some of the Romans owned 20,000
each.   Of Marcus Crassus, the wealthiest Roman of the last
century of the republic, Plutarch says: "Though he had
many silver mines, and much valuable land, and many
laborers on it, still one would suppose that all this was of
little value, compared with the value of his slaves; so many
excellent slaves he possessed—readers, clerks, assayers of
silver, house managers, and table servants; and he himself
superintended their education, and paid attention to it, and
taught them; and, in short, he considered that a master was
mainly concerned in looking after his slaves, who were the
living instruments of domestic economy." [1]   Gibbon estimates
the number of Roman slaves as high as 60,000,000, for at
the height of her power Rome had slaves from Britain, Gaul,
Scandinavia, Sarmatia, Germany, Dacia, Spain. the different
countries of Africa, from Egypt to the Troglodytes of
Ethiopia, the Western Mediterranean islands, Sicily, Greece,
Illyria, Thrace, Macedonia, Epirus, Bithynia, Phrygia, Cap-
padocia, Syria, Media, and almost every other country to
which ambition or avarice could lead the soldier or the
trader to penetrate. [2]   We doubt whether they ever heard of
the "curse on Canaan."   We doubt whether they cared anything about it, and we doubt whether any one can prove to
us the "divine sanction" of Roman slavery.   They spared
no nations, but all races furnished their contributions to the
greatest population of slaves that ever existed under one
dominion, from the most cultivated Greek to the most stupid

---

[1] Plutarch's Lives—"Crassus."   Longhorne's Edition, p. 358.
[2] Decline and Fall of Roman Empire, vol. iv, p. 296.

Cappadocian. Unlike the Greeks, the Romans "acknowledged the general equality of the human species, and confessed the dominion of masters to flow entirely from the will of society;" but this did not prevent them from enslaving all men upon whom they could lay their hands.

It has been asserted that liberty is unknown among the Hindoostanese. As far back as reliable history and reasonable tradition runs, that country and people have been enthralled. First came the Persian conquerors, then the Greeks, then the Syrians, and then the Mohammedans. Genghis Khan and Tamerlane lorded it over them; then came the Mogul Empire established by Sultan Baber, until finally, the British seized and enjoyed dominion. Thus from generation to generation they owned a foreign sway, and so permanent has been their servility that "not a word denoting freedom is known to their vocabulary." The explanation of all this the Pro-slavery theologians attribute to Hamitic extraction, but they fail to prove the point in leaving unexplained the dynasty of Maha-Rajah, which existed for seven hundred years before the arrival of the Persians, as well as other points too numerous to mention.[1]

But let us draw another picture. In the valleys of the Caucasus, between the Black Sea and the Caspian, we may distinguish, in the Caucasian family, those features which ethnologists, without exception, agree are the nearest to perfection. These people have long been noted for the beauty of the women, and for imposing stature, elegance and activity of the men. It is the pride and the boast of the great Aryan family that we sprang from this family—that here is the very fountain of purity. Yet those people are to-day and have been for ages, practicing the very worst sort of slavery —selling their own beautiful women to lives of damning degradation in the harems of the lustful Turk. Dr. Burgess, who has written a volume on "Blushing," affirms that a Circassian maid who *blushes*, brings a higher price in the slave market. Apply the test here. Would any one blaspheme the Redeemer by saying He *justifies* this?

All this may horrify a certain class who have worshipped at this shrine so long that their knee-caps are horny. But let them be patient. We are not laying down a doctrine, but stating facts, which they may disprove if they can. Let them

[1] Baldwin's Dominion, pp. 331, 382.

remember, that all the slavery which they delighted to find in the Bible was the slavery of *white* men, and that the Roman slaves in the time of Christ, whose bondage, we have been told, he and his Apostles approved, were held by the right of war. Other white slaves have been held by the same tenure. We shall present a case very near home to us.

It is a fact, although not generally known, that the conversion of England to Roman Catholicism was due to the sympathy for some English slaves shown by St. Gregory the Great, (who occupied the pontifical throne from 590 to 604.) Touched by the youth and physiognomy of some English children exposed for sale in the market at Rome,[1] Gregory, before becoming Pope, ransomed and instructed them, and prepared them to become the apostles of their country. On becoming sovereign pontiff, he did more; "their progress was slow and his zeal impatient," says Lingard;[2] he sent St. Augustine and his companions to convert the island, where the Saxon, more ferocious than the savages of Africa, who sell their captives taken in war, trafficked even in their fellow-countrymen and their own children.

Thus we might multiply instances, but have room only to mention a few others. In 1513, when the Barbary corsairs ruled the Mediterranean, the *white slaves* in Tunis alone amounted to twenty thousand. Cervantes, the immortal author of Don Quixote, who had himself been a slave in Algiers, says in his writings, "For liberty we ought to risk life itself; slavery being the greatest evil that can fall to the lot of man." In 1793, there were one hundred and fifteen *white American slaves* in Algiers captured by these pirates, and held by a Scriptural tenure, we suppose. We suppose so.

Then what can be said in defense of the slave-traders and man-stealers whether Dutch or Spanish—whether Portugese or English—whether from New England or from the Southern States, who by all sorts of wicked devices kidnapped the ignorant and inoffensive Negroes and transferred them to lives of servitude and degradation. We have not the art to speak decorously of indecorus things, and do not wish to lower our tone, but in this enlightened age will it be overreaching the case to employ a little of the clear-cut truth in characterizing

---

[1] Bede's Eccl. Hist., Lib. ii, chap. i.
[2] Lingard's Antiq. Anglo-Sax., chap. c. i.

them as assassins of liberty, and bold, unscrupulous despoilers
of human freedom?—and will any one give his conscience to the belief that they stole Negroes in accordance
with the curse upon Canaan? Do we plead in extenuation
that the Negro in Africa was in the lowest depths of degradation, of mean and ignoble savagery—and given over to feti-
chism and cannibalism? "I am willing," says Cochin with
power and with truth—"I am willing to believe that the
Negro was more unhappy in Africa; but the question is, not
to know how he was treated in the land of Mahomet, but how
should he be treated in the land of Jesus Christ." [1] Do we
argue that by enslaving the Negro we have lifted him up to
Christian civilization? Oh, yes, we may say that. But we
must acknowledge also that God never justifies evil, though
He sometimes overrules evil that good may follow. Trans-
port missionaries to the Soudan, to the East and the West
coast of Africa, go instruct these heathens, "Go ye into all
the world and preach the gospel to every creature"—that was
the command of Jesus. But to ravish them of all the gifts
of God, of country, of family and liberty, and say to them—
with or without whip in hand "Work! work or starve! work,
for the curse of labor is upon you and not upon us," then, with
the same breath exhort them to "pray!"—do we call this horrible constraint conversion? Strange compensation! Compulsory labor without wages, religion without liberty, a dish
of pottage for a birthright.

Can anything *whatever* be said in defense of the buccaneer
gentry who roamed the high seas a century back—men who
seemed to have formed league with Satan and gloried in the
wicked federation? The word Humanity has had wonderful
effect on the hearts of the noble and the good; it has checked
the ambition and the despotism of modern nations; it is a
word very dear to Christian hearts, for it is preparing the
world for the coming reign of Peace and Love—but what did
eighteenth century pirates care for that? Sighs, and tears,
and agony—the pleas of want and the plaints of woe—seem
to have given but renewed zest to their remorseless greed.
Cold, cruel, stern and pitiless, they struck down the weak and
staggering prosperity of a continent that they might clutch
the fragments of its wreck. "Robbery, by the strong hand,
is as old as man; the plunderer's creed is, 'thou shalt suffer

---

[1] Results of Slavery, p. 79.

ere I suffer;' the spoil changes hands, but the robber's gain is the measure of the robbed one's loss.   Larceny is as old as man ; the child instinctively appropriates whatever it covets, and careful training is necessary to implant or cultivate the moral principle, yet even then, imperious necessity will often condone an act of theft.   Oppression is as old as man ; but the world's greatest scourges, half demon and half god, have yet left the blazon of their public virtues to illume their darkest crimes."   But what shall be said of the robbers of human rights who stole the liberties of a race and turned their tears and blood into filthy gold? who desolated, decimated and crushed the lowest races of Africa? who sullied, divided, and imperilled the highest races of the New World? who blighted germs which might have taken root? who withered the fruits of conscience, and warped the work of reason, courage, virtue, wealth and liberty?   They fill up the full measure of human baseness, and become, we had almost said, joint-heirs with Judas Iscariot.   And yet these are the men who left to us the fatal heritage which the South dragged after it, as the convict drags his ball and chain.

Still, numerous apologies are put forth.   One man convinced of a large self and a small world, feeling his personal superiority over the entire balance of the human race, argues with settled conviction, that somebody, some race *had* to be enslaved.   Another, looking alone to the welfare of society thinks it positively necessary that we should have a permanent laboring class in absolute and perpetual subjection, and still another, bringing the matter home, actually believes that God foreordained that *we* should be free and rich and powerful through the misery and the toil of the Negro.   Away with such shallow apologies!   That sort of argument will not stand the test—will not fit in the exacting scales of justice, but must fly away from the broadening sense of Right as night evanishes before the invincible advance of morning.   It reminds us forcibly of Hogarth's caricature of fat men and lean men.   It is necessary to the equilibrium of the world that every fat man should have a lean man—otherwise human society would be in perpetual revolution, the world would be overturned—antipodes would not be antipodes, and the green globe would lose its equipoise.

But who would consent to be for a single day the *slave* of even his most loving friend?   What man is happy if he be the slave of his own passions, and not of those of another weak and sinful mortal whom God gave over to a reprobate heart when Humanity fell? No one finding himself free would wish to become a slave; no one finding himself a slave but would wish to be free. This settles that question.

On the question of labor, God commanded man to labor, but not to serve. Therefore, we cannot escape the command to labor by imposing that labor upon another. Noah cursed Ham, but Ham does not labor—the curse, so they say, falls on innocent Canaan. Still if Ham was cursed or if Canaan was cursed, what malediction was powerful enough to outlive the pardon of Jesus Christ?

There is no need to argue this question more, though we cannot resist making one more extract from Dr. Baldwin's beautifully written but exceedingly lugubrious—nay, terribly ominous book. He says (pp. 376–377):

"The prophetic history of Ham is brief but mournful. As the second member of the human trinity, a curse is on his fortunes, and the form of a servant on his gloomy generations. Isolated and inferior, he is the national or personal bondman, first of Shem, and then of Japheth. Without political supremacy or divine right to social equality, he is an appointed 'servant of servants to his brethren,' till 'made perfect through sufferings.' The malediction of Jehovah is the comprehensive description of his rights and destiny from Noah to the Judgment. His brethren may advance to dominion, and he also may ascend from primordial degradation; they may exchange relations and rights, and Ethiopia may stretch forth her hands to God, but his political relation remains intact and unaltered. Unlike Esau, he shall not 'rise to dominion, nor break from his neck the yoke of his brothers.' To him dominion and equality are unpledged by the Lord, and what is unpromised is precluded from hope. Barbarism may be banished, amelioration may be realized, and the race may be useful to all nations, but full emancipation can only transpire when nature is re-organized, and the great era of the kingdom dawns on the earth, like immortality on the grave. At the trumpet of jubilee he may leap to liberty, and shout full redemption when the curse, like a tempest, shall fly from creation; till then he will serve, till then be a slave; so the Lord has declared; so the Lord will fulfil."

There is a dense opacity or rather an air of delicious mysteriousness, about this prediction, as there is about much that Dr. Baldwin prophesied. It should not detract from our sincere reverence for that gentleman's memory if we venture to say it is a very convenient, self-adjusting, "back-action" mode of prophesying (and ought to have been patented) to declare startling things couched only in the potential mood; though it reminds us of the old Greek prophet, quoted by Rabelais, who by way of preface used to say, That what he was to tell would either come to pass or not. No matter for that

What is most objected to in this extract is the exaltation of
the mortal, as is implied in the phrase, "the human trinity."
Aside from the syntactical error, it is a phrase belonging
alone to our high and holy Divinity, whose Godhood should
be regarded as too sublimely sacred even for contrast. And,
again, as to the Negro being made "perfect through sufferings" is employment of a similitude not warranted. We
must in all our doings keep ever in view the fact that the
tyranny man imposes upon man is not and cannot be charge-
able to God. We must remember that if a nation is conquered or enslaved through the fortunes of war, it comes from
the avarice, the arrogance or the ambition of the one or the
debasement of the other, and that we cannot justify the
bondage of a distant, unknown, unoffending people by any
such plea. More than this, we must remember that the God
of Christians is love, benevolence, justice; that He is the
Creator of the whole of mankind, and wishes for universal
happiness; that He gives the same laws to all, makes no exceptions, and pays no attention to the appearance of persons;
that He is a Spirit that cannot be confined to temples—is not
confined to nations, but is to be adored by every person
—Jew and Gentile—white and black, in spirit and in truth.
Or to put it still stronger—God is our Father, and not our
Master: we are His children and not His slaves. How is it
possible, then, that we dare assume for political power, what
we refuse to divine Omnipotence?

After the manner, then, of the Wise Man, let us sum up
the argument. "Let us hear the conclusion of the whole
matter."[1]   And permit us to present it in the words of M.
Cochin, whom one is never weary of citing:

"Christianity has destroyed slavery.

"Yes, He who is pre-eminently the Redeemer, he who
has ransomed woman from degradation, children from abandonment, subjects from tyranny, the poor from contempt,
reason from error, the will from evil, the human race from
punishment, Jesus Christ has restored fraternity to mankind
and liberty to man, Jesus Christ has destroyed slavery.

"I find this fact established or affirmed by the most impar-
tial, the most severe, the most renowned writers; it is written
in a long series of laws, decisions and canons, in an uninter-

---

[1] Eccles. xii, 13.

rupted train of historical monuments. This imposing unanimity of testimony confirms the presentiments of universal instinct. Before all demonstration, we comprehend, we divine that Christianity must abolish slavery, as daylight abolishes darkness, because they are incompatible.

"Yes, Christianity has destroyed slavery," [2]

A GLANCE AT AFRICAN HISTORY.

Suppose, however, it could be proven that the Negroes are descendants of Canaan, is there anything in history that justified their enslavement, or marked them *ab origine* as an inferior race? We propose to inquire into these points, and shall dive down into the pages of the past and bring up facts that cannot be controverted. Readers of history and scholars in general are well acquainted with what we shall have to say, but there is such widespread and lamentable ignorance on prominent historic truths, one should not begrudge the space. This ignorance cannot be charged to the lack of educational facilities, and must follow from the taste of the day, though from whatever cause, it does not matter, we all know that truth lies neglected on the book shelves, while grace and fiction occupy the centre-table.

Our proposition then, is this, not to assert that the Phœnicians descended from the Canaanitish tribes, but to say that the weight of proof is that they did, and that if they did, the Negro may boast a lineage and an ancient glory as grand even as that of the Greek and the Roman. Indeed, the Phœnicians deserve to be commemorated in history by the side of the Greek and Latin nations as pre-eminently the diffusers of civilization. They were a race essentially materialistic and commercial. They were the most renowned and the earliest merchants, carriers and colonizers, and might be called the Yankee nation of the ante-Christian ages. Ancient Sidon, the mother-city, was made "very glorious in the midst of the seas," for many isles bought merchandise of their hands; and of far-famed Tyre, the Hebrew prophet has said, "The harvest of the river is her revenue; and she is a mart of nations—the crowning city, whose mer-

---

[1] Results of Slavery, Book vii, p. 282.

chants are princes, whose traffickers are the honorable of the earth."—Isaiah xxiii, 3–8.

Phœnicia—a name derived from the Greek word *phœnix*— a palm-tree,[1] is the name given by the Greek and Roman writers to the narrow region which lies between the hills of Palestine and the mountains of Syria on the east and the Mediterranean on the west.   By the Phœnicians themselves thier country was called Canaan.   The Phœnicians were, almost without doubt, Canaanites by descent.[2]   A portion of the posterity of Canaan left the shores of the Red Sea, and settled in Phœnicia, or the immediate neighborhood.   The descendants of Canaan were Heth, and the Jebusite, (who laid the foundation of the city of Jerusalem), the Emorite, the Girgasite, the Hivite, the Arkite, the Sinite, the Arvadite, the Zemarite and the Hamathite, "and afterwards (as is stated in Genesis x) were the families of the Canaanites spread abroad."   Well, what of that?   Does by being "spread abroad" signify that they were enslaved? or does it justify their enslavement?   Has not the whole of mankind spread abroad until now all of the continents and the remotest islands are peopled.   One portion of Canaan's descendants we may say spread abroad in the direction of interior Africa, while the Phœnician branch in the course of civilization colonized along the Mediterranean, occupying the islands of Cyprus and Crete—along the shores of Northern Africa, establishing themselves at Carthage, Leptis and Utica—along the coasts of Sicily and Sardinia—beyond the Pillars of Hercules—to the Western and Northern coasts of Spain, and even to the British islands and the borders of the North Sea—here and there, they founded cities, planted colonies and built naval stations.   In the East their richly freighted vessels sailed down the Persian and Arabian Gulfs, and thus, as Humboldt says, "The Tyrian flag floated simultaneously in the British and Indian seas,"[3] while their bold and enterprising circumnavigators, according to Herodotus,[4] made the voyage around the continent of Africa.

They lived in walled cities at the gates of which public

---

[1] Some writers derive its name from Phœnix, one of its ancient kings, and the son of Agenor.   The above though, is commonly accepted.

[2] In the Scriptures they are always termed Canaanites, and are classed among the descendants of Ham.   They were of darker complexion than the other Syrians, and the Greek writers frequently speak of them as Ethiopians.

[3] Cosmos ii, 499.   [4] Herodotus iv, 42,

business was transacted. They cultivated the earth, raised corn and made wine. They used silver as a medium of exchange, and were very prosperous in all their dealings. They were also distinguished for their skill in manufactures; the textile fabrics of the Sidonians, and the purple cloths of the Tyrians, were celebrated from remote antiquity. They also manufactured glass and were excellent metallurgists—their bronzes, their gold and silver vessels, and other works in metals had a high repute. As hewers of timber and stone their skill was remarkable, and their knowledge of the solid, great and ornamental in architecture was very superior. Indeed, the fame of the people of Sidon for elegant taste, for arts of design, and ingenious invention, was such, that whatever was elegant, neat or pleasing to the eye, in apparel, utensils, ornaments or toys, was distinguished, by way of eminence, with the epithet of "Sidonian." Their artisans were among the chief builders of Solomon's Temple. The friendship and alliance of Hiram their king, and the wise Monarch of Israel, and the voyages of their fleets to Ophir in search of gold, are fully recorded in Scripture. But their chief glory perhaps, was the invention of the letters of the alphabet. And thus as they extended the triumphs of commerce they transplanted on foreign shores the fair flowers of their wonderful genius, and contributed incalculable benefit to the art and the literature of the world.[1]

Pretty soon Carthage, her favorite daughter flashes like a jewel on the bosom of the Dark Continent. Carthage the classic and the glorious. Carthage, the famous republic, the envy of all the falling kingdoms of later times. A narrow

---

[1] Humboldt says of this people: "Although circumscribed in many spheres of mental cultivation, and less familiar with the fine arts than with mechanics, and not endowed with the grand form of creative genius, common to the more highly gifted inhabitants of the valley of the Nile, the Phœnicians as an adventurous and commercial race, and especially by the establishment of colonies (one of which far surpassed the parent city in political power), exerted an influence on the course of ideas and on the diversity and number of cosmical views, earlier than all the other nations inhabiting the coast of the Mediterranean. . . . . But that by which the Phœnicians contributed most powerfully to the civilization of the nations with which they came in contact, was the general spread of alphabetical writing, which they had themselves employed for a long period. Although the whole mythical relation of the colony of Cadmus in Bœtia remains buried in obscurity, it is not the less certain that the Hellenes obtained the alphabetical characters long known as Phœnician symbols, by means of the commercial intercourse between the Ionians and Phœnicians."—[Cosmos, vol. ii, pp. 490-91.

To this we may add the testimony of Strabo : "The Sidonians are described as industrious inquirers in astronomy, as well as in the science of numbers, to which they have been led by their skill in arithmetical calculation, and in navigating their vessels by night, both of which are indispensable to commerce and maritime intercourse."—[Strabo, lib. xvi, p. 75.

strip of light fringing the sea, but losing its rays in the mysterious and unknown waste beyond—she rose, she sunk, amid a blaze of peculiar and exceeding glory.   Her whole history is one of beautiful interest—whether we read from the scanty pages of authenticity or from those which are involved in obscurity and mixed with fable.   The story of Pygmalion's tyrrany in Phœnicia—the exile of his sister Dido—the founding of Carthage—the romantic visit of Æneas and the love of the beautiful queen for the Trojan hero—all readers of Virgil are familiar with as their recital forms one of the most entertaining portions of the Æneid.   Thus living a life of alternate splendor and misfortune ; opulent and enlightened ; boasting its sages, generals, artists and musicians—Carthage stands out brilliantly conspicuous on the motley pages of the past. No wonder haughty Rome looked across the sea with envy and alarm.   No wonder Cato thundered in the Senate, "Carthage must be destroyed!"   But Carthage was not to die without a desperate struggle · for the mastery.   For more than a hundred years she defied the legions of the "mistress" and plucked the plumage of conquest from her hungry eagles. Her armies led by Hamilcar, Hasdrubal and Hannibal, the latter one of the greatest military geniuses that ever lived, crossed the Pyrenees—crossed the Alps, and waved the banners of the African Republic above the snowy crags.   Descending thence to the plains of Italy, moving hither and thither, out-generaling Scipio and Flaminius, wary Fabius and bold Marcellus, they scattered the Romans like chaff, exhausted the finances of the State, detached the Italian nationalities from their allegiance, and came near making an end of Rome.   But alas, for Carthage, the tide of battle turned against her, and ere long the beautiful city was given to sword and brand, and thus the lust of conquest—the greed of Rome, put out the camp-fires of liberty on the coast of Africa, and drove her children back into melancholy silence.

Vicissitudes also visited Phœnicia.   Her wars with the Assyrians, under Shalmaneser ; with the Babylonians, under Nebuchadnezzar, whose siege of Tyre lasted for thirteen years, and is one of the most celebrated in history ; her final subjugation by the Persians under Cyrus and his successor Cambyses ; the invasion by Alexander ; the conquest of the country by the Romans since which time Phœnicia has shared the fate of Syria—all of these facts are well known to students of history.   During the Crusades Tyre was a port of consequence, but under the depressing rule of the Turks, and especially since the commercial changes consequent upon the passage to India by the way of the Cape of Good Hope, it became what it remains to this day, "a rock for fishermen to spread their nets upon."

Admitting all this, we see no reason for the enslavement of the Africans in America. If they are with the Phœnicians and the Carthagenians, descendants of Canaan, they have been an unfortunate but none the less glorious people. If their land was conquered—their cities leveled, their nations subdued—what is all this but a part of the world's history? Like things have occurred in other quarters of the earth since remotest antiquity. Remorseless Rome bent her neck when the Hun, the Goth, and the Vandal sacked her provinces, laid waste the plains of Lombardy, and wrecked and pillaged even the Imperial city without mercy. Athens—"mother of arts and eloquence" is now but the shattered and crumbling monument of Grecian greatness. Thebes and Memphis, Nineveh and Babylon—Babylon "the glory of the Chaldee's excellency" all tell the same sad story. Even Jerusalem, the Holy City, has felt the blight of war and travail, and withered away with decay. Like the stars of heaven they rose to shine for a season. Like the stars they have set—perhaps to re-appear with renewed brightness when the star of God's empire dawns on earth " and He shall set up an Ensign for the nations, and shall assemble the outcasts of Israel, and gather together the dispersed of Judah from the four corners of the earth."

If then we find nothing in history peculiarly ignoble and condemnatory charged against the immediate descendants of Canaan, certainly the " curse" does not rest upon the descendants of the other sons of Ham. It is interesting research and perhaps not beyond our province to look into history on these points also. The descendants of Cush are a remarkable and eminently distinguished people. Nimrod, "the mighty hunter before the Lord," was a son of Cush. He was a man of great courage and address; and, in fact the first king of whom we read in authentic history as waging war to extend his conquests, and enlarging his acquisitions by violence. He founded the Assyrian empire, and built the magnificent cities of Babylon and Nineveh. The Book of Genesis reveals to us the existence of a Tetrapolis or confederation of four cities, that ruled over the Empire established by Nimrod, namely: 1. Babylon; 2. Erech; 3. Accad; 4.

Calneh—all of which places have been identified in modern times. After Nimrod came Ninus, who conquered Babylon, Armenia, Media, and other countries. At his death his infant son, Ninyas succeeded, nominally, to the crown; while the real sovereignty was exercised by the queen mother, Semiramis in her capacity of regent. Semiramis appears to have been one of the greatest female sovereigns in history. She strengthened and adorned the capital of the empire; built walls around Nineveh, and embellished it with costly structures. Having finished these monuments of her power and grandeur, she determined to augment it by conquest, and commenced making war upon her neighbors. Her most famous campaign was against India, in which she signally routed her enemy and penetrated into the heart of his dominions. She also marched in the direction of Africa, and it is said, added Ethiopia to her possessions. After the reign of Semiramis came Ninyas and Sardanapalus who were the beginning of a long line of effeminate monarchs. For thirty generations, the empire remained in such a state of tranquility as to offer nothing worthy the notice of history. It afterwards passed into the hands of the Medes and the Persians.

We may next examine briefly the history of Ethiopia. Many writers are of opinion that Ethiopia received its first inhabitants from the countries east of the Red Sea. According to these authorities, one portion of the descendants of Cush, having settled in Arabia, gradually migrated to the south-eastern part of Africa. This is plausible, for in addition to Nimrod, Cush had other sons: "Seba, and Havilah, and Sabtah, and Raamah, and Sabtecha," all mentioned in Genesis. Bruce mentions a tradition among the Abyssinians, which they say, has existed among them from time immemorial.[1] It is to this effect: Cush, the grandson of Noah,

---

[1] Bruce's Travels to Discover the Source of the Nile, vol. ii, pp. 303-305 ; see also Herodotus on same point, lib. ii, cap. 29.

Sir Roderick Murchison, the learned devotee of science, and President of the Royal Geographical Society, holds the opinion, we believe, that the Africans are not of Noachian descent, though he grants them Adamic extraction. He maintains that they were not destroyed by the Deluge, but took themselves to the "mountains of the moon," and thus escaped the dreadful destruction. Late explorers, however, have determined that there are no "mountains of the moon," that the chain of mountains which was supposed to run east and west separating Central from Southern Africa, do not run in that direction, and are but a continuation of the plateau of Abyssinia running north and south. However, this is of no consequence to us, as we only wished to remark, if Sir Roderick's view is leastways correct, it would seriously interfere with the curse on Canaan. For, if the Africans were not in the Ark, and are not descendants of Noah, they certainly are not under Noah's curse.

with his family, passed through a country destitute of inhabitants, called *Albara*, till they came to a ridge of mountains which separates it from the highlands of Abyssinia. Here, still terrified with the remembrance of the deluge, and apprehensive of a return of the same calamity, they took up their abode in caves among the mountains, rather than trust themselves in the plains. Here the Cushites, with unparalleled industry, and by the help of instruments utterly unknown to us, formed commodious yet wonderful habitations in the heart of mountains of granite and marble, which remain entire, in great numbers, to the present day, and promise to remain so till the consummation of all things. Here they built the superb city of Axum, and their magnificent and renowned capital, Meroe. Here they made improvements in architecture, cultivated commerce, agriculture and the arts; applied themselves to the study of astronomy, and the natural history of the winds and seasons. Less is known of the arts and sciences of Ethiopia than of the Egyptians. The pyramids of Meroe, though inferior in size to those of Egypt, are said to surpass them in architectural beauty; and the sepulchres evince the greatest purity of taste. But the most important and striking proof of the progress of the Ethiopians in architecture, is their knowledge and employment of the arch. The Ethiopian vases depicted on the monuments, though not richly ornamented, display a taste and elegance of form that has never been surpassed. In sculpture and painting, the edifices of Meroe, though not so profusely adorned, rival the choicest specimens of Egyptian art. They were also a great commercial people—their country, situated at the intersection of the leading caravan routes—was the headquarters for an immense trade with India, and with the interior and west coast of Africa. These people were undoubtedly of Hamitic descent. They differed from the Indians and other Asiatic people in color, hair and language. Their complexion was very dark, and the hair of the Western Ethiopians was *frizzled*. It appears also, that Judaism was, at one time, the prevalent religion with them.[1] From the time of Moses to that of Solomon, there is a chasm in their history. In the reign of

---

[1] In Acts viii, may be found an account of the conversion and baptism by Phillip of "a man of Ethiopia, an eunuch of great authority under Can lace, Queen of the Ethiopians, who had the charge of all her treasure, and had come to Jerusalem for to worship."

the latter monarch, the Queen of Sheba, noted for her wealth, wisdom and beauty, paid him a visit in Jerusalem. The Ethiopians affirm that she had a son by King Solomon. Among other noted sovereigns Zerah and Queen Candace were most celebrated. Indeed, according to all accounts, the Ethiopians must have been a nation of first importance in the world. The ruins of cities and monuments south of the Lybian Desert in Ancient Ethiopia; the vast armies that came up from them, like that of Zerah's, who went forth against King Asa of Judah, with a million men and three hundred chariots—all these facts have led many to believe that civilization had its origin on the banks of the Nile in Negroland. In fact, Herodotus wrote for us four hundred years before the annunciation that the Egyptians came up from Ethiopia; however this may be, there is no doubt as to the early existence of a very powerful Egyptian civilization. Inasmuch, then, as the Egyptians are also descendants of Ham, we will next speak as concisely as possible of their career.

We are well aware that a class of writers deny that the Negroes are entitled to rank with the Egyptians, or to claim Hamitic honors in that direction. They seem determined to claim for Shem and Japheth all the good there is in humanity and give all that is bad to Ham. Even in the ordinary text-books of our common schools we find such statements as the following: "The Hamitic family were the ancient people of Palestine, the Nile basin, and the shores of the Arabian Sea and Persian Gulf. They have either passed away or have so blended with their Semitic and Japhetic conquerors as to be scarcely distinguishable."[1] And, again, "the Egyptians were not *Africans*, as we understand the term. They belonged to the Caucasian race. Still, they were neither Aryans nor Semites, and hence scholars call them by a special designation, namely, Hamites, or Khamites. *Khame* (literally the Black Land) was the native name of Egypt."[2] Nevertheless, Ham is the name by which Egypt is repeatedly called in Scripture, as "Jacob sojourned in the land of Ham," "wonders in the land of Ham," "Mizraim was glad when they departed." Dr. Lardner — good enough authority — says, "The name of Ham is identical with that of *Cham*, or

---

[1] Guyot's Physical Geography, p. 118.
[2] Swinton's Outlines of History, p. 16.

Chamia, by which Egypt has, in all ages been called by its
native inhabitants; and *Mizer*, or *Mizraim*, is the name by
which it, or rather the Delta, is still called by the Turks and
Arabians."[1] This is further strengthened by Humboldt, who
says "It is not at all improbable that 'the Ethiopians of
the sun-rising' mentioned by Herodotus were diffused much
further towards the north-west than at present," and gives it
as his firm conviction that the inhabitants of the ancient Egyptian empire were "the actual woolly-haired negro races."[2]
Then, again, the Scriptures plainly say,[3] Mizraim was the son of
Ham, and "Mizraim begat Ludim, and Ananim, and Lehabim,
and Naphtuhim, and Pathrusim, and Calushim, (of whom came
the Philistines), and Caphthorim." The coincidence of
family names and the names of their countries are too striking
to pass unnoticed. We accept, therefore, the Bible account
in preference to any other, and confidently refer to it as our
authority, defying the production of a better. Indeed, as
Bishop Patrick has well said, "No book in the world shows
the original propagation of mankind, but only the Holy
Scriptures. They who are ignorant of them, having nothing
of true antiquity, devised senseless fables of their descent
they knew not how, nor from whom. . . . This was the
peculiar glory of the Jewish nation that they alone were able
to derive their pedigree from the first man that God created;
of which no other nation could boast or make a shadow of
pretense."

So we come now to speak of Egypt, that wonderful land
involved in so much obscurity and uncertainty, as to appear
almost fabulous. But Egypt, as we certainly know it—the
cradle-land of science, the nursery of art, the "homestead of
the nations."[4] Older than any known organized government
on earth—older than Chaldæ and India—rich in wisdom,
famous for abundance, and renowned for elegance long before the Israelites, the Greeks or the Romans can begin
record of their civilization. "When Greece was under the
tumultuary sway of a number of petty chieftains, Homer
already celebrates the hundred gates of Thebes and the

---

[1] Credibility of Gospel History, vol. iii, chap. iv, 2.
[2] Cosmos, vol. ii, p. 531.   [3] Genesis x and 1 Chronicles i.
[4] One of the most charming works on Egypt lately published is Edward L. Clarke's
"Daleth, or the Homestead of the Nations"—a work we have consulted with much
pleasure.

6

mighty hosts which in warlike array issued from them to battle." "Before the faintest dawn of science had illumined the regions of Europe, the valley of the Nile was the abode of learning, and distinguished for its incomparable works in sculpture, painting and architecture." What a land! What a history! Centuries there are but as a day. Time, the bald-pated ruler of the centuries, who needs must travel swiftly in this age of steam, could, however, well afford to lay aside his scythe and reverse the old-time hour-glass to tell to us, his anxious but ignorant children, the multiplied wonders of those far-off ages. And yet, that which we do know is glorious. This is Egypt—the kingdom of the Pharoahs—a powerful monarchy as far back as the time of the patriarch Abraham. The land to which the merchants of Gilead took Joseph a captive and sold him as a slave. The land where Jacob went to buy corn—the land of Israel's bondage—birthland of Moses and of Aaron, and after-refuge of God's Holy Child, our gentle Lord and Savior.

What brilliant dynasties of kings she boasted! Saophis and Menes, Cheops and famous Sesostris—the latter com-memorated in the hieroglyphical paintings, under the name of Rameses the Great. And in after centuries, what a gorgeous panorama of events! This was the kingdom of the Ptolemies. And yonder the classic waters whence came the galley of Cæsar—"the foremost man of all the world," and after, that of Mark Antony, throbbing with the impulse of an hundred impatient oars, yet moving too slowly toward the colonnades of Cleopatra's palace, which, like long ranks of marble sentinels in silence guard the sacred shore. Ah, indeed, this was Egypt with her magnificent cities of Mem-phis and Heliopolis, and Thebes with her four millions of people; Egypt with her vast armies, her massive walls, and her knowledge of geometry, astronomy and many an art that has since been lost. Egypt—with her vocal statue of Mem-non, her pyramids and sphinx, temples and tombs, obelisks and monoliths—now scattered along her fertile valley, as if this had been the burial ground of grandeur for a "nation of gods." Here, too, is where Thales, the Greek astronomer was taught by the Egyptians six centuries before Christ. Here Anacreon borrowed some of his sweetest strains, and here Pythagoras learned from the Egyptian priests—" in the land of Ham" the *fact* that "the square of the hypothenuse is equal to the sum of the squares of the two other sides."[1] Here, too, in later times were built the cities of Alexandria and Grand Cairo, the former for seventeen hundred years the chief maritime city of the world, the seat of the largest library of ancient days, and of a magnificent lighthouse, built by the Ptolemies, and which for ages was recognized as one of the wonders of the world. However, to add to these evidences of an African civilization not only most remote but most powerful, Alexandria is also dear to the hearts of Christians as the birthplace of Clement, Apollos and Origen—for as the poet Herbert has beautifully said—

> "Now with the cross as with a staff alone,
> Religion, like a pilgrim westward bent,
> Knocking at all doors ever as she went
> To Egypt first she came."

The descendants of Phut are the Mauritanians and the present Berbers of North Africa. Very little is known of their history though they are believed to have been the inhabitants of ancient Libya. The prophet Jeremiah (in chapter xlvi,) predicting the destruction of Pharoah-necho's army, says, "Come up, ye horses; and rage ye chariots; and let the mighty men come forth; the Ethiopians and the Libyans, that handle the shield; and the Lydians, that handle the bow." Commentators are of opinion that these were the Egyptians' allies, which makes it probable that they were all Africans. They were famous for the use of the bow. By consulting Ezekiel (xxvii: 10) it will be observed that they were also allies of the Tyrians—" in thine army, thy men of war." For many long centuries they were lost to sight— buried as it were in the bosom of the wilderness. But when the Saracen sway swept across from Asia, "even remote Mauritania, which seemed doomed to be forever the inheritance of a barbarous and nomadic race, was converted into a civilized empire, and its capital, Fez, became a distinguished school of learning." The Saracen invaders introduced the camel from the sandy wastes of Arabia, opened paths through wilds which had hitherto defied all human effort, and formed a trade in gold and slaves with countries which had not been known. There in the territory distinguished

---

[1] Here, too, perhaps, Plato first learned of the immortality of the soul—for Herodotus (somewhere, we do not remember exactly) makes the remarkable statement—" The Egyptians are the first of mankind who have affirmed the immortality of the soul."

on our maps as Soudan, several flourishing kingdoms were
founded, which Europeans vainly sought to reach until within
a comparatively recent date.   Ghana, a kingdom boasting
unrivaled splendor, whose royal master rode out attended by
obedient elephants and camel-leopards—a kingdom which,
after various fortunes as subject to Timbuctoo, Kashna, and
Sackatoo, came to be identified in the present Kano.   There
too was Tocrur or the present Sackatoo, and Kuku, the Bor-
nou of to-day.   Farther South was the ancient city of Kangha,
famous for its industries and arts, which modern historians
have recognized in the city of Loggun, celebrated by Major
Denham, for "its ingenuities, its manufactures, and its witty
women."

Thus we see ancient Africa is rich in history.   Even as the
terra incognito of mythology it is described in picturesque
terms in the legends of the classic bards.   Northern Africa
which we now know as one vast connected sea of sand, and
lying there like a withered arm of the ocean, was invested by
the ancients with strange, weird interest.   Mt. Atlas, rising
like a solitary aerial pillar—upholding the heavens over the
region once so famous, but now so downcast and lonely is
known from the traditions that run through the songs of the
poets.   In the deathless epic of Homer we read of an Atlas
who bore upon his shoulders the great columns which separate earth from heaven.[1]   Here too was the land whither Hercules went in search of the golden apples of Hesperides.[2]
Here were the Elysian Fields[3] and the Islands of the Blessed,
mentioned by Herodotus, and which the ancients believed
were destined to be the abode of good men after death.[4]
Thither, also, according to Diodorus, the "ancients referred
the early reign of Saturn under the appellation of Ouranus
or Heaven; the birth of Jupiter and his nursing by Amalthæa;
the impious race of Titans and their wars with the gods;
Cybele with her doting love for Atys and frantic grief for his
fate."   And there were placed the hideous Gorgons, and the
serpents hissing in the hair of Medusa.   And thence came
the stories of those dreadful Amazons, "gallant viragoes,"
who ravaged all the region and carried victorious arms, according to the historian, into Syria, and Asia Minor.

" But mingled with so much fable the ancient writers had

[1] Odyssey, i, 52.   [2] Iliad, iv, 561.   [3] Theog, v, 517.
[4] Op. et Dies, v, 167.

also some just conceptions of this region, and many things mentioned by Herodotus, Diodorus, and particularly by Strabo, who wrote after the Roman sway was fully established over Africa, indicate that greatest care was used in treasuring the scraps of knowledge which floated up out of the deeper wilderness beyond. Yet that wilderness kept its secrets so jealously that the diligence of historians and the eagerness of explorers and the power of armies were equally ineffectual in extending the range of precise knowledge beyond the narrow confines on the north and a limited extent of western coast. The light struggled to penetrate the gloom, its blunted rays rested against an opacity, and rose in towering brilliancy, and stood awhile flashing like a resisted sun, then paled and quivered and fell, and left the continent, a heritage of darkness to the future!"

Wonderful Africa! Hapless Africa! The soldiers of Cambyses and Solomon and Alexander, the legions of Greece and Rome, of Saracen and Christian, have contributed to the story of its sorrows, but even these tales were written in the sand. Great pageants have crossed its plains. Great processions to Jerusalem and Babylon and Mecca have crept over its hills. Yet the desert has no historian—no resting place—no resting place for the departed save in the flying sand that forms its ever-shifting sepulchres. Thus for six thousand years Africa has stretched forth her hands to God. Thus for nearly two thousand years she has stood with open and empty arms longing to clasp therein the blessed Redeemer. But oh! shame upon the world, she has been crowded back to the outer edge of the swarming millions that have pressed forward if but to touch the hem of His garment.

There are islands in the Pacific which it is said had no vices until the Christians went there. And of Africa it may be said that the cup of her sorrows was not full to overflowing until the modern white man set foot upon her soil. Hence the history of Central and Southern Africa is brief and obscure; consisting chiefly of an account of the modern discoveries made, and colonies founded, by the Europeans. Abyssinia, the ancient Ethiopia, was imperfectly known during the middle ages, although it had been converted to Christianity in the third century; but we must pass over its history till the Portuguese mission of Covillan, about 1490; whose reports hastened the discovery of the southern passage to India. In 1516, the Portuguese aided the native king, David, in recovering his throne from the Turks; and, in 1543, they extended like aid to Claudius, the next *negus* or king. The Roman Catholic religion was established there in 1604; but overthrown in 1632, by the negus *Basilides* or Facilidas. The country has since been involved in civil war, and is now divided into the states of Amhara, Tigre, and Shoa-Efat. Melinda, in Eastern Africa, was taken by the Portuguese, about 1500; but re-captured by the Arabs in 1698. Mozambique, taken by the Portuguese in 1508, still remains in their possession; and the Portuguese settlements in Lower Guinea were founded at about the same time.[1]

The Cape of Good Hope was colonized by the Dutch, in 1615. It was taken by the British in 1795; and again in 1806; since which time it has remained in their possession. In 1797, the "African Association" was formed in England, by Sir Joseph Banks and others, for the purpose of exploring the interior of Africa. In the same year Sierra Leone was colonized by Negroes from England, and being surrendered to the British crown in 1807, it has since been made the home of Negroes rescued from slaveships. The "American Colonization Society," was formed in 1816; to colonize in Africa the free Colored people of the United States. Liberia was purchased by it in 1821; and settled by the first emigrants in 1822, under Governor Ashmun. The delta of the Niger, and other lands have since been settled by English people.

But there is hope, bright hope, that Africa will be restored to the waiting world. For we behold evidences of a restoration drifting out from those dark shores, as the seaweed of the New World floated out to meet Columbus. To those nations that have awaited the son of God for so many long and dreary centuries, we have borne alas! a divided truth. To them it has not been the message of love, and everywhere there has been grievous obstacle to the propagation of the Gospel. "But the men who have the courage to spread it in the centre of Africa, whatever be their communion," nobly says Cochin, "are men who honor humanity and serve it." It is impossible to read their narratives[2] without emotion. Livingstone admirably remarks, that "all classes of Christians find

---

[1] See Pantology, or A Systematic Survey of Human Knowledge. By Roswell Park, A. M., Philadelphia, Hogan & Thompson, pp. 216–217.

[2] Twenty-three years in the South of Africa, by Robert Moffat, 1864; Les Bassoutos, by M. Cazalis, Paris, 1860; Life and Labors of David Livingstone, 1876; Stanley's Across the Dark Continent, etc., etc.

that sectarian rancor soon dies out when they are working together among and for the real heathen."

Thus, these men went forth rivals, precursors of missionaries or missionaries themselves, ambassadors of civilization,
heralds announcing to the world the coming of truth, preparing the path, making "straight in the desert a highway for
our God." In Abyssinia and Eastern Africa, Bruce, Baker,
Grant, Speke, Burton, Kraff, New, and Dr. Schweinfurth,
the German botanist; while in the South, the heroic travelers,
Barth, Vogel, Hope, Barrow, Lichtenstein, Campbell, Trutter,
Somerville, Moffat, Richardson, Overweg, Baikie, Gullain,
the brothers d'Abbadie and Raffanel, intrepid rivals of
Mungo Park, Hornemann, Lander, Andresson, Du Chaillu,
Denham and Clapperton, have explored Central Africa,
Soudan, the source of the Nile, the course of the Niger, the
shores of Lake Tchad, of Victoria Nyanza, and Albert
Nyanza, in every direction; from Bernghazi to the Cape of
Good Hope, they have marched from one coast to the other,
teaching Africa the worth of Christian civilization, and the
outside world what is contained in Africa. But of all the
travelers who have excited most interest—possibly because
nearest our day, most prominent are David Livingstone, the
martyr to duty, Lieut. Cameron of the Royal Navy, and our
own heroic American journalist, Henry Moreland Stanley,
who has "flashed a torch of light across the Dark Continent."
These men have crossed South Africa from east to west, explored the Nile, the Zambezi and the Congo rivers, and
reached the Nyassa lake and the Shire country. They have
traced the great Lualaba river through the Bangweolo, the
Moero, and the Kanalondo to its junction with the Lomame.[1]
They have penetrated to the very heart of the continent,

---

[1] The writer recently had the pleasure of listening to a lecture on "Africa," by the
venerable Dr. J. Leighton Wilson, who was for eighteen years a missionary on the West
Coast, but is now at the head of the Presbyterian Board of Foreign Missions, Baltimore. He spoke most glowingly of the work performed by Livingstone, Cameron and
Stanley in determining the course of the Lualaba river, and among other bright anticipations for Africa, predicted that before twenty years shall have passed steamers will
be loaded at Liverpool, and in two weeks time discharge their freight in the very heart
of Africa. Afterwards, in a private interview with Dr. Wilson, we learned much that
was interesting in regard to that wonderful African language the *Mpwongwe* or *Pongwe*,
which has some three or four hundred inflections of the verb, far surpassing the Greek,
which has only about seventy. And this reminds us that Latham speaks of the Tumali,
a truly Negro language of Kordofan, which in respect to the extent to which its inflections are formed by internal changes of vowels and accents, it is fully equal to the
Semitic tongues of Palestine and Arabia. [See Latham's Man and his Migrations,
p. 155.]

south of the equator, visited mountains, lakes, rivers and
people before unknown in the annals of the civilized
world.   We wish we could speak more fully of their
brilliant exploits ; a sketch so imperfect only aggravates both
reader and writer.   But space forbids.   Enough to say the
eyes of the whole world are now fixed on Africa.   More
books are being written on this subject that most any other.
Newspapers, magazines, reviews, are taking up the torch of
enlightenment in her behalf, and they will pass it into the
hands of, the next generations.   Africa will—she must be
saved!   Not only the curiosity of the world calls for her redemption; commerce calls for it; there may be vast treasures concealed there ; there may be nations easily advanced
in industrial interests.   Philanthropy calls for it; there are undoubtedly wrongs crying to the world for redress; there are
evils of ignorance and superstition which must be mitigated.
Science calls for it; her commission embraces the whole
world, and while there is a rock unbroken or a star without a
name, she must not rest.   But, most of all, religion calls for
it—Christianity—there are in that region souls to be saved.[1]

ETHNOLOGICAL STATUS OF THE NEGRO.

Having satisfactorily settled the foregoing points we may
next inquire into the ethnological status of the Negro.   Much
has been said—much has been written on this important
question of the human races—one of the most difficult and
the most delicate the science of nature and history can
propose to itself.   It is not intended, even if we felt able, to go
into extensive discussion here, but we shall present a number
of facts, gathered from eminent and learned authorities, put
in popularized form, establishing the black man's just claims
to honorable position among the peoples of the earth.   One
reason for thus seeming to step out of the way, is, that in a
certain city, which is to-day the very centre of culture, where
the black man is in an advanced state of civilization—blessed
with colleges that are admirably conducted—blessed with a
score of churches whose spires are "like pencils on the sky
tracing silently life's changeful story"—blessed with social
advantages and by material advancement—only twelve years

---

[1] Chambliss' Life of Livingstone, p. 44.

since a book was issued to prove that the Negro is not the progeny of Ham, not a descendant of Adam, but is *a beast in God's nomenclature, and has no soul!*

We make it a point to exaggerate nothing, and yet how can we do violence to the truth by withholding it? We would much rather be silent altogether, but the truth must be told. And, therefore, we calmly submit, that as a perfect chrysolite of welded error and polluted prejudice; nay, as a bold, heartless, immoral and blasphemous libel on the whole human race that pamphlet stands unequalled and unapproached. We do not intend to reply to it. What honor would a man gain? We have too much respect for ourself, for the Colored man, and for humanity in general, to dip into such matters. We fling it aside, for the measure of its influence was limited—its defenders are few; but, as the culminating outgrowth of an isolated prejudice, baneful and blighting in its evil intentions, it seems to have been vomited forth upon the world from the very "belly of hell" itself.[1]

However, very many very ridiculous hypotheses have been assumed on this subject. Some of them, perhaps, attributable partly to the fact, that every man thinks himself superior to every other man, and his particular race superior to every other race, or as the metaphysicians state the idea, it is "the ego and the non-ego, or that which is myself, and that which is without me." There have been persons who have most earnestly protested against their own noble selves being placed in a natural system in one common species with Negroes and Hottentots. And again, there have been other people who have had no compunction in declaring themselves and the orang-outang to be creatures of one and the same species. Thus, the renowned philosopher and caprice-monger, Lord Monboddo, says in blunt words, "The orang-outang are proved to be of our species by marks of humanity that, I think, are incontestable." On the other hand, another but not quite so candid a caprice-monger was the German doctor, whom Blumenbach calls *Theophrastus Parcelsus Bombastus*, who could not comprehend how all men can belong to one and the

---

[1] Shortly after the appearance of this libelous pamphlet a distinguished clergyman published a " Reply." While it was undeniably correct on ethnological questions, and able and pointed in many particulars, the Doctor's " Reply" did not squarely meet expectation. The trouble seems to have been it ran in the same old rut worn deep by the Pro-slavery writers; hugged the phantom of "divine sanction" too closely, and, we are sorry, on his account, to say it, fell " flat and unprofitable."

same original stock, and contrived on paper for the solution of the difficulty, his two Adams—one white and the other black.   Then again, Lord Kames, one of the principal champions of the theory that there are different species of man, was of the opinion that the Giagas, a nation in Africa, could not have descended from the same original with the rest of mankind, because, unlike others, they are void of natural affection; kill all their own children as soon as they are born, and supply their places with youths stolen from neighboring tribes.   This is absurd, for "common sense," as has been well said, "would answer, that if such a species were created, it could not continue longer than ,the primitive stock endured. The stolen youths would resemble their parents, not those who adopted them, and would soon be the sole constituents of the nation." [1]

Coming down to later times, we are confronted by the variformed, subtle and perplexing theories of cotemporaneous scientists.   For, as Prof. Schmidt says, "with the exception of the ecclesiastico-political question, no sphere of thought agitates the educated classes of our day so profoundly as the doctrine of descent.   On both sides the cry is, 'Avow your colors!'" [2]   Thus, Mr. Darwin, Mr. Matthew Arnold, Prof. Tyndall, and others, give us some knotty points in the "evolution" idea, the "struggle for existence," "survival of the fittest," "selection," etc.   Then, Prof. Huxley comes forward and advises us to go deep into biology, and promises, *entre nous*, "we shall see, what we shall see."   Next, Hæckel, concludes that "the human race is a branch of the catarrhine group; he was developed in the old world, and sprang from apes of this group, which have long been extinct." [3]   And so it goes.   But the result and the fact is this; that all theories as to primitive man must necessarily be very uncertain.   Granting the doctrine of evolution to be true— even then can men tell what their common ancestor was like?   Moreover, a possible descent or ascent from an ape or orang-outang does not lower but heightens the attributes of a developed humanity, and whether evolution be a correct theory or not, it does not demonstrate the non-existence of that incumbrance called *Conscience*—which Shakspeare has

---

[1] Spurzheim's Education of Man, p. 25.
[2] Schmidt's Doctrine of Descent and Darwinism—preface.
[3] History of the Creation of Organized Beings.

truthfully declared "doth make cowards of us all." Nevertheless, our scientists, leaving the physical, soar aloft to psy-
chologic fields. Thus, Mr. Spencer traces all morality back
to our inherited experience of utility. Mr. Darwin ascribes
it to an inherited sympathy, while Mr. Mill, with characteristic courage undertakes to build up the whole moral nature
of man with no help whatever either from ethical intuition or
from physiological instinct. Here we are content to leave
them, to return to our immediate subject, and also for fear we
might, as Sir William Hamilton used to say, "truncate a
problem which we cannot solve."

We do not deny that it has been customary with many
writers to place the Negro lowest in the scale of humanity,
but this is easily explained. Blinded by tradition, there are
eyes that cannot see; hardened by prejudice, there are hearts
that cannot feel; and, beclouded by ignorance, there are
minds that will not be convinced. So, whether it results from
tradition, prejudice or ignorance, the conclusion is incorrect
and unjust, as we shall see by examining the best authors on
the subject. The one grand and salutary fact, however, has
been established and cannot be denied, viz.: *the unmistakable*
evidences of the unity of mankind. A comparison of the different tribes and races of men, reveals the fact of a gradual
modification of types, on every side of the central and highest
race, until, by insensible degrees, the lowest and most
degraded forms of humanity are reached. But even then,
in the central race—among the individuals of which there is
greater diversity in form, features, temperament and mental
characteristics, than in any other—there are persons of pure
blood who show almost every distinguishing feature of each
of the lower races. These facts, although they seem to show
that the White is the normal race, from which the others have
gradually deviated, also establish a *bond of union* among all
the varieties of mankind, however remote they may appear to
be from the most noble type.

The main point ethnologists have raised is, that a wide difference in the physical qualities of the races exists. Complexion, it is said, is the most easily changed. Climate, diet
and the manner of living, may change the whole human constitution. In his history of ancient art, Winckelmann seems
to attribute all to climate; not only the perfection of form in
the inhabitants of Greece, but their serenity of mind, sweet-
ness and love of beauty. The only objection to this we have

come across is that of Sir Charles Bell, who in his "Anatomy and Philosophy of Expression," says, "It is strange that Winckelmann should attribute so much to the influence of climate, seeing that where the olive still ripens, in the long summer of Greece, not a vestige of those virtues which were the admiration of the world now exists; and centuries have passed without a poet or philosopher appearing in the country of Homer and Plato." This, though, refers more especially to the mental degeneration of the Greeks, and we merely interposed this view here in order to give all sides of the question. There can be no doubt that climate does operate on the physical man, and to great extent makes him what he is *physically*. The Portuguese in Africa become black, but preserve their original configuration. The Jews in northern countries are fair, but become brown and tawny towards the south, while their configuration does not undergo proportionate changes. Zimmermann shows how color is changed by climate — heat producing Negroes, and cold Esquimaux; cites the old traveler Benjamin, of Tudela, for Jews turning black in Abyssinia, and credits a story related by Caldanus, how once he saw, at Venice, a negro who, brought there in childhood, had, in his old age, become *yellowish!* Thus, says Zimmermann, "The white man can become black, and the black man on the contrary white, and this change is again carried on through the different degrees of heat and cold"—his conclusion being that—"man possessing himself thus little by little of all climates, becomes through their influence—here a Georgian, there a Negro, elsewhere an Eskimau!"[1] Indeed, arguing from this point, as a distinguished writer has said, "It seems difficult to say whether the original color of man was white or black, but it is certain that white people grow black sooner than Negroes becomes white."[2]

Authors have however labored most in endeavoring to explain the color of the Africans which above all other national colors from the most remote period has struck the eyes of naturalists and excited their minds to inquire. Nor is it surprising that with that object all sorts of hypotheses should be elaborated. A heap of authors could be cited, and indeed we have waded through a formidable array of volumes in

---

[1] Zimmermann's "The Earth and its Inhabitants," vol. iii, p. 384, London.
[2] Spurzheim's Education of Man, p. 26.

search of the truth, but limited space only permits us to notice briefly without quoting *verbatim* in every case. One writer attributes the tawny skin of the Greenlanders to their particularly oily diet. Another declares that the skin of Europeans in the East Indies becomes yellow from copious meals of dishes prepared from the calipash of turtles. Among the Indians those who inhabit the northern part of America are so much whiter than others, that they nearly lose the red color altogether.[1] The Chinese are of all colors between brown and white; in the south, brown; towards the north, white. The Ethiopians on the north shore of the Senegal are tawny, on the south, black. We are told expressly about the Malabars that their black color approaches nearer to tawny and yellow the further they dwell towards the north. Thus we might quote from a cloud of witnesses who have observed the same well-known effects of climate, and mode of life in other parts of the world, but a few other examples out of the many will suffice. The women of Biscay are of a brilliant white, while those of Granada on the contrary are brownish, so that in this southern province the pictures of the Virgin Mary are painted of the same national color. The Moors are by no means naturally black, spite of the proverb, though many persons think so; they are born white and remain white all their lives, when their business does not expose·them to the heat of the sun. In the towns the women are of such a brilliant whiteness that they eclipse most Europeans; but the Mauritanian mountaineers, burnt unceasingly by the sun and always half-naked, become, even from infancy, of a brown color, which comes very near to that of soot. Many inhabitants of Timur are of a copper color with red hair; and Marcgrav, the traveler, reports having seen an African woman with an undoubted red skin and red hair. Raynal says, "The circumstances that seem to confirm the opinion, that the color of the Negroes is the effect of the climate, of the air, of the water, and of the food of Guinea, is, that this color changes when the inhabitants are removed into other countries. The children they procreate in America are not so black as their parents were. After each generation the difference becomes more palpable. It is possible that after a numerous succession of generations, the men come from

---

[1] Catlin in his History of the North American Indians, has contended that the red man is of Jewish origin.

Africa would not be distinguished from those of the country into which they may have been transplanted."[1]

Then again, Dr. Geo. S. Blackie, of Nashville, a distinguished graduate of the Universities of Edinburgh and Bonn, and one of the most learned scientists in the South says:

"It is authoritatively stated that the third generation of our late household slaves lost much of the flattened nose, and acquired longer head and beard, while the ugliness of a field-hand is proverbial. Bojesman, the lowest type, perhaps, give evidence of the ugliness produced by moral degradation and external circumstances. These facts have illustrations everywhere. Among the Irish, the French, the Germans, and the Spaniards we find the same. Coarse, unwholesome diet, and ill-prepared food will make the human race degenerate. All people who live miserably are ugly and ill-made. On the other hand, luxury and good living have a tendency to develop beauty, as well as long life and refinement, as we see in the aristocratic families of England."[2]

These views are correct, and we dare assert as a fact, and therefore call the attention of *savants* to it, that the Negroes of the South are improving in physical characteristics since their emancipation. Freedom, education, better food, more of the luxuries of life, less work, and more leisure are bringing this people out. It is so in the cities and towns, and discoverable also in the country districts. But we will continue citing authorities, for they are numerous. In 1845, Sir Chas. Lyell, President of the Geological Society of London, made a tour of the United States and noted that "the Negroes in America are undergoing a manifest improvement in their physical type. He had no doubt that they will, in time, show a development of skull and intellect quite equal to the whites." Dr. Nott, of Mobile, commenting on this in 1855 has this to say, though it must be remembered he wrote under the slave regime:

"That Negroes imported into, or born in the United States, become more intelligent and better developed in their *physique* generally than their native compatriots of Africa, every one will admit; but such intelligence is easily explained by their ceaseless contact with the whites, from whom they de-

---

[1] See the Abbe Raynal's Philosophical and Political History of the West Indies, vol. iv, book xi, p. 35.
[2] See Dr. Blackie's letter to Dr. Young on the "Ethnological Status of the Negro," Nashville, 1867, p. 45.

rive much instruction; and such physical improvement may also be readily accounted for by the increased comforts with which they are supplied. In Africa, owing to their natural improvidence, the Negroes are, more frequently than not, a half-starved, and therefore half-developed race; but when they are regularly and adequately fed they become healthier, better developed, and more humanized."

This is all very well so far as it goes, and but for the fact that Dr. Nott allowed his prejudice to carry him into the following sneering conclusion which, from all appearances, was evidently done to bolster up the institution of slavery. He says:

" Wild horses, cattle, asses, and other brutes, are greatly improved in like manner by domestication; but neither climate nor food can transmute an ass into a horse, or a buffalo into an ox.

" One or two generations of domestic culture affect all the improvement of which Negro-organism is susceptible. We possess thousands of the second, and many more of Negro families of the eighth or tenth generation, in the United States; and (where unadulterated by white blood) they are identical in physical and intellectual characters. No one in this country pretends to distinguish the native son of a Negro from his great-grandchild (except through occasional and ever-apparent admixture of white or Indian blood); while it requires the keen and experienced eye of such a comparative anatomist as Agassiz to detect structural peculiarities in our few African-born slaves. The 'improvements' among Americanized Negroes noticed by Lyell, in his progress from South to North, are solely due to those ultra-ecclesiastical amalgamations which, in their illegitimate consequences, have deteriorated the white element in direct proportion that they are said to have *improved* the blacks." [1]

Ah, there was the point. Amalgamation, which was the *bete noir* of Messrs. Nott, Gliddon, *et id omne pecus*—explains much of this thinly veiled sarcasm. But before proceeding further we shall state emphatically that this being by no manner of means a matter of our business we do not propose to discuss it. What we shall say in this paragraph shall be " the butt and very sea-mark of our utmost sail." It is a question that regulates itself. And for the relief of many, we will remark that amalgamation has not taken place to any very great extent in the North, nor is it more likely to take place in the South unless the South invites it, and in that case a man should be like Von Moltke, who is passive if any man ever was passive; who is "silent in seven languages."

Let us turn now to the further discussion of the question in

---

[1] Nott and Gliddon's Types of Mankind, p. 260.

hand.   We have not been very particular to arrange our cita-
tions in chronological order, for this would be useless waste
of time, seeing there are so many " standing, waiting to be
heard." However, for the sake of a little contrast—light and
shadow as it were, permit us to introduce the opinion of M
Quatrefagas, who is among the very latest authorities, being,
we believe, at present, Professor of Anthropology in the Mu-
seum of Natural History, Paris:

"There still exist *Whites* in a distinctly savage state.   We need only read
the details given by Cook, La Perouse, Meares, Marchand, Dixon, Dr.
Scouler, and others, upon some *Kolushes*, whose women besmear themselves
with grease and soot, and wear a girdle, as both *true Whites* and *true Savages*,
who in many respects must rank below the Negro of Ardra or Juida.   On the
other hand, enough is known to prove that the most strongly characterized
Negro, the *typical Negro*, has the power of raising himself to a considerably advanced social condition.   It has been said, that, without being a *savage*, he
has remained a *barbarian*, as was the case with our German or Gaulish ancestors.   This view is not a just one; the Negro has risen much higher.
The annals of Amed Baba show that in the Middle Ages the basin of the
Niger contained empires very little inferior in many respects to European
kingdoms of the same epoch.   As to the *yellow* races, it will be sufficient to
remember that the whole of the Aryan race was plunged in barbarism at the
time when China was acquainted with the calendar, had determined the
form of the earth, and recognized the flattening of the poles, had woven
materials in silk, and possessed a coinage." [1]

But it may be said there are other racial peculiarities
among the blacks that make them of a different species.   To
this we answer that there are racial peculiarities among other
peoples as well.   The Calmuck Tartars are nearly all bandy-
legged from being accustomed, as is said, from riding horse-
back from tender age.   The great artist, Benj. West,
President of the Royal Academy of Arts, was of the opinion
that the racial face of the Jews, above all others, had something particularly goat-like about it, and was of further opinion that this peculiarity " lay not so much in the hooked nose
as in the transit and conflux of the septum, which separates
the nostrils from the middle of the upper lip."
Perhaps it will contribute something to the tranquilization
of many upon this common family affair (and there is really
no need of so much ado about a mere family matter) if we
name three philosophers of quite a different kind, who however much they may have differed otherwise in many of their
ideas, still were completely of accord with each other on this

---

[1] Quatrefagas, "The Human Species," New York, D. Appleton & Co., 1879, p. 88.

point ; possibly because it is a question which belongs to natural history, and all three were the greatest naturalists in the world at their time—Haller,[1] Linnæus,[2] and Buffon,[3] all these three considered man different by a whole world from the orang-outang and all other brute creatures, and on the other hand all true men, Europeans, Negroes, etc., as mere varieties of one and the same species. And to which Blumenbach adds this valuable testimony:

" I am acquainted with no distinctive bodily character which is at once peculiar to the Negro, and which cannot be found to exist in many other and distant nations; none which is in like way common to the Negro, and in which they do not again come into contact with other nations through imperceptible passages, just as every other variety of man runs into the neighboring populations. The color of the skin they share more or less with the inhabitants of Madagascar, New Guinea and New Holland. And there are imperceptible shades, up from the blackest Negroes in North Guinea to the Moors; amongst whom many, especially the women, according to the assurance of Shaw, have the very whitest skin that it is possible to imagine. The curly, woolly hair is well known not to be common to all Negroes, for Barbot says, even of those in Nigritia itself, that some have curly and some have straight hair ; and Ulloa says just the same of the Negroes in Spanish America. Secondly, this so-called woolly hair is very far from being peculiar to the Negroes, for it is found in many people of the fifth race, as in the Yglotes in the Phillippines, in the inhabitants of Charlotte Island and Van Diemen's Land, and also in many of the third variety who are not reckoned as Negroes. Many Abyssinians have it, as the famous Abbe Gregorius. To this may be added the testimony of Le Maire, who says in his travels through Senegal and Gambia, that there are negresses, who, abstraction being made of the color, are as well formed as European ladies. So also Adamason, that accurate naturalist, asserts the same of the Senegambian negresses; ' they have beautiful eyes, small mouth and lips, and well-proportioned features; some, too, are found of a perfect beauty; they are full of vivacity, and have especially an easy, free and agreeable presence.' As to the good disposition and faculties of these our black brethren, as well as in natural tenderness of heart, they can scarcely be considered inferior to any other race of mankind taken altogether."[4]

This is the weighty testimony of Blumenbach, the illustrious naturalist, in whom the whole scientific and cultured world has acknowledged the very father of anthropology. We have quoted from his writings in several places already, and intend to make draft on his vast treasure-house of knowledge elsewhere, but we here entreat the reader's permission to step a little out of our way to say a word about Blumenbach himself. At the time when the Negroes and the savages were

[1] Elements of Physiology.   [2] Mat. Med. Reg. Anim. vol. i p. 276.
[3] Natural History, vol. ii, p. 185.
[4] Anthropological Treatises of Johann Friedrich Blumenbach, edited by Thomas Bendyshe, London, 1865, pp. 64, 65.

7

still considered as half animals, and no one had yet conceived
the idea of the emancipation of the slaves, Blumenbach raised
his voice, and showed that their physical qualities were not
inferior to those of the Europeans, that even amongst the
latter themselves the greatest possible differences existed, and
that opportunity alone was wanting for the development of
their higher faculties.   His connections with the learned were
both numerous and honorable.   His pupils were such distinguished men as Alex. von Humboldt, Hornemann, Langsdorf,
Seetzen, Sibthorp, and others.   His studies upon various subjects were taken up by great thinkers—Kant, Fichte, Schelling
and Goethe—and were made use of, though with alterations
of expression and manner of representation, as foundation
for further development.   Indeed as Marx says in his memoir,
" it might be sufficient to mention that seventy-eight learned
societies elected him as a member.   There was scarcely any
scientific body of reputation in the wide extent of cultivated
nations which did not send him its diploma by way of testifying their respect." [1]   And this from M. Flourens:

"He raised the science out of chaos, and drew a distinction everywhere
between what belongs to the brute and what belongs to man.   A profound
interval, without connection, without passage, separates the human species
from all others.   No other species comes near the human species; no genus
even, or family.   The human species stands alone.   Guided by his facial
angle, Camper approximated the orang-outang to the Negro.   He saw the
shape of the skull, or more precisely, the form and prominence of the upper
jaw, [2] which gives an apparent resemblance; he failed to see the capacity of
the skull, which makes the real difference.   In form nearly, the skull of the
Negro is as the skull of the European; the capacity of the two skulls is the
same.   And what is much more essential, their brain is absolutely the same.
And, besides, what has the brain to do with the matter ?   The human mind
is one.   The soul is one.   In spite of its misfortunes the African race has
had heroes of all kinds.   Blumenbach, who has collected everything in its
favor, reckons among it the most humane and the bravest men; authors,
learned men and poets.   He had a library entirely composed of books
written by Negroes.   Our age will doubtless witness the end of an odious
traffic.   Philanthropy, science, politics, that is true politics, all join in attack-
ing it; humanity will not be without its crusades." [3]

It affords us peculiar gratification to be able to quote from
so wise and distinguished an author.   It will stop the
wagging tongues of rattle-pated scribblers, and lead the
superficial into water clear over their shallow heads.   And,

---

[1] Marx's Memoir of Blumenbach, p. 31.
[2] See Hist. des t. et des i. de Buffon, p. 183.
[3] Flouren's Memoir of Blumenbach, p. 57.

besides, it is an admirable thing that science—though maligned and perverted in many quarters, seems to add to Christian charity, or, at all events, to extend it, and invent what may be called *human charity.*

Some one, however, may say, give us examples of the Negro's condition to-day. Well, we will. We have before us a copy of the "Life and Labors of David Livingstone," with the adjunct explorations of Henry M. Stanley, the American journalist. We shall quote examples as they come:

Of the Zulus, Livingstone (p. 332) says: "They have the lofty forehead, the prominent nose, and high cheek bones. They are a good humored, generous and independent people, and love to number among the excellencies of their king, that 'he chooses to be black, he might have been white, but would not.'"

Of the Baulungu men, he says, (p. 522), "They are in general tall and well formed. The facial angle is as good in most cases as in Europeans, and they have certainly as little of the 'lark-heel' as the whites."

Of the people of the district of Hara, (p. 528), he says, "The only difference between them and Europeans is color. Many of the men have very finely formed heads, and so have the women; and the fashion of wearing the hair sets off the forehead to advantage. The forehead is shaved off to the crown, the space narrowing as it goes up; then the back hair is arranged into knobs of about ten rows. They are quite intelligent and evince considerable quickness of perception."

The people of Itawa he describes (p. 546) as follows: "Many of the men have as beautiful heads as one could find in an assembly of Europeans. All have very fine forms, with small hands and feet. None of the West Coast ugliness, from which most of our ideas of the Negroes are derived is here to be seen. No prognathous jaws nor lark-heels offended the sight. My observation deepened the impression first obtained from the remarks of Winwood Reade, that the typical Negro is seen in the ancient Egyptian, and not in the ungainly forms which grow up in the unhealthy swamps of the West Coast. Indeed, it is probable that this upland forest region is the true home of the Negro."

Stanley, writing of the Wanyamwezi, says, (pp. 661, 662):

"They are generally splendid specimens of the genus homo, so far as physical proportions make it up; tall and manly-looking, and endowed with re-

markable strength and powers of endurance.   But they are genuine sons of
Ham notwithstanding; the deep brown hue and negroid features are unques-
tionable. . . . Like all negroes they are great lovers of music, and
among them there are artists, who, in spite of the barbarous monotony of their
strains, furnish real amusement.   Many of these individuals are great impro-
visators, and delight to weave the latest political news or personal scandal
into their merry songs."

The Wanyamwezi, he says, (pp. 666, 667):

"Are the typical race of Central Africa, and their industry and commercial activity have won for them quite a reputation.   These are the people
whom we have seen among the hills of Itawa, in the forests of Lunda, on
the banks of the Lualaba, in the wilds of Manyuema, on the banks of all
the lakes—who are found in the mountains of Kavangerah, on the plains of
Uvinza, on the barren plateau of Ugogo, in the park lands of Ukonongo, in
the swamps of Useguhha, in the defiles of Usegara, in the wilderness of
Ubena, among the pastoral tribes of the Watuta, trudging along the banks
of the Refugi, and in slave-trading Kilwa, everywhere; weighted with the
bales of Zanzibar, containing cottons and domestics from Massachusetts,
calicoes from England, prints from Muscat, cloths from Cutch, beads from
Germany, and brass wire from Great Britain.   In caravans they are docile
and tractable, on trading expeditions of their own they are keen and clever;
in their villages they are a merry-making set.   As Ruga Ruga or forest men,
the Wanyamwezi are unscrupulous and bold; in Ukonongo and Ukawendi
they are hunters; in Usukuma they are drovers and iron-smelters; in Lunda
they are energetic searchers for ivory; on the coast they are a wondering,
awe-struck people."

But one of the most curious, and indeed wonderful facts related by Stanley, is concerning the "king of mountains"—
Gambangara, which attains an altitude of between 13,000 and
15,000 feet above the ocean.   He says, (pp. 835, 836):

" On the summit of this high mountain we came across a strange pale-
faced tribe of natives, complexion almost European, a handsome race, some
of the women being singularly beautiful.   Their hair is kinky, but inclined
to brown in color.   Their features are regular, lips thin, but their noses,
though well-shaped, are somewhat thick at the point.   Several of their descendants are scattered through Unyoro, Ankori and Ruanda, and the royal
family of the latter powerful country are distinguished by their pale com-
plexions.   The Queen of Sasua Islands, in the Victoria Nyanza, is a descendant of this tribe." . . . " This discovery is of very great interest in an
ethnological point of view, establishing the fact that there are as many different types of the African family in Africa as there are of the Caucasian race
in Europe."[1]

Still another curious discovery was made by Stanley in
Usongora, the great salt fields of Central Africa.   Here the

---

[1] This fact is corroborated by the recent discovery of a race of " White Negroes " in
the heart of the continent, by Major Serpa Pinto, the Portuguese explorer of Africa,
an account of which recently appeared in the Paris journals.

sole occupation of the natives consists in watching their cows, of which they have an immense number. Like the inhabitants of Ankori, they care for nothing but milk and goat skins, and are "a race of such long-legged natives that ordinary mortals regard them with surprise and awe. The Waganda, who have invaded their country for the sake of booty, ascribe a cool courage to them, against which all their numbers and well-known expertness with shield and spear were of little avail. They are, besides, extremely clannish, and allow none of their tribe to intermarry with strangers, and their diet consists solely of milk." (p. 838.) Here, then, are two instances showing conclusively the effect of climate and diet on complexion and physical form.

Facts are stubborn things, and practical demonstration constitutes incontrovertible testimony. Science, however, backs these examples, and the most eminent scientists of this enlightened century stand in solid phalanx to prove them. We could quote at length from such distinguished naturalists as Cuvier, the two Humboldts, Bunsen, Muller, Lepsius, Agassiz, Owen, Lavater, Bachmann, Pritchard, Latham, Martin, and others, but a few must suffice. Let us take them at random.

First, Agassiz, who says, "I still hesitate to assign to each race an independent origin. Man is everywhere the one identical species." And again, "I cannot repeat too emphatically, that there is not a single fact in embryology to justify the assumption that the laws of development, now known to be so precise and definite for every animal, have ever been less so, or have ever been allowed to run into each other. The philosopher's stone is no more to be found in the organic than the inorganic world; and we shall seek as vainly to transfer the lower animal type into the higher ones by any of our theories, as did the alchemists of old to change the baser metals into gold."[1]

Next we quote from Prof. Richard Owen, of the Royal College of Surgeons—the foremost among comparative anatomists of the world. He says, "In reference both to the unity of the human species, and to the fact of man being the latest, as he is the highest, of all animal forms, upon our planet, the interpretations of God's works coincide with what has been revealed to us, as to our origin and zoological relations in the

---

[1] Agassiz's Methods of Study in Natural History, p. 319.

world. Man is the sole species of his genus, the sole representative of his order." And again, Dr. Owen ˙says with
truth, "If the physiologist and pathologist had done no
more than demonstrate the universal law of our being, they
would deserve the gratitude of the Christian world."[1]

Prof. Muller, of Berlin says: "The different varieties of
species (*not excepting man*) may be accounted for by supposing the original existence of a pair of individuals of opposite
sexes, belonging to the same species, and the constant action
of different-external modifying agencies, such as climate, upon
several, or many successive generations."

Buffon says: "Upon the whole, every circumstance con-
curs in proving that mankind are not composed of species
essentially different from each other; that, on the contrary,
there was originally but one species, which, after multiplying
and spreading over the whole surface of the earth, has un-
dergone changes from the influence of climate, food, mode of
living, diseases, and mixture of dissimilar individuals; that at
first these changes were not so conspicuous, and produced
only individual varieties; that these varieties became afterward more specific, because they were rendered more general,
more strongly marked, and more permanent by the continual
action of the same causes, and that they are transmitted from
generation to generation."

To which we add a quotation from Dr. John Bachman's
" Unity of the Human race"—the same made use of by Dr.
Young:

"In the number of separate bones composing the human skeleton—
amounting to two hundred and forty—in the peculiar structure of the breast-
bone, there being eight pieces in infancy, three in youth, and but one in old
age; in the dropping out of the milk-teeth, between the sixth and fourteenth
year, which are replaced by thirty-two permanent teeth, there is perfect uni-
formity in every variety of man. So also in the period of gestation—the
number of young at a birth, generally one, very rarely two; the period of
longevity, etc., the different varieties of men present a perfect similarity.
They all possess those high prerogatives of man, the attributes of speech and
the faculties of the mind, with capacities for transmitting any improvement
to their descendants. In all there is a capacity to acquire the languages and
songs of other tribes, whilst they may forget those of their forefathers. Thus
whole nations have forgotten their languages, and adopted those of other
nations. But no species of quadruped or biped has ever lost its native notes,
and adopted the notes of another species. In all we discover the same instincts; in all, the power of conscience, the recognition of truth, and a sense of

---

[1] Richard Owen's Comparative Anatomy and Physiology of Vertebrates, vol. iii, p. 825.

right and wrong; in all, some sentiment of religion, some recognition of a higher power; in all, the hope of immortality; in all, the idea of a happier life, and the dread of punishment beyond the grave. Positive Atheism is excluded from the creed of all nations."

Then comes Quatrefagas, who says:

"These human groups, however different they may be, or appear to be, are only *races of one and the same species* and not distinct species. Therefore, there is but *one human species*, taking the term Species in the acceptation employed when speaking of animals and plants. . . I wish that candid men, who are free from party spirit or prejudice, would follow me in this view, and study for themselves all these facts, a few of which I have touched upon, and I am perfectly convinced that they will, with the great men of whom I am only the disciple—with Linnæas, Buffon, Lamarck, Cuvier, Geoffroy, Humboldt and Muller, arrive at the conclusion that *all men belong to the same species*, and that there is but *one species of man*." [1]

Such an accumulation of evidence ought to satisfy the most skeptical, but we desire to add here the opinion of our Dr. Blackie: "The origin of the Negro, as I have been taught at the great seminaries of learning which I have the honor to be an *alumnus*, and have satisfied myself in my researches in the study, and in the two great books of Nature and of God, is the same as that of the Caucasian."

However, there is an answer conclusive and final to this portion of our subject, and we are enabled to present it in the succinct and powerful language of Spurzheim, whose eminent ability is held in the highest esteem by scholars everywhere. He says:

"If there be several species of Man, there can be no universal principles of human conduct; human nature cannot be included in any one system; and the rules which are suitable for one nation will not be fit for another. If, on the contrary, there be only one species, general principles of education, general rules of conduct and national laws, may be established. Moreover, if there were several species, and one superior to the others, the White to the Negro, for example, slavery might be contended for as an institution of Nature; but if the species be only one, neither the primitive moral character, nor Christianity can excuse this most selfish of all barbarities." [2]

And yet still another argument to prove that there is only one species of man—a point hitherto not sufficiently understood in education, nor taken into due consideration in ethnology, concerns the organic conditions on which the manifestations of the mind depend. The general fact should be admitted that the great proportion of mankind can be modi-

---

[1] The Human Species, p. 88.
[2] Education of Man, p. 19.

fied by education and circumstance; and that there are some so constituted, inefficiently or powerfully, that no circumstance or training in the one instance shall ever turn them aside from realizing their burning impressions, or, in the other ever elevate them to produce anything. But this has only a relative value, and does not hold good universally. It applies individually, not collectively; to families, not to races. Everywhere, and at all times, the same primitive faculties, however modified the actions flowing from them may be, are to be observed.

It will not be at all superfluous to point out here some not so well known, though remarkable examples of the perfectibility of the mental faculties and the talents of the Negro, which, of course, will not come unexpectedly upon any one who has perused the accounts of the most credible travelers about the natural disposition of the Negro. Thus, the benevolent Bishop Gregory,[1] and Herder,[2] and Raynal, in various passages of their works, quote instances of extraordinary talents, virtue and morality, observed among the savage and barbarous nations. And thus the classical Barbot, in his great work on Guinea, expresses himself as follows:

"The blacks have, for the most part, head and understanding enough; they comprehend easily and correctly; and their memory is of a tenacity almost incomprehensible; for even when they can neither read nor write, they still remain in their place amidst the greatest bustle of business and traffic, and seldom go wrong. . . . Since they have been so often deceived by Europeans, they now stand carefully on their guard in traffic, and exchange with them, carefully examine all our wares, piece by piece, whether they are of the samples bargained for in quality and quantity; whether the cloths and stuffs are lasting; whether they were dyed in Haarlem or Leyden, etc. . . . In short, they try everything with so much

---

[1] The celebrated Abbe Gregoire, Bishop of the Department of Loire et Cher, and Deputy of the National Assembly of France, wrote a work entitled *"De la litterature des Negres,"* containing sketches of the lives and writings of Negroes, "who have distinguished themselves in science, literature and the arts," the object of which was to demonstrate the moral and intellectual capabilities of the African race. This work has been translated into English, and published both in Great Britain and the United States, but we regret not being able to obtain a copy. However, in a work entitled " Historical Survey of the French Colony in the Island of St. Domingo," written by Bryan Edwards, member of the British Parliament, and Fellow of the Royal Society, we find a letter addressed by Gregory to the inhabitants of St. Domingo, from which we make the following significant extract; "God Almighty comprehends all men in the circle of his mercy. His love makes no distinction between them, but what arises from the different degrees of their virtues. Can laws, then, which ought to be an emanation of eternal justice, encourage so culpable a partiality? Can that government, whose duty it is to protect alike all the members of the same great family, be the mother of one branch, and the stepmother only of the others?"

[2] Herder is a Dutch writer of renown, but unfortunately, few of his works are to be found in the United States.

prudence and cunning as any European man of business whatever can do. Their aptitude for learning of all sorts of fine handy-work is well-known. It is estimated that nine-tenths of the ordinary craftsmen in the West Indies are Negroes."

However, what Blumenbach has to say is still more interesting :

"With respect to their talents for music, there is no necessity for me to call attention to the instances in which Negroes have earned so much by them in America, that they have been able to purchase their freedom for large sums, since there is no want of examples in Europe itself of blacks, who have shown themselves true virtuosos. The Negro Freidig, was well known in Vienna as a masterly concertist on the viol and the violin, and also as a capital draughtsman, who had educated himself at the academy there under Schmutzer. As examples of the capacity of the Negro for mathematical and physical sciences, I need only mention Hannibal, the Russian colonel of artillery, and the Negro Lislet, of the Isle of France, who, on account of his superior meteorogical observations and trigonometrical measurements, was appointed their correspondent by the Paris Academy of Sciences. Dr. Rush, of Philadelphia, wrote a history of the Negro, Fuller, of Maryland, who became so famous through his extraordinary capacity for calculation. In order to test him on this point, he was asked in company how many seconds a man would have lived who was seventy years and so many months, etc., old. In a minute and a half Fuller gave the number. Others, then, calculated it, but the result was not the same. 'Have you not forgotten,' said the Negro, 'to bring into account the days of the leap years?' These were then added and the two calculations coincided exactly. Benjamin Banneker, a Negro of Philadelphia, acquired considerable astronomical knowledge without oral instruction, and entirely through private study of Ferguson's works and Mayer's tables, etc. Boerhaave de Haen, and Dr. Rush have given the most decided proofs of the uncommon insight which Negroes have into practical medicine. Negroes have also been known to make very excellent surgeons. Madox, the Wesleyan Methodist preacher, became famous in England, and so also did Ignatius Sancho and Gustavus Vasa, all Negroes. Sancho was a great favorite both of Garrick and Sterne, and Vasa made himself a name by his interesting autobiography."

Blumenbach had a library of English, Dutch and Latin poems, written by Negroes, and declares Phillis Wheatley, the Negro poetess of Boston, justly famous for her scholarly poems. Some particularly beautiful selections from them are to be found in the famous prize essay of Clarkson on the "Slavery and Commerce of the Human Species." However, let Blumenbach continue :

"In 1734 a Negro, Ant. Wilh. Amo, was created Doctor of Philosophy in the University at Wittenberg, Germany, and in an account of Amo's life, printed in the name of the University Senate, great praise is allotted to his exceptional uprightness, his capacity, his industry, and his learning. It says of his philosophical lectures, 'he studied the opinions both of the ancients and the moderns; he selected the best, and explained his selections clearly and at full length." Still another Negro, Capitein, by name, studied theology at Leyden, and became widely known through his sermons and poems, but more especially his famous *Dissertatio Politico-theologica de Servitute Libertati Christianæ non contraria*, which ran through several editions, and was translated into Dutch, English and German.

"Finally, I am of opinion that after all these numerous instances I have brought together of Negroes of capacity, it would not be difficult to mention entire well-known provinces of Europe, from out of which you would not easily expect to obtain off-hand such good authors, poets, philosophers, and correspondents of the Paris Academy; and on the other hand, there is no so-called savage nation known under the sun which has so much distinguished itself by such examples of perfectibility and original capacity for scientific culture, and thereby attached itself so closely to the most civilized nations of the earth, *as the Negro.*"[1]

It is, perhaps, needless to strengthen a fortress already so impregnable, except that we desire to add a few names of distinguished Colored men in the United States, and elsewhere, at the present time, to prove for one thing, that the black race, at least, has not degenerated intellectually since Blumenbach wrote. Our list is taken from memory, and is, therefore, necessarily, abridged: Frederick Douglass, the celebrated Americo-African orator; Prof. John M. Langston, United States Minister to Hayti; ex-Governor Pinchback, of Louisiana; United States Senator Bruce, of Mississippi; Congressman Rainey, of South Carolina; Prof. Greener, a graduate of Harvard University, and now in charge of the Law Department of Howard University, Washington; Rev. C. H. Thompson, D. D., of the Protestant Episcopal Church, New Orleans; Bishop Payne, ex-President of Wilberforce University, Ohio:—all men of national and some of more than national fame for intelligence and culture. To give a list of the Colored men who possess local reputation for intellectual ability, would necessarily swell this into a large volume, for, indeed, there is scarcely a city or county in the United States, and we dare say in the South, that cannot present a creditable list of ministers, physicians, teachers, merchants—much more than ordinary in intelligence.. In Louisiana, Mississippi, and other Southern States, the professions, the mercantile branches, and the trades, are well represented, while not a few Colored men are possessed of great wealth. Nearly all are liberally educated; some are scholars of a high order.

Among celebrated Negroes abroad, there is the highly educated native black Bishop Crowther, of West Africa;

[1] Blumenbach's Anthropological Treatise, pp, 305-312.

Prof. Blyden; Rev. Barnabas Root, of the A. M. A., who graduated among the highest in a Western College, and the Chicago Theological Seminary; and last, but not least, Rev. Alexander Crummell, formerly of the United States but now of Liberia. He is one of the brightest examples of the black man, and we are glad to quote the following concerning him: " Blood unadulterated, a tall and manly figure, commanding in appearance, a full and musical voice, fluent in speech, a graduate of Cambridge University, England, a mind stored with the richness of English literature, competently acquainted with the classical authors of Greece and Rome, from the grave Thucydides to the rhapsodical Lycophron, gentlemanly in all his movements, language chaste and refined, Mr. Crummell may well be put forward as one of the best and most favorable representatives of his race. He is a clergyman of the Episcopal denomination, and deeply versed in theology."

Then, again, the world renowned French novelist, Alexandre Dumas, may be set down as one-eighth Negro; his father, the black Gen. Dumas, a quadroon, commanded a legion of horse composed of blacks and mulattoes, under the great Napoleon. Pushkin, the most celebrated of Russian poets had Negro blood through his mother. Diaz, the black commander in Brazil, is extolled in all the histories of that country as one of the most sagacious and talented men, and experienced officers of whom they could boast. Hannibal, (the African mentioned by Blumenbach,) gained by his own exertions a good education, and rose to be a lieutenant-general and director of artillery under Peter the Great. Don Juan Latino, a Negro, became teacher of the Latin language at Seville. James Denham, an imported Negro, was considered by Dr. Rush as one of the ablest physicians in New Orleans. Placido, the Negro poet of Havana, wrote elegant and finished verses, that were set to music and sung in the drawing-rooms of the most refined companies which assembled in that city; he was afterwards executed for attempting to incite an insurrection among the slaves by his "songs of freedom."

Among actors, the name of the late Ira Aldridge, "the African Roscius," is at once recognized. Though at one time he lived in the United States, he was a native of Senegal, in Africa, where his forefathers were princes of the Foulah tribe. He was a graduate of the Glasgow University, obtained several premiums and the medal for Latin composition. He adopted the stage as a profession, and played only the leading *roles* of the standard drama. He appeared in a number of Shakspearian characters in all the great cities of Europe—first at Edinburgh, Glasgow, Manchester, then Paris, Berlin and Drury Lane and Covent Garden, London. His "Shylock," the London *Morning Chronicle*, placed among the "finest pieces of acting that a London audience had witnessed since the days of the elder Kean."

It is said that "when a bloody revolt occurred in a province of Ethiopia a few years ago, the Turkish officials tried in vain to control the soldiers and restore order and quiet to the country. A Negro Bey, who, when a boy, had been sold as a slave into Egypt, arrived, and by his masterly shrewdness and ability quelled the insurrection, and His Highness, the Khedive, made him commander-in-chief of the troops of the Soudan." "The Negroes have exhibited as much inventive genius in Africa as was displayed by savages in Europe and America until the people of these climes came in contact with the civilization of the East. One of them, on the West Coast, invented an alphabet, and another has become, doubtless, the most learned man on the continent, either native or foreign."

So many examples of the Negro's intellectual and moral capacity ought to satisfy the most exacting, and it does seem like piling Pelion upon Ossa to beg permission to add a few more names. Since compiling the above, the writer has had the pleasure of hearing a lecture from the highly cultivated colored orator, Dr. William Wells Brown, of Boston, who chose for his theme, "Hannibal, the Carthagenian Hero," and handled it in a masterly manner—presenting a fine literary treat—eloquent, philosophic and finished, and, besides, showing extraordinary culture as an elocutionist and rostrum speaker. Afterwards we had the additional pleasure of meeting Dr. Brown personally, and learned from him that he has already written a number of volumes concerning his people, chief among which are "The Rising Sun" and "The Black Man."[1]   This latter work is before us—a most interesting book—abounding in fact and argument, replete

---

[1] The Black Man : His Antecedents, His Genius and His Achievements. By William Wells Brown. Published for Jas. M. Symms & Co., Savannah, Ga.

with eloquence, logic and learning, and containing biographical sketches of about sixty colored individuals—men and women, who have distinguished themselves in the higher walks of learning. Some of these we have already briefly mentioned, those which follow are from Dr. Brown's book, condensed and arranged by the writer, as follows:

Among distinguished orators and lecturers may be found Charles L. Remond, of Salem, Mass.; Geo. T. Downing and Samuel R. Ward, of New York—the latter called "the black Daniel Webster;" Robert Morris, the Boston lawyer; Henry Highland Garnett, born a slave in Maryland, but afterwards a writer and orator of far more than ordinary ability; Jeremiah B. Sanderson, of New Bedford, Mass., a scholar and lecturer, well versed in history, theology and the classics; Frances Ellen Watkins, the Negro poetess of Baltimore, who was before the public some years as an author and lecturer.

Of the Colored *literati* and educators mention is made of the following: James M. Whitfield, the "barber-poet" of Buffalo, a man noted for his scholarly attainments, as well as native genius; Charles L. Reason, Professor of Mathematics and Belles-Lettres in New York Central College; Prof. George B. Vashon, A. M., a graduate of Oberlin College, and afterwards called to a professorship in New York Central College—well-known as a lawyer, literateur and astronomer; John Sella Martin, born in Charlotte, N. C.—three times sold as a slave, but who finally escaped, educated himself, and became a writer of both prose and poetry, and a preacher of decided ability in Boston; Charlotte L. Forten, of Salem, Mass.—poetess, author and teacher; Henry Bibb, of Windsor, Canada; William Still, of Philadelphia; Prof. William J. Wilson and William Nell, of Boston—all Negroes, and all intellectual and cultivated.

The medical profession is not without its able men. Martin R. Delany, M. D., is the name of another distinguished pure blooded Negro, widely known as a traveler, discoverer and lecturer. He accompanied Prof. Campbell in the "Niger Valley Exploring Expedition" and made an official report on the climate, soil, diseases, and natural productions of Africa. He lectured in the United States and Great Britain; was presented at the Court of St. James, and in many ways has made himself a man of mark.

Dr. James McCune Smith, graduated with distinguished honors at the University of Glasgow, Scotland, where he received his diploma of M. D. ˙For more than twenty-five years he has been a successful practitioner in New York, and yet has done besides much literary work. "History, antiquity, bibliography, translation, criticism, political economy, statistics—almost every department of knowledge—receive emblazon from his able, ready, versatile and unwearied pen."

Dr. John S. Rock, graduated both in medicine and dentistry at the American Medical College, Philadelphia. Afterwards, on account of ill health he studied law, passed his examination before the Superior Court of Massachusetts, and was admitted to practice as an attorney and counsellor in all the Courts of that State. He has also made reputation as a lecturer, and in 1860 by invitation of the Massachusetts Legislature delivered a lecture on the "Character and Writings of Madame DeStæl." Of this lecture *Der Pionier*, a German newspaper in Boston, said: "This thinking, educated German and French speaking Negro, proved himself as learned in German as he is in French literature."

Among colored artistes there are Edwin M. Bannister, of Boston, who began life as a hair dresser, and is now a landscape painter; while William H. Simpson, of the same city, has exhibited marked ability and consummate genius as a portrait painter. Hon. Chas. Sumner, gave Simpson a "sitting;" and portraits from Simpson's studio are to be found in many of the Northern States, California, Canada, Hayti, and Liberia.

The clergy claims numerous brilliant, learned and eloquent men. Rev. Wm. Douglass, rector of St. Thomas church, Philadelphia, and Rev. J.ʼTheodore Holly, of New Haven, Conn., also of the Protestant Episcopal Church, are men of finished education, versed in Latin, Greek and Hebrew; forcible and logical writers, of varied talents and undoubted culture. Rev. Elymas Payson Rogers, of Newark, New Jersey, clergyman of the Presbyterian order, is highly educated—a forcible writer of prose, and possessed of poetical talent. Rev. Dr. J. W. C. Pennington, was born a slave in Maryland, and served as plantation blacksmith on the farm of Col. Gordon. He had no early opportunities for learning, and was ignorant of letters when he made his escape to the North. Through intense application, he gained an education, studied theology and became a Presbyterian preacher. He afterwards visited Europe several times, was a member of the Peace Congresses held at Paris, Brussels, and London. While in Germany the degree of Doctor of Divinity was conferred upon him by the University of Heidelberg, and on his return to the United States he was settled as pastor over Shiloh Church, New York city. Dr. Pennington has been a good student, and is a ripe scholar, and not only a theologian but a linguist—understanding Greek, Latin and German. He is of unmixed African blood, and with strongly-marked African features.

Ex-President Roberts, of the Republic of Liberia, a native of Virginia, is a Negro. Sir Edward Jordan, born a slave in Kingston, Jamaica, became premier of the Island, and president of the privy council, and in 1860 was elevated to the dignity of the knighthood by the Queen of England. In a literary point of view he is considered one of the first men in Jamaica. Joseph Jenkins, the wonderful and most versatile genius whom Dr. Brown met in London—who distributed hand-bills in Cheapside in the morning, swept crossings in Chelsea in the afternoon, sold religious tracts and sung psalms at Kensington in the evening, played Othello at the Eagle Theater at night, and preached on Sunday—was nothing but a Negro.

The West Indies are well represented in Dr. Brown's book. Among the celebrated Colored men mentioned are Toussaint L'Overture, the military chieftain of St. Domingo; Vincent Oge, his famous deputy; Andre Rigaud, well educated, and of cultivated manners; Henri Cristophe, who was master of the French, English and Spanish languages, and was thought to be the most polished of all of Toussaint's generals. Also, Jean Jacques Dessalines, the African, the savage, the slave, the soldier, the general, the president, and lastly the Emperor of Hayti. President Geffrard, President Jean Pierre Boyer, and President Alexandre Petion, of the Republic of Hayti, were all highly educated Negroes. Petion, was a graduate of the Military School of Paris, was a skillful engineer, and perhaps the most scientific officer and the most erudite individual among the people of Hayti.

And lastly, we will mention two most curious and interesting historical facts. By a striking coincidence, the same year, 1620, which witnessed the landing of the Pilgrims at Plymouth Rock, also witnessed the landing of the first Negro slaves for sale by the Dutch, at Jamestown, Virginia. The other fact is this, the first blood shed in the American Revolution was that of a Negro named Crispus Attucks, who led the

Boston populace against the British soldiers who were drawn up in line on King (now State) street, March 5, 1770. So that if we have shown the Negroes are not wanting for intellectual representatives neither are they without their Revolutionary hero.

With these multiplied and overwhelming testimonies in favor of the Colored man, we may as well leave the subject with all fair-minded people. But in order that there may not be a stone unturned, we are constrained to add a few more points in their behalf. The investigations we have pursued, and the corroborative proof of wisdom—acquired and natural —establish beyond controversy the grand points we have been aiming at, viz : the unity of the human species, and the just claims of the black man to respectful consideration from his brother man. We dare assert the fact, that no candid man, thoroughly acquainted with comparative anatomy, no candid man, capable of intelligent opinion, will make use of stupid and nonsensical objections to the black man, simply on account of his color. In their general economy, in the plans ordained for their government, in the construction as well as offices of their principal parts, there exists between all men a close resemblance, whether they be white or black, or red or brown. In all, life is sustained and the body nourished by the same apparatus, The heart, the lungs, the stomach ; the flesh, the bones, the viscera, and all the internal parts, are of the same color in Negroes as in the Whites. The same fluid (for no distinction of blood has been discovered even under the most powerful and searching microscopic tests), the same fluid circulates through their vessels and in precisely the same order. The lymph is equally white and limpid ; and the milk of the nurses is everywhere the same. In this latter connection let us state one fact, which has excited the admiration and caused the constant wonder of anatomists, viz: the lacteal system of animals. Dr. Paley notes " that the number of teats and paps in each species is found to bear a proportion to the number of the young. In the sow, the rabbit, the cat, the rat, which have numerous litters, the paps are numerous, and are disposed along the whole length of the belly ; in the cow and mare they are few. The most simple account of this," says he, "is to refer it to a designing creator,"[1] But the point we aim at, though Dr. Paley may not have over-

---

[1] Paley's Natural Theology, p. 147.

looked, yet failed to mention, just here is, the lacteal system of the human being—placed as it is over the lungs and the heart, as if the good God had intended to remind the sons of women that the storehouse of sustenance lies near the seat of life, and the child imbibes the distilled liquor from the very fountain of the mother's love. But in this respect there is no difference between the white and the black mother.

Then again, man alone is destitute of what are called *instincts*, but he has *reason*. Brutes have not reason, but have instinct. *Instinct* always remains the same, and is not advanced by cultivation, nor is it smaller or weaker in the animal than the adult. *Reason*, on the contrary, may be compared to a developing germ, which, in the process of time, and by the accession of a social life and other external circumstances, is as it were developed, formed and cultivated.

> " Before his horns adorn the calf, they're there,
> All weaponless he butts, and furious beats the air." [1]

But not so with man. He is born naked, has no hair on his back ; is born weaponless, furnished with no instinct, and is enterely dependent on society and education. On this point Dr. Paley says : " The human animal is the only one which is naked, and the only one which can clothe itself. This is one of the properties which renders him an animal of all climates, and of all seasons. He can adapt the warmth or lightness of his covering to the temperature of his habitation. Had he been born with a fleece upon his back, although he might have been comforted by its warmth in high latitudes, it would have oppressed him by its weight and heat, as the species spread towards the equator." [2]

Man brought up amongst the beasts, destitute of intercourse with man, may lose much of his manhood, but does not come out a beast. On the contrary, beasts which live with man never lose their brute instincts, and never gain anything of manhood. Neither the beavers, nor the seals, who live in company, nor the domestic animals who enjoy our familiar society, come out endowed with reason.

Man alone possesses *speech*, or the voice of reason. Beasts have only the language of affection. On this point let us quote from Prof. Daniel Wilson, of Toronto, Canada : " We habitually designate all other living creatures as *dumb* an-

---

[1] Lucret, v. 1033.
8

[2] Natural Theology, p. 123.

imals, discriminating in this between the inarticulate cries of the lower animals, and the intelligent utterances of human speech. Hence the legitimate selection of language as the most essential and unvarying index of man. No race of men has ever been found devoid of language. No other race of animals has been known to possess language in its most rudimentary form. We have, indeed, speech in a certain sense, in the parrot, starling, etc., but this is no more than another phase of the capacity for imitating sound, familiar to us in the natural imitations of the mocking bird, and dependent in part on physical structure. Neither in the one case nor in the other, are the sounds symbols of thought or vocal signs of objects or ideas." [1]

Just here let us introduce an important point from Dr. Latham, who, in speaking of the efforts to place in proper rank of a standard, the families of mankind, refers to the investigations of philologists, thus:

"The Caucasians had been put in a sort of antithesis to the Negroes; and hence came mischief. Whatever may be the views of those able writers who have investigated the Sub-Semitic Africans, when pressed for definitions, it is not too much to say that, in practice, they have all acted as if the moment a class became Semitic, it ceased to be African. They have all looked one way; that being the way in which good Jews and Mahometans look—towards Mecca and Jerusalem. They have forgotten the phœnomena of correlation. If Cæsar is like Pompey, Pompey must be like Cæsar. If African languages approach the Hebrew, the Hebrew must approach them. The attraction is mutual; and it is by no means a case of Mahomet and the mountain. I believe that the Semitic element of the Berber, the Coptic and the Galla are clear and unequivocal; in other words that these languages are truly Sub-Semitic. . . . But unequivocal as may be the Semitic element of the Berber, Coptic and Galla, their affinities with the tongues of Western and Southern Africa are more so. I weigh my words when I say, not *equally*, but *more*. Changing the expression for every foot in advance which can be made towards the Semitic tongues in one direction, the African philologist can go a yard towards the Negro ones in the other." [2]

Let us proceed then to other considerations. The erect portion of man declares him *not* a beast. One of Blumenbach's great endeavors was to illustrate the difference between man and beast; and he insisted particularly upon the importance of the upright walk of man and the vertical line.

> "Mankind alone can lift the head on high
> And stand with trunk erect."

---

[1] From an address delivered by Prof. Wilson, before the American Association for the Advancement of Science, at Nashville, Tenn., Sept. 3, 1877.
[2] Man and His Migrations, pp. 155, 156.

Man has two hands—beasts have none. Man is a perfect biped, beasts are quadrupeds. The immobility of the ears; the shape of the brain in man differs for all the world from the brute. Mankind cannot, like brutes be fattened. "Man," as Franklin says, "is the tool making animal." Man cooks his food, brutes do not. Man sows and reaps, brutes do not. All of this and much more leads us to conclude that the white man is not a brute.[1] It also leads us to conclude that the black man is his brother. "God's image too," as Fuller says, "although made out of ebony."

So, then, God speaks to the black man, as well as the white man, not only through the robe of flesh and blood and bones that fits upon his undying soul—a perfect net-work of moral teaching tissues—not only in the administering faculties of sense, reason and feeling, but in the blind and voiceless elements that fill the solid and insensible world, as well as in every motion and harmony of the spheres, in the gorgeous banners spread upon the boundless air and sky, and in

"The book of Nature, and the print
Of beauty on the whispering sea."

Talk then, of the black man having no soul! Why? Because no man has ever *seen* it? Has any man ever seen a white man's soul? No. It is strange, then, that even so bold an infidel as Voltaire would admit, "it is hazardous to assert, that because we never beheld a thing, it does not exist," "No man hath seen God at any time," but only "the fool hath said in his heart there is no God."

Here, then, are humanitarian sentiments worthy to be reflected upon—the soul-inspiring thoughts of the Humboldts —which, powerful and charming and profound—basing their high moral value on their touching eloquence—all but rival St. Paul's eulogia of "love" in boundless charity towards all mankind: "Without doubt," says Alexander von Humboldt, "there are families of peoples more susceptible of culture, more civilized, more enlightened; but there are none more noble than others. *All are equally made for liberty*, which, in a state of society but little advanced, appertains only to

---

[1] Of course we except here such special pleading, or rather we recognize the rebutting testimony which was illustrated in the examination of a ladies' class in Scotland recently, as follows ; *Instructor.*—" What does Condillac say about brutes in the scale of being ?" *Young Lady.*—He says a brute is an imperfect animal." *Instructor.*—" And what is man ?" *Young Lady.*—" Man is a perfect brute."

individuals; but which, among those nations called to the enjoyment of veritable political institutions the right of the whole community."

Then, the idea of humanity is beautifully developed by his brother William: "This is what tends to break down those barriers which prejudices and interested motives of every kind have erected between men, and to cause humanity to be looked upon in its *ensemble*, without distinction of religion, of nature, of color, as one great brotherhood, as a single body, marching towards one and the same goal, the free development of the moral forces. . . , Rooted in the depths of human nature, commanded at the same time by its most sublime instincts, this beneficent and fraternal union of the whole species becomes one of the grand ideas which preside over the history of humanity."

We now leave this subject for good and all, but we leave it with a feeling of triumph, the satisfaction of a man who has performed a conscientious duty with credit to his subject and credit to himself. However, we cannot resist making one more point, submitting to those who are curious of establishing the ethnological status of the Negro—who is nearly as strong physically as the European, and superior to the Australian and the South Sea Islander, and more vigorous than the Tartar and the Chinese races—submitting the privilege of contrasting the black man with the Indian, the so-called noble savage. The Indian is of a melancholy, cold, insensible race. The Negro light-hearted, affectionate, impressionable. The Indian, says a traveler, is "foreign to our hopes, our joys, our griefs; it is rarely that a tear moistens his eyes, or that a smile lights up his features." The Negro is ardent and impulsive, his emotions respond with the vivacity of childhood to every impression, whether joyous or sad. The Indian is passive, as in old age, alike indifferent to pain or pleasure —let us call the Indian, the dotard of the ages, and his life the sunset of an epoch that is passing away. But the Negro, we hail and christen the child of the new civilization just coming up—his rising, to use a metaphor, the gray dawn of the brighter centuries. The most barbarous tortures cannot extort from the Indian a single complaint, and his stoical indifference is disturbed only by vengeance or jealousy. If he sometimes exhibits a display of prodigious muscular force, he is yet without endurance. "Who knows not," asks Guyot, "that when the first invaders of the New World endeavored to compel the inoffensive Indians, who had received them as gods, to the rude labors of the mines and the cultivation of the soil, these men of the woods, incapable of enduring fatigue, perished in agony by thousands? And it was thereupon that the Europeans substituted for the Indian the robust and vigorous native of the Old World, the Negro, who still, to this day, used as the instruments of the white man's labor, endures, I had almost said, gayly, a degree of toil equal to that which destroyed the native of the country."

And yet for the Indian, when the guns of the army are not turned upon his breast, we have eulogia and romantic notions of his native nobility, while for the Negro, we have had nothing but sneers and cuffs and kicks. Our country's flag with its "stars and stripes"—what did it symbolize? Were the stars for the white man? and the stripes for the black? But which race has shown true progression? In three hundred years the social condition of the Indian, instead of advancing, has retrograded, for it must be remembered that in the path of development, not to advance is to go back; it is impossible to remain stationary. He has seldom elevated himself above the condition of the hunter. He has never even ascended to the rank of the pastoral man—much less sought nourishment from the generous bosom of mother earth. What service has he performed for the nation? What service had we the right to expect? And yet contrast this with the enforced labors of the Negro—who felled forests, redeemed waste places, built roads and barns and farm-houses, toiled in the mills and the brick-yards—worked with ringing trowel on temple and edifice, and made our beautiful South, with her far-stretching fields, wave her harvests, like the banner of divine benevolence. Take into account, too, the rapid civilization of the African just come from the jungles, his fine capacity for improvement, and he advances proudly and rightly to a higher position in the scale of humanity. Even as the tropical man of the Old World, the Negro possesses a native vigor of vital energy, manifested by his sanguine temperament, by his gaiety, by his lively affections and by his muscular strength, placing him higher than the Indian of tropical America. His social state, even there, has made a step in advance. The Negro tribes of Congo and Soudan had formed commonwealths, and were quite well acquainted with agriculture before visited by the Europeans.

But the Indians—nomadic bands, in undisturbed possession of fruitful pasture lands for thousands of years, knew nothing of pastoral life, scarce anything of agriculture, but lived, and hunted, and battled, and died on the very plains whereon the European pioneer and his African co-laborer founded the most illustrious nation of modern ages—and built up the magnificent Republic of the New Times.

COLORED EDUCATION IN THE SOUTH.

That point in our labors is reached where we must speak of the Colored man as a citizen under the new order of things. It is a delicate subject to handle and requires *nerve*, from the fact, that most unfortunately for all, nearly everything relative to the Negro has heretofore been made to bear political significance, and become a question of party rather than a question of humanity. But we started out with the intention of writing only truth, and, as we have purposely repeated this, it arms us with stout and stable confidence for the task. So far our treatise is fortified with the opinions of eminent and learned men. We have swept over a wide range of history and science, and touched upon subjects capable of great elaboration. This, however, seemed unavoidable—*first*, to get somewhat obscure though important facts before the public in succinct and simplified form, and, *secondly*, to show the overwhelming and seemingly insurmountable obstacles—the multiplied difficulties, prejudices and proscriptions that weighed down the black race and acted as effectual barriers to their progress. In the further investigation of this subject we shall pursue a similar plan—not to excite controversy, but to remove error. We shall continue writing history, (though the true history of the Colored race in this country is only of few years growth), and, therefore, except where it becomes necessary to state a truth we shall peremptorily order *individual opinions* to the rear. Seventeen years only have elapsed since the black man was freed, the old system disappeared forever, and the fundamental principles of our laws were changed. Seventeen years only since the Proclamation of Emancipation was issued, and we shall see directly whether the black man is proving in any way worthy of a struggle that cost billions of treasure and rivers of blood.

When the echo of the death-dealing guns had died away, when the smoke of conflict had lifted from the scene, the old ship Constitution that had so long breasted the bloody waves of the battle-sea, lay stranded, with battered hulk, on the ever-shifting sands of Time. Daylight revealed a ghastly picture. The South prostrate and bleeding ; the North crippled and in want. And more than that, the country awoke to the fact that between four and five millions of poor, homeless and ignorant Negroes had suddenly become the " wards of the nation." What was to be done with them? It would have been unjust, as it was impossible for the South to take charge of them, though there are persons who seemed to think otherwise. Education was the measure and the remedy, but education is of slow growth, and was attended by many disadvantages and discouragements. It has been said also that " there never was a class of people, who were more heartily abused than those who first came South to teach," and that Colored pupils were " assailed with annoyances, taunts and jeers." We do not deny this, nor do we affirm it. Even if it is true, it is not unnatural. To consider this subject with justice and equity, the people of the North must also practice forbearance, must put themselves in our place, and then if they would have acted differently, then, and not until then, would they be justified in condemning. Let it be remembered that the South was suffering under the bitter pain of deep and galling wounds. Let it be remembered that the North was very aggravating, and that new-found freedom made the Negro aggressive and tantalizing. Put all these things together, and the conclusion will be that if it was wicked in the South to rebel, it was wicked in the North to turn Spanish Matadore, and so to speak, flourish a red rag in the face of a gored and maddened bull. True victory is not to crush an opponent, but to make him a friend. A little more of Christian patience and forbearance, on both sides, will bring matters once more into harmony, and cement relations between the sections stronger than ever.

There was then, and there is but one solution of this gigantic problem. *The Colored man must be educated.* He is no longer an enigma—no longer as a dumb, driven brute. He is a thinking, reasoning man—a man with a soul, and capable of the highest culture. An eloquent, straightforward, manly statement of the needs of the race was set forth by Rev. Dr. Strieby, Secretary of the American Missionary

Association, in an address delivered at the dedication of Fisk University, Nashville, Jan. 1, 1876, and from which we extract the following :

⚬ "They are 'a nation born at once,' born in their helplessness, unskilled in the arts of industry, economy or of thrift; born with almost nothing on the face of the earth; with no land, no home, no capital, no skill. Their ignorance—while they are citizens and voters—gives a startling preponderance to the illiteracy of the South, as compared with any other section of the Union. The census of 1870 shows that while the West had only 409,175 persons over 10 years of age who cannot read, the South has, including both whites and blacks, 3,550,425—an excess of *over three millions!* It shows that of the *voters*, the West has only 217,403, who cannot read, but the South has, including both races, 1,137,303, or nearly *one million* more! If we are alarmed at the prevalence of ignorance through the incoming of foreigners in the North and West, what should be the alarm at the dense illiteracy in the South! What a theatre for demagogues of both parties and of both colors! What a range for the growth of the vices begotten of slavery! The Negro is not a communist—the danger is not of violence and blood; it is rather of stagnation. The malaria in the low-lands hangs heavy and close to the ground. It is only dissipated by the sun's rays and the influx of the pure mountain winds, which, mingling with it, and lifting it up, render it harmless. So is this Southern problem to be met. These colored people must have the rays of the sun of knowledge and the pure air of divine truth to dissipate their ignorance. There is no hindrance. They can be educated. They must be helped to develop whatever of talent or manhood God has given them. They are to take their place among men, not by compulsion, but by showing their fitness for it.

"The American Missionary Association comes to lend a helping hand. We claim not to be alone in this work. We recognize gladly the institutions and labors of kindred societies from the North and the co-operation of the people of the South. We come not with Force Bills, Civil Rights enactments, nor with denunciation. We come not to seek office nor public emoluments, but we have come simply to aid in the education and Christian culture of the people—to help to develop in them all the manhood, the talent, the genius and the piety with which God has endowed them. This Christian work is the surest bond of union between the North and the South. Men talk of political unity, but there is a far more tender and endearing tie —that of Christian love and labor. When the Christian people of the South see that our sole purpose in coming here is to lift up this people by educational and religious culture, they will extend to us the hand of welcome, and say, 'Brothers of the North, if you come for this, we are with you heart and soul?'"

And so they are. Enough to say that much of the opposition to Colored Schools has passed away, and the spirit of prejudice and bitterness that once prevailed now no longer exists. The best citizens of all parties and sects admit that it is better for all concerned that the Colored people should be educated, than to remain in ignorance, and liberal provisions by city, county and State have been made for establishing and supporting Colored schools.

Education is the grand problem of the age, not only with this country, but with the world. History not only affirms the necessity of education to the permanence and progress of every administrative system—ecclesiastical, political and popular, but the *present* declares education to be the very breath of existence. Senator Lamar, recently said, "Questions of Constitutional law, the relations of the States to the Federal Government, and the relations of the people to their State Government, will soon cease to play any very conspicuous part in the issues of American politics. Questions of tariff, trade, commerce, currency and transportation, will soon take their places, are beginning to engross the attention of the people, and will tax the intellect of American Statesmen." But the Senator, who is himself an educator, surely could not have forgotten the greatest of all social, if not politico-economic questions, which is bringing eminent educators and other students of social science to the fore-front in the magnificent work of lifting up and enlightening the masses.

Gen. John Eaton, United States Commissioner of Education, in his Report for 1877, presents the following views of the question of Colored Education in the South, which demand more than a passing notice:

"In order to comprehend the difficulties encountered by the friends of universal instruction in the States where slavery has been more recently abolished, certain facts should be remembered.

(1.) That the interests of slavery did not permit the instruction of the Colored people.

(2.) That during the existence of slavery the universal education of the whites was felt to be in some sense a source of danger to the progress of slavery.

(3.) That, as a consequence, the philosophy of education in its comprehensiveness was not understood; the facts which illustrated the benefit of universal education could not and did not exist in those communities.

(4.) When, therefore, slavery passed away, and the several States where it had existed attempted to establish universal education, there was (*a*) a lack of its methods, (*b*) of its philosophy, and (*c*) of its results, either upon individuals or upon society, as regards its advantages in promoting virtue and social order, or in producing wealth.

(5.) All the questions that arose were complicated by the influence of race prejudice. This is nothing new; it is only what has occurred in other lands, and, indeed, elsewhere in our own country, as, for example, will be found in studying the history of the efforts to educate the Colored people in New York city.

(6.) The Colored people on their part entertain erroneous anticipations of what education is and what it was to do for them; and not a few intelligent whites were influenced by the idea that education as offered to the Negro would destroy him as a laborer. Indeed, they were not familiar with the effect of education upon the laborers of any race.

(7.) Added to all these was the feeling of extreme poverty.

(8.) The progress noted in the summaries given should be studied in the light of these facts. It is plain that those results could not have been accomplished without a change of position on the part of many leading minds. Indeed, it has been true that an honest study of the facts has been followed with the approval of the great principle which underlies the most successful system in the country.

"The many questions of race discussed among us, render of peculiar interest all facts in regard to the progress of education among the Colored people."[1]

Are the views of the Commissioner correct? Is it true that "the interests of slavery, did not permit the instruction of the Colored people?" These are questions we have asked ourself—and which many Southern people will ask themselves. At first glance it seems like a sweeping assertion, perhaps is too much so, for there were hundreds and indeed thousands of Southern masters who had their slaves taught. The Colored ministers were, as a rule, men of education, and a great many house-servants were instructed in reading and writing. But as for general education the statement is true. We regret to do so, but must again quote from Dr. Baldwin, who says, (p. 443): "The North calls upon the South to educate their slaves, and this they should do. But the kind of education really demanded is quite another matter. The Bible prescribes the education obligatory upon Southern masters. It says not 'teach reading, writing, arithmetic, mathematics, pneumatics nor politics,' but 'teach them all things whatsoever I have commanded you; repentance toward God, and faith in our Lord Jesus Christ.' As for *literary* education, the South cannot give it—at least while the North will encourage slaves to desert their masters. Would Northerners do like St. Paul—send back the fugitive slave to his master—the South could then educate without loss; the North prevents the Negro from literary improvement."

How or in what manner the North prevented the Negro, still in slavery, from literary improvement does not appear, but if Dr. Baldwin spoke authoritatively, it is plain to be seen the observations of the Commissioner are correct. To the foregoing statement of Gen. Eaton, as showing a more

---

[1] Report of the Commissioner of Education for 1877, p. 33.

recent phase of the question, is attached the following foot-note :

"The attitude of the struggle is well illustrated by the discussion between Hon. W. H. Ruffner, Superintendent of Public Instruction for the State of Virginia, and Rev. Dr. R. L. Dabney, an eminent citizen of that State. Dr. Dabney having published an article against Negro education and the school system generally, in a Virginia newspaper, a discussion ensued, in the course of which Mr. Ruffner maintained, first, that 'Unless we propose to abolish education wholly we must employ the public system, because we are too poor to do without it;' secondly, Dr. Dabney errs in holding that 'If our civilization is to continue, there must be at the bottom of the social fabric a class who must work and not read,' since the history of prominent industrial nations points to a different conclusion; Virginia's greatest statesman, moreover, have persistently urged the policy of widespread popular education ; thirdly, admitting religious instruction to be necessary to the proper development of the child, and conceding that the State has no right to teach anything of a sectarian character, yet the State 'may formally teach the recognized morality of the country;' fourthly, illiteracy is not so prevalent in countries having systems of popular education as in those without such a system; fifthly, ignorance and crime are closely related; sixthly, the hope of prosperity in the South is to be based on the Negro's elevation and development, and not on his extermination."

Superintendent Ruffner's points are well taken and are capable of the strongest support. Let us prove these facts as we advance. There was a time, not very far back, when men decried the advantages of education and were outspoken in their opposition. About the middle of the 16th century, the old Duke of Norfolk said, " I never read the Scripture, nor never will read it. It was merry in England before the new learning came up ; yea, I would all things were as hath been in times past." Two centuries ago, when the English Commissioner of Foreign Plantations, inquired of the Colonial Governors, with regard to the condition of their respective settlements, the Governor of Virginia, replied: " I thank God there are no free schools or printing presses, and I hope we shall not have these hundred years." And though these were very good old times in which these dear good old gentlemen lived—it is plain

" The old order changeth, and yieldeth place to new,
And God fulfills himself in many ways,
Lest one good custom should corrupt the world."

Contrast these opinions with those held upon the subject by the fathers of the Republic : Ex-President John Adams, in his work on government, says, " Laws for the liberal education of youth, especially of the lower class of people, are so extremely wise and useful, that, to a humane and generous mind, no expense for this purpose would be thought extravagant." Ex-President Madison, says, " Knowledge will forever govern ignorance; and a people who mean to be their own governors must arm themselves with the power which knowledge gives. . . . Every class is interested in establishments which give to the human mind its highest improvement. . . . Learned institutions ought to be favorite objects with every free people. They throw that light over the public mind which is the best security against crafty and dangerous encroachments on the public liberty." These views are admirably supported by the opinions of many other eminent men, but we shall only quote one more : Judge Aldrich, of Massachusetts, who wisely says : " It is too late to deny that superior education is *necessary* to the State, and it is precisely on this ground of State necessity that the grants to, and public support of, schools should be made and given, and not on the ground that they are made benefactors to the grantees."

Beyond question it is both more effectual towards promoting the welfare of society, and more humane and agreeable, to correct morals, than to punish crimes. There is nothing more true than the homely old adage, " An ounce of preventive is worth a pound of cure." To that end it ought to be a serious aim with governments and States, to adopt such means as will exclude idleness and intemperance from society. There can be no doubt that governments are wrong in licensing numberless drinking saloons, and in affording great facility and immunity to pawn-broking establishments. At any rate, the most important way of preventing crime, is that of improving mankind by every possible means, and especially by education. Moreover, let ignorance and idleness, intemperance and inexcusable poverty, which are the principle causes of crime, be prevented, and there will be less need for prisons and police. On this point the Commissioner of Instruction has the following to say :

" The expenditure for police in our cities brought into comparison with the expenditure for education, presents many interesting contrasts. It would naturally be thought that all the items necessary for such comparison could be furnished from the records of every city annually; unfortunately this is not so. It is universally admitted that education which develops aright the whole man, must bear a close relation to the evils in human condition, and among them to crime. The most enthusiastic would hardly claim that education at its best could perfect human condition ; they believe, however, in its power to modify and improve. From the present imperfect condition of records and statistics, a fair mind can hardly reach a different conclusion ; but a thorough investigator will scarcely be satisfied until the data before him shall include a fair statement of all the conditions involved in the statement. The police expenditure is but a single item in the cost of crime ; there is also the destruction of life and property, with the evils arising from their constant peril, to which must be added the cost of courts, of jails, of penitentiaries, and all other expenditure on account of crime." [1]

The Commissioner then gives a tabulated comparison of municipal expenditure for police and education in various cities, from which we take the following :

CITIES.	Year.	Population.	Police Expenditure.		Educat'l Expend'ure.	
			Total	Per Capita.	Total	Per Capita.
Chicago,	1876	425,000	$ 564,398	$1.32	$ 829,429	$1.95
Louisville,	1876	125,000	168,079	1.34	285,302	2.28
Baltimore,	1877	302,839	599,110	1.97	699,514	2.30
Boston,	1877	341,919	833,706	2.43	1,816,615	5.31
Detroit,	1877	110,000	135,000	1.22	213,214	1.93
St. Louis,	1877	500,000	464,584	92	1,007,830	2.01
Albany,	1877	69,422	117,689	1.69	129,125	1.86
New York,	1877	1,200,000	3.292,400	2.74	3,316,889	2.76
Cincinnati,	1877	267,000	271,627	1.01	673,036	2.52
Philadelphia,	1876	750,000	1.437,546	1.91	1,991,364	2.65
Washington,	1877	106,000	300,000	2.83	333,766	3.15

From the foregoing, it will be seen that in proportion as the educational expenditure is large the police expenditure is small. Take, for instance, the figures given for New York— where the police expenditure is $2.74 per capita, and the educational expenditure $2.76 per capita, or take those given for Chicago $1.32 per capita for police and $1.95 per capita for education—and no one will attempt to say this does not explain much of the wickedness of those two cities. In Detroit also, where $1.22 per capita is paid for police, and only $1.93 per capita for education—the whole number of arrests for 1877 was 4657. Of these, 701 could neither read nor write, and 107 others could read only.

But the fact is patent to all that the district school-house and the ward school-house are more efficient agents of progress than the corner grocery—the polical caucus—the blue-coated policeman, or the grim-visaged walls of a prison.

[1] Commissioner's Report for 1877, pp. 65, 66.

Menace and punishment, moral suasion and religion have their uses, but none separately or together, seem able to check or withstand the present tendency of the age to immorality, vice, and crime of almost every description. We are all, every one of us, largely the creatures of impulse, under opportunity. "Chance makes rogues" is a threadbare saying, but time has proven it literally true, and in quarters we least expected. The sons of clergymen and other upright persons, above all taint of character, frequently become the most abandoned of criminals. Neither by heredity, nor necessity, nor by the lack of education in themselves, but by their surroundings in society—it may be at college or university, where they are far removed from the restraints of home—or battling with the world where no friendly hand is stretched out to save, and the joy that love once kindled has died out in bitter disappointment. We all know these things, for the world is brimful of dejected and heart-broken examples. And we all know, too, that the greatest, the wisest, the most sublime, the purest of all philosophers—He who was God and philosopher in one, based His religious system upon the knowledge that we are all poor, erring beings, without help in or of ourselves. He it is who tells us in that prayer which must ever be a consolation and inspiration to humanity —we must with all the power of heart and mind and soul struggle, and pray, "Lead us not into temptation," "Deliver us from evil."

It is, therefore, to the interest of all good citizens, as it is the duty of a wise and paternal government, to diffuse instruction as widely as possible, according to the capacities of the people; and whoever wishes to promote the moral conduct of mankind, to make dutiful citizens of them, and insure their happiness, will favor public institutions for useful information. Understanding, education, indeed, is the first condition of civil and religious, as well as of personal and moral liberty, and, therefore, ignorance ought to be remanded back to darkness along with superstition and slavery. The Germans expressing civilization by the word *aufklaerung* (enlightening) indicate that they consider intellect as the basis of improvement. But knowledge is not virtue—neither are charity and justice sciences, and hence more attention than hitherto has been given, must be paid to the moral improvement of the race.

There is also the vastly important question to be considered, whether education is useful, or in other words, whether it is better to leave the common people in ignorance, or to instruct all classes of society. There can be no opposition on this point from enlightened sources, and just here we have in mind the opinion of Dr. Spurzheim, which is so admirable, we shall set it down at length:

" In following the history of mankind, we observe that in proportion as nations cultivate their moral and intellectual powers, atrocious actions diminish in number; the manners and pleasures become more refined, the legislation milder, the religion purified from superstition, and the arts address themselves to the finer emotions of the mind. By observing also the different classes of society, and the inhabitants of different provinces, we learn that ignorance is the greatest enemy of morality. Wherever education is neglected, depravity, and every kind of actions which degrade mankind, are the most frequent. Among ignorant persons *cæteris paribus*, rapacity, cheating and thieving, drunkenness, and sensual pleasures are prominent features in the character. Those, then, who object to the instruction of the lower orders, can merely act from selfish motives. Being aware of their superiority, they may wish the inferior classes to be obedient to their arbitrary regulations; for unquestionably, it is much easier to lead the ignorant and uncultivated than the instructed and reasoning people. Knowledge, too, and the habit of reflection, detect abuses and errors, which selfishness and pride may wish to keep concealed. But whoever thinks it right to cultivate his own mind, cannot with justice desire others to remain in ignorance. He, therefore, who is versed in history, or understands the law of Christian charity, will join those who contend for the benefit of an instruction, adapted to every class of society. This, then, will not be confined to reading and writing, but particularly extended over the moral conduct, and all duties and rights in practical life."[1]

There remains but one point in this connection to notice, viz.: the absurd idea that education will destroy the efficacy of the Negro's labor. And although it is a widespread opinion, we shall only combat it with figures taken from the educational progress of other nations.[2] Let us first give the countries where popular education does not prevail:

The school population of Russia is 12,213,558, viz.: 5,803,656 boys, and 6,409,902 girls. Of this number only 6.9 per cent. attend school. What wonder that Nihilism flourishes, and the Czar's life is threatened three times a day?[3]

---

[1] Education of Man, pp. 34, 35.

[2] For these valuable statistics we acknowledge indebtedness to the Report of United States Commissioner Eaton.

[3] It is a curious fact that in 1875, Japan had 1,828,474 pupils who received instruction, while Russia in 1877, had only 1,074,559 pupils. This contrast is more striking when it is stated that the population of Russia is 85,000,000, while that of Japan is 32,000,000.

In Turkey, a law relating to public instruction, designed to spread over the empire, was issued by the government in October, 1869; but there has been no attempt of any kind made to execute the law in subsequent years. Consequently, no one dare claim Turkey as a model government for morality, intelligence or industry.

Look next at the enlightened States. Saxony has made the so-called complementary schools compulsory for every youth below the age of 17. In the Grand Duchy of Baden gymnastic exercises are compulsory in the public schools. Baden has also had very good industrial schools in operation for many years, and these have had marked influence on the industries of the country.

Belgium has its royal athenæums, including two sections— a classical course of six years, and an industrial course of four years. In 1876, of the 46,000 conscripts examined in Belgium only 8000 could neither read nor write, 2000 could read only, while 19,000 could read and write, and 15,000 had received a high education. In addition to schools of fine arts, and military schools, Belgium also has schools of agriculture, horticulture and veterinary surgery.

Denmark, with a population of less than two millions, has 208,000 children under instruction, and for special instruction has a royal veterinary and agricultural school, a polytechnic school, two academies of fine arts, a technical school, eight navigation schools, a military academy, and the usual institutions for the unfortunate.

Next comes France with its lyceums and commercial colleges—the former maintained by the State and the latter by municipalities—affording in both classical and modern instruction. Then there are schools of art and manufacture:—the course of instruction limited to three years, during which it is obligatory; including lectures, daily examinations, drawing and graphic exercises, chemical manipulations, working in stone and wood, physics and mechanics, and the construction of buildings and other works; and, in addition to which, the students are expected to visit the workshops and manufactories. For agricultural education, France has a farm school in each department, a higher agricultural (central) school, and a national agronomic institute, a sort of normal school of agriculture. These farm schools are intended to furnish a good example of tillage to the farmers of the district, and to form agriculturists capable of working intelligently as farmers or overseers. This special course extends through three years.

Look next to England, Her great endowed universities, her ancient and honorable private institutions, her night schools, industrial schools—all show the wisdom of wide-spread and non-exclusive education. The public schools of England do not give gratuitous instruction to their pupils, as do the schools called public in the United States, but for elementary education the most ample provisions are made, and compulsory laws have been enacted throughout the king-dom of Great Britain

Next, we would mention Germany, with its twenty-one great universities—or more especially Prussia—which is in advance of all States, where the universities and the Gymnasien not only give scientific and literary culture to their students, but develop the physical and moral power to the highest standard. In 1876, Prussia had 34,988 primary schools, with 57,936 teachers, and 4,007,776 pupils; 176 teachers' semin-aries; 37 schools for deaf mutes; 13 schools for the blind; 215 higher female schools; 90 higher burgher schools; 17 Realschulen of the second order, and 79 of the first order; 33 Progymnasien, 228 Gymnasien, 81 Agricultural and Hor-ticultural schools; 6 schools of forestry; 35 schools of mining; 45 technical and industrial schools; 9 schools of building, 12 of commerce; 31 navigation schools; and several military and naval schools. Now, mark the influence and the work of popular education: At the examination for the army in 1876, only 2749 recruits out of 77,194 were without a sufficient primary education.

Austria has a splendid system of elementary and indus-trial schools. These latter include schools for weaving, schools for lace making, schools for watch making, for giving instruction in the art of working in wood, marble and ivory, for instruction in making toys, baskets, mats, arms and other articles in metal, while there are schools and workshops for the whole group of mechanical industries. Several of these schools have been acknowledged a public benefit by the rural population of the empire. The schools for wood carving, for instance, have created a new kind of business in the moun-tainous districts of Bohemia, Austrian Silesia, and Moravia, where great quantities of cheap toys for children are manufac-tured. In the Tyrol, the school of sculpture at Imst is especially designed to develop artistic cabinet work and orna-

9

mental furniture; at Innsbruck, the industrial school applies itself to figures; that at Mondsee to groups of animals; that at St. Ulrich, to the sculpture of religious statues, and that at Wallern, to the commoner kinds of furniture, and to cases for clocks.

Not to prolong this subject, we abbreviate additional points. Primary education is compulsory throughout Italy, Brazil and Australasia; while Spain, Portugal, Sweden, the Netherlands and Switzerland, all pay especial attention to primary and industrial instruction, and no one has yet appeared so stupid, or so audacious, or so incrusted with hidebound prejudice, in the face of contrary facts, to declare education has ruined the labor of any of the numerous countries mentioned.

Nor will it jeopardize labor in this country. The total number of children enrolled in public schools in the United States, according to latest reports, is 8,954,478; and the average daily attendance 4,919,408. The amount and the quality of moral and mental instruction received by these young Americans—white and colored—is a question of transcendent interest. Yet no pseudo philosopher comes forward to demonstrate visible decadence of our labor system. Somebody does the work, somebody will always do it. In the language of the campaign poet, "The work goes bravely on." The greatest cause for alarm is, that while the Negroes are receiving their share of mental culture, the whites are devoting a good deal of time to "muscle culture." We have had the rowing mania, long swimming matches, base ball and pedestrianism. We have seen the man who poises and gyrates on a tight rope fifty feet above the heads of the people; the man who swam the strait of Gibraltar; we have seen the "Man with the Iron Jaw." And these accomplished gentlemen, almost without exception, were members of the great Aryan family.. We have introduced the Olympic games of Greece, but are lacking in Grecian art and philosophy. We have the Turn-Verein of Germany, but where is the culture? Physical development, if not carried to absurd lengths, is desirable. But this worship of muscle will have a tendency to dwarf the intellect—muscle will soon be worth more than mind, and men will be valued by brawn instead of brain. Nevertheless, it is true, that if a vessel should arrive in New York, having but two passengers, the one the most famous and erudite of European philosophers, the other the "Champion Pedestrian of the World"—the former, with his mind stored with valuable information concerning such lofty themes as the stars, the firmament, the ages, the seasons, the wonders of the universe, the grandeur of eternity, and the majesty of God, would be forced to wend his way quietly and unseen to the hotel, while the latter, with nothing but a robust chest, strong arms, and elastic and sinewy nerves, would be received as a conquering hero.

Or to take another view, it is safe to say the fault is with the false ideas of education rather than with those who are to be educated. It is a lamentable fact, but none the less a fact, that the whole tendency of modern education is to lift boys and girls to places they are not fitted to fill, to disgust them with work which they are fitted to do, which must be done, and which can easily be obtained. Our theory of education is continually losing sight of a fact which never permits itself to be ignored, and teaching the young to lose sight of it, that the mass of people in every generation and under whatever form of government must be laborers, but should be intelligent laborers. The old heresy that every boy has a chance to be President of the United States has done more mischief in the small brains of boys who, when they attain manhood's strength, are fitted to dig trenches and do nothing else, than it has even in the larger brains of public men who, once infected with the idea, are good for nothing afterward. Education should not be exclusive, nor built on foundations of sand, nor warped, perverted or biased. When completed it should make the subject better fitted to pursue well the work for which he is fitted, should make him not ashamed to do it, and thus he adorns labor while labor dignifies him.

Then, give the Negro a chance. Help him to be a man. If he has talent, help him to improve. If he has genius— the country stands in need of geniuses. If he has love of learning and desire to do something good and useful—encourage him, lift him up. Aid him to be something, anything, everything but a bad man. It is not a matter of speculation, it is a clear, fair, mutual business transaction. It is not a matter of charity. It is justice. It is our duty, and woe unto us if we shirk duty. Our country, great and powerful as she is, does not refuse the labor of the Colored man in time of peace; she would not ignore his courage in time of war, and therefore should not withhold from him education and enlightenment—the ability to make himself a useful and happy citizen. Education will teach him to reflect, will give him better and sounder judgment, and more accurate discrimination. Beneath the lighter layer of orna ment and accomplishments there will be a solid substratum of piety, intelligence, good sense, manly suavity, moral consciousness and social virtue. But we anticipate. Education can do that for the Colored man, and it is already having its effects. The seed has been planted, already it is budding and blossoming.

We shall now present some very valuable statistics showing the astonishing progress made in educating the Colored people of the South since the close of the late war. These tables are copied *verbatim* from the admirable and accurate "Report of the Commissioner of Education for the year 1877," the last report made. In thus acknowledging our indebtedness to Gen. Eaton for his kindness and courtesy, it may not be inappropriate to publish the following:

DEPARTMENT OF THE INTERIOR,
BUREAU OF EDUCATION,
WASHINGTON, D. C., October 16, 1879.

CHARLES EDWIN RôBERT, ESQ.,
Nashville, Tenn.:

My Dear Sir:—Your letter of the 30th ult., came duly to hand, and has given me great pleasure. I am gratified to know from yourself, personally, what you have already so well accomplished, and also the excellent object you propose. I shall be happy to render you any aid in my power. I find your letter, with a great number of others, waiting for me on my return from a recent absence, and send you a Report for 1877, and ask you to look over the points on which you are specially interested, and let me know further what additional items you desire. The tables of contents and index may relieve somewhat your labor and research. Do not fail to let me know with the greatest freedom what you desire, and I will aid you to the utmost.

I hope that all fears that your work may not be favorably received in certain quarters of the South may prove unfounded. There is more thought in the direction you are thinking than is generally known.

Very respectfully, your obedient servant,
JOHN EATON,
Commissioner.

Table showing the comparative population and enrollment of the white and colored races in the public schools of the recent slave States for 1876-'77.

States.	White.			Colored.		
	School population.	Enrollment.	Percentage of the school population enrolled.	School population.	Enrollment.	Percentage of the school population enrolled.
Alabama	a236,520	86,485	37	a168,706	54,745	32
Arkansas	143,949	b23,895	17	43,518	b7,255	17
Delaware	31,849	22,398	70	3,800	1,663	44
Florida	40,606	b14,948	37	42,001	b16,185	39
Georgia	218,733	107,010	49	175,304	48,643	28
Kentucky	c459,253	228,000	50	c53,126	19,107	36
Louisiana	d88,567	b45,000	51	d108,548	b40,000	37
Maryland	e213,669	125,737	59	e63,591	24,539	39
Mississippi	150,504	84,374	56	174,485	76,154	44
Missouri	692,818	381,074	55	32,910	13,774	42
North Carolina	267,265	128,289	48	141,031	73,170	52
South Carolina	83,813	46,444	55	144,315	55,952	39
Tennessee	330,935	171,535	52	111,523	43,043	39
Texas	f135,430	85,620	63	f30,587	23,432	77
Virginia	280,149	140,363	50	202,640	65,043	32
West Virginia	a178,780	a120,657	a67	a5,980	a2,847	a48
District of Columbia	20,671	15,310	74	11,000	5,954	54
Total	3,573,511	1,827,139	....	1,513,065	571,506	....

a For 1875-'76.
b Estimated by the Bureau.
c For whites the school age is 6-20; for colored 6-16.
d Exclusive of that of New Orleans.
e Census of 187̃.
f The school age in Texas at our last report was 6-18; it has been made 8-14, considerably lessening the school population.

Statistics of institutions for the instruction of the colored race for 1877.

Name and class of institution.	Location.	Religious denomination.	Instructors.	Students.
NORMAL SCHOOLS.				
Rust Normal Institute	Huntsville, Ala	Meth	2	60
State Normal School for Colored Students	Huntsville, Ala			81
Lincoln Normal University	Marion, Ala		3	120
Emerson Institute	Mobile, Ala	Cong	4	147
State Normal School for Colored Students	Pine Bluff, Ark		2	83
Normal department of Atlanta University	Atlanta, Ga	Presb		168
Lewis High School	Macon, Ga	Cong	3	89
Haven Normal School	Waynesboro', Ga	Meth	4	125
Peabody Normal School	New Orleans, La		5	95
Baltimore Normal School for Colored Pupils	Baltimore, Md		3	134
Centenary Biblical Institute	Baltimore, Md	Meth	4	77
Tougaloo University and Normal School	Tougaloo, Miss	Cong	8	106
Lincoln Normal Institute	Jefferson, Mo		6	122
State Normal School for Colored Students	Fayetteville, N. C		3	71
Bennett Seminary	Greensboro', N. C	Meth	2	75

Statistics of institutions for the instruction of the colored race for 1877—Continued.

Name and class of institution.	Location.	Religious denomination.	Instructors.	Students.
St. Augustine's Normal School...................	Raleigh, N. C........	P. E........	4	127
Shaw University............................	Raleigh, N. C........	Baptist. ...	5	240
Avery Normal Institute..	Charleston, S. C.....	Cong	9	315
Fairfield Normal Institute........................	Winnsboro', S. C....	Presb......	......	340
Freedman's Normal Institute	Maryville, Tenn......	Friends. ..	13	204
LeMoyne Normal and Commercial School....	Memphis, Tenn......	Cong	9	295
Hampton Normal and Agricultural Institute..	Hampton, Va.........	Cong *a*....	14	274
Richmond Institute..........................	Richmond, Va........	Baptist.. ..	5	104
Richmond Normal School for Colored Pupils.	Richmond, Va........	....	6	232
Miner Normal School...........................	Washington, D. C...	....	2	27
Normal department of Howard University....	Washington, D. C...	Non-sect..	3	74
Normal department of Wayland Seminary....	Washington, D. C...	Baptist....	(*b*)	(*b*)
Total........................	....	....	119	3785

INSTITUTIONS FOR SECONDARY INSTRUCTION.

Name and class of institution.	Location.	Religious denomination.	Instructors.	Students.
Trinity School..........................:	Athens, Ala..........	Cong	......	139
Talladega College........	Talladega, Ala.......	Cong	10	236
Cookman Institute...............................	Jacksonville, Fla....	Meth	3	62
Clark University............ ....---...............	Atlanta, Ga..........:	M. E	4	110
St. Augustine's School............................	Savannah, Ga.........	P. E........	3	75
La Teche Seminary................................	Baldwin, La..........	Meth	......	......
St. Francis Academy for Colored Girls.........	Baltimore, Md.......	R. C.......	......	95
Scotia Seminary...................................	Concord, N. C.......	Presb... ...	8	128
St. Augustine's School............................	Newbern, N. C......	P. E.......	2	224
Williston Academy and Normal School.........	Wilmington, N. C ..	Cong	5	84
Albany Enterprise Academy......................	Albany, Ohio.........	Non-sect..	......	23
High School for Colored Pupils.................	Charleston, S. C.....	P. E.?.....	4	224
Wallingford Academy.............................	Charleston, S. C.....	Presb.	......	220
Brainerd Institute	Chester, S. C........	Presb.	3	277
Benedict Institute...............	Columbia, S. C......	Baptist.. ..	4	117
Brewer Normal School	Greenwood, S. C....	Cong	......	49
Claflin University.......	Orangeburg, S. C...	M. E	4	120
Canfield School..................................	Memphis, Tenn,.....	P. E.......	1	100
Nashville Institute.............	Nashville, Tenn.. ...	Baptist. ...	6	195
Wiley University.................................	Marshall, Tex........	M. E	2	53
St. Stephen's School..............................	Petersburg, Va.......	P. E.......	5	150
St. Philip's School..............................	Richmond, Va.......	P. E.......	2	86
St. Mary's School................................	Washington, D. C..	P. E........	......	40
Total...........................	....	....	66	2807

UNIVERSITIES AND COLLEGES.

Name and class of institution.	Location.	Religious denomination.	Instructors.	Students.
Atlanta University...	Atlanta, Ga..........	Cong	5	33
Berea College.............................	Berea, Ky.............	Cong	*c*13	129
Leland University.................................	New Orleans, La....	Baptist. ...	- 4	......
Straight University................................	New Orleans, La....	Cong	7	223
New Orleans University...........................	New Orleans, La....	Meth	*c*12	110
Shaw University...................................	Holly Springs, Miss.	Meth	6	130
Alcorn University.................................	Rodney, Miss.........	Non-sect .	5	86
Biddle University............	Charlotte, N. C......	Presb..	*a*7	126

a In addition to the aid given by American Missionary Association, this institute has an appropriation from the State.   *b* Reported under schools of theology.   *c* For all departments.

*Statistics of institutions for the instruction of the colored race for 1877—Universities ana Colleges—*Continued.

Name and class of institution.	Location.	Religious de-nomination.	Instructors.	Students.
Wilberforce University.....	Xenia, Ohio............	M. E	16	145
Lincoln University........................	Oxford, Pa............	Presb.	9	134
Central Tennessee College........................	Nashville, Tenn....	M. E	8	24
Fisk University........................	Nashville, Tenn......	Cong	9	69
Howard University........................	Washington, D. C...	Non-sect..	7	57
Total........................	....	....	108	1270

SCHOOLS OF THEOLOGY.

Rust Biblical and Normal Institute.............	Huntsville, Ala......	Meth	......	......
Theological department of Talladega College	Talladega, Ala.......	Cong	2	18
Institute for the Education of Col'd Ministers	Tuscaloosa, Ala......	Presb	......	......
Augusta Institute........................	Augusta, Ga.	Baptist. ...	2	85
Theological department of Leland University	New Orleans, La....	Baptist. ...	2	28
Thompson Biblical Institute (New Orleans University)	New Orleans, La....	M. E......	......	18
Theological department of Straight University	New Orleans, La....	Cong	......	14
Centenary Biblical Institute........................	Baltimore, Md.	M. E	5	24
Theological department of Biddle University.	Charlotte, N. C......	Presb	3	9
Theological department of Shaw University...	Raleigh, N. C..	Baptist. ...	2	50
Theological Seminary of Wilberforce Univer'y	Xenia, Ohio............	M. E	6	8
Theological department of Lincoln Univer'y..	Oxford, Pa............	Presb	5	20
Baker Theological Seminary (Claflin Univer'y)	Orangeburg, S. C.....	Meth	......	......
Theological course in Fisk University...........	Nashville, Tenn......	Cong	2	33
Theological department of Central Tennessee College...	Nashville, Tenn......	M. E	5	35
Theological department of Howard Univer'y.	Washington, D. C...	Non-sect ..	4	32
Wayland Seminary........................	Washington, D. C...	Baptist. ...	6	88
Total...	....	....	44	462

SCHOOLS OF LAW.

Law department of Straight University........	New Orleans, La....	....	4	8
Law department of Howard University........	Washington, D. C...	.........·*····	2	6
Total........................	....	....	6	14

SCHOOLS OF MEDICINE.

Medical department of New Orleans Univer'y	New Orleans, La....	....	5	8
Meharry Medical department of Central Tennessee College........................	Nashville, Tenn......	....	......	18
Medical department of Howard University...	Washington, D. C...	....	7	48
Total........................	....	....	12	74

SCHOOLS FOR THE DEAF AND DUMB AND THE BLIND.

Institution for the Colored Blind and Deaf Mutes......	Baltimore, Md........	....	c11	31
North Carolina Institution for the Deaf and Dumb and the Blind (colored department).	Raleigh, N. C.......,	....	a14	68
Total........................	....	....	25	99

a For all departments.   W
b This institution is open to both races, and the numbers given are known to include some whites.
c Includes other employes.

Summary of statistics of institutions for the instruction of the colored race for 1877.

States.	Public schools,		Normal schools.			Institutions for secondary instruction.		
	School population.	Enrollment.	Schools.	Teachers.	Pupils.	Schools.	Teachers.	Pupils.
Alabama	168,706	54,745	*4	9	408	2	10	375
Arkansas	43,518	7,255	1	2	83			
Delaware	3,800	1,663						
Florida	42,001	16,185				1	3	62
Georgia	175,304	48,643	3	7	382	2	7	185
Kentucky	53,126	19,107						
Louisiana	108,548	40,000	1	5	95	1		
Maryland	63,591	24,539	2	7	211	1		95
Mississippi	174,485	76,154	1	8	106			
Missouri	32,910	13,774	1	6	122			
North Carolina	141,031	73,170	4	14	513	3	15	436
Ohio						1		23
South Carolina	144,315	55,952	2	9	655	6	15	1007
Tennessee	111,523	43,043	2	22	499	2	7	295
Texas	30,587	23,432				1	2	53
Virginia	202,640	65,043	3	25	610	2	7	236
West Virginia	5,980	2,827						
District of Columbia	11,000	5,954	3	5	101	1		40
Total	1,513,065	571,506	27	119	3785	23	66	2807

States.	Universities and colleges.			Schools of theology.			Schools of law.		
	Schools.	Teachers.	Pupils.	Schools.	Teachers.	Pupils.	Schools.	Teachers.	Pupils.
Alabama				3	2	18			
Georgia	1	5	33	1	2	85			
Kentucky	1	13	129						
Louisiana	3	23	337	3	2	60	1	4	8
Maryland				1	5	24			
Mississippi	2	11	216						
North Carolina	1	7	126	2	5	59			
Ohio	1	16	145	1	6	8			
Pennsylvania	1	9	134	1	5	20			
South Carolina				1					
Tennessee	2	17	93	2	7	68			
District of Columbia	1	7	57	2	10	120	1	2	6
Total	13	108	1270	17	44	462	2	6	14

Summary of statistics of institutions for the instruction of the colored race for 1877.—Cont'd.

States.	Schools of medicine.			Schools for the deaf and dumb and the blind.		
	Schools.	Teachers.	Pupils.	Schools.	Teachers.	Pupils.
Louisiana	1	5	8	....	....	....
Maryland	....	....	....	1	11	31
North Carolina..	....	....	....	1	14	68
Tennessee.................	1	....	18	....	....	....
District of Columbia	1	7	48	....	....	....
Total..	3	12	74	2	25	99

Table showing the number of schools for the colored race and enrollment in them by institutions without reference to States.

Class of institution.	Schools.	Enrollm'nt
Public schools..	a10,792	a571,506
Normal schools	27	3,785
Institutions for secondary instruction............................	23	2,807
Universities and colleges...	13	1,270
Schools of theology	17	462
Schools of law..	2	14
Schools of medicine..	3	74
Schools for the deaf and dumb and the blind.................	2	99
Total..	10,879	580,017

a To these may be added 315 schools, having an enrollment of 16,548, in reporting free States, making total number of colored public schools 11,107 and total enrollment in them 588,054 ; it will be observed that this augments the total number of schools above given by 315, and the enrollment by 16,548, making the total number of schools, as far as reported to us, 11,194, and total number of the colored race under instruction in them, 596,565; this, however, does not include the colored public schools of those States in which no separate reports are made.

Here then, is the grand exhibit—most astonishing—most gratifying. These tables show that in 1877, nearly *six hundred thousand* Colored pupils were under instruction in the Schools of the South, which is a larger number than the total of white pupils, (581,861) in the South in 1850. It will be seen, however, that these tables were made from reports returned three years ago, and at a time when there was great political distress in the South. The Commissioner's report for the subsequent years is not yet completed, but we dare say the total number of pupils for 1879, will show considerably *over seven hundred thousand pupils.* This estimate is not mere guess work ; we have been able to get figures from but two States—Tennessee and South Carolina, but the increase

in those States justify our figures.   Gov. Simpson, of South
Carolina, in his late message, shows that there were 64,095
Colored children in attendance in his State for 1879, which is
an increase of 8,143, since 1877, and gives an attendance of
45 per cent. of the entire scholastic population.   Superintendent Trousdale, of Tennessee, in his report for 1878, gives the
increase of Colored pupils for that year, as 11,299; increase
of Colored teachers 147; increase of Colored schools 177,
and an actual attendance of about 50 per cent. of the scholastic population.   The figures for 1879 although not def-
initely ascertained, Col. Trousdale states, will show an equal
increase, and this notwithstrnding the school-tax was levied
later in the year.   In Tennessee the school ages is from 6 to
18 years, hence no correct estimate can be made for more
advanced scholars in the higher schools.   Whatever else may
be said, these statistics demonstrate beyond controversy, the
growth of a healthier public sentiment, increased efficiency in
the management of public affairs, and the rapid abatement of
the evils that held sway over the people during the long years
of a mis-named reconstruction.

But let us bear in mind that these schools are not merely
for the purpose of teaching the three "R's," ('readin', 'ritin',
and 'rithmetic,") which were formerly declared " the limit of
Negro-Organism," but as we see they are gaining rapidly in
Normal Schools, in institutions for secondary instruction, in
Universities and Colleges, and in schools of theology, law,
and medicine.   Graduates are being turned out in Literature,
Mathematics, in Sciences, in Languages—ancient and modern,
and in all the branches of ornamental accomplishments.   We
have not the figures, but risk the assertion that *not less than
one million Colored people have learned to read and write in
the South since the close of the late war*—only fifteen years since.
These apt and willing pupils were not all children, but many
of them men and women in middle life, and even grey-haired
and half blind old men and women, have learned a little—
enough to write their names and to "spell out" the wondrous
truths in God's Holy Book.   And, moreover, we are bold
enough to say, that the white man who cannot see that the
Colored people are advancing in intellectual power, is blind
because he will not see—nay, more, he is thick-skulled—as
thick-skulled as a plantation Negro in slavery times.

There are secrets explaining the Colored peoples' advancement, which we shall proceed to divulge.   In the first place,

they are ambitious. The colored urchin is deeply impressed with the important fact, that there is something valuable between the lids of books, and he is going to find out what it is. Secondly, Colored children, are obedient, tractable, more docile than is generally supposed, and hold in affectionate honor and reverence the man or woman who will teach them something, and treat them with kindness. The Colored boy will arise betimes, earn his wages, run errands, do chores, "pick up chips" and not be ashamed; but when the school bell taps, he bounds away with light step and lighter heart, and thus completely reverses the received opinion of Shakespeare's school boy:

> "With his shining morning face,
> Creeping like snail, unwillingly to school."

But there is another, and a more important characteristic in Negro-Organism which our philosophers all seem to have overlooked. To state it fully, we will say, that there is nothing in which men differ so much as in their customs. They are of innumerable origin, climate, soil, diet, occupations, laws, religion, individual men, government, the institution of monarchy or a republic, with a thousand other things, create and alter their customs. But however various the causes may be, which create and alter the customs of men, there is but one which can make them lasting, stable, and, as it were eternal. This is *imitation,* the most powerful principle in man. By this we acquire customs, manners, and almost everything. Sometimes indeed its power is such that against our will we are compelled to imitate others. From this source depends the resemblance of customs in the family, the city, or in the whole nation. This was well known to the great poet, who had seen through the whole range of the human mind. In the drama of King Henry IV., we find Falstaff thus philosophizing: "It is a wonderful thing to see the semblable coherence of his men's spirits and his; they, by observing of him, do bear themselves like justices; he, by conversing with them, is turned into a justice-like serving man. Their spirits are so married in conjunction, with the participation of society, that they flock together in consent like so many wild geese. It is certain, that either wise bearing or ignorant carriage is caught, as men take diseases, one of another." This imitative faculty is perhaps one of the most important gifts of Heaven, and to the Colored race it has been given with the lavish love of God. It is one of the chief characteristics of the black race. *By nature they are imitative.* If well directed, this faculty is capable of the noblest efforts of human intellect. It has been well and forcibly observed that a boy without power of imitation is destined to remain all his life a one-sided character. " He has no range of sympathies, he has been fused only once in life, and been poured into a mould, and *there* he cools and will never be other than you see him. His creed on all matters is already formed, and you no more need hope to see him change beneath the generous and genial sympathies of opinion or of truth, than to find platina melt before an ordinary parlor fire. The most promising boys are the most imitative; in this lies their capacity for education."

There is another important matter to be touched upon in this connection, viz: the relative mental capacity of White and Colored children. In considering a question like this, theories and opinions are worth but little, unless supported by facts. The relative intellectual ability of the two races can only be ascertained by a careful comparison of the advancement made under similar conditions. The public schools of Nashville, furnish such a test; controlled, as they are, by the same Board of Education; the pupils pursuing the same studies, and passing from one grade to another by the same examination. The following statistics are for the scholastic year ending June, 1878–79, and are taken from the published report of Superintendent S. Y. Caldwell, of the Nashville City Schools:

	White Schools.	Colored Schools.
Total Enrollment for 1878–9	3,217	905
Per cent of attendance	95.33	96.80
Average Scholarship	69	67
Cost of tuition per pupil	$15.24	$11.97

It should be stated that the white pupils are admitted to the higher grades and that the general average of scholarship is thus advanced. The Colored children mentioned in these reports are those admitted to the lower grades, their education generally being completed in the Colored Colleges, Universities, etc. This will explain also the average cost of tuition per pupil.

In 1874, Prof. G. W. Hubbard, Principal of the Belle View Colored public school, made a report on this subject, from which we quote the following interesting points:

" A careful comparison of pupils of almost unmixed African descent with those who are nearly white, shows that there is but little, if any difference in their intellectual capacity. For more than two hundred years the colored race in this country were held in bondage, and, in most cases, their intellectual faculties systematically repressed. To be seen with a spelling-book in their hands was an offense of no ordinary magnitude, and the number of colored people in 1860 who were able to read and write was so small that it might fairly be said that the whole race was in a state of total ignorance. The hereditary transmission of intellectual and moral qualities is generally believed; and if we accept this doctrine, how long will it take to overcome the degrading influence of so many generations, supposing that the Caucasian and the African originally possessed the same natural abilities?

It is not easy to estimate the influence of home culture. A large proportion of the white children live in what might be called an intellectual atmosphere. Books, papers and magazines abound, and the parents are both able and willing to give their children all necessary assistance. With regard to the colored children, the reverse is equally true; their parents have neither the time nor ability to aid them in preparing their lessons. In addition to this, a majority of the colored children are obliged either to make their own living, or assist their parents, so that they have but little if any time to study out of school. Taking all these things into consideration, the advancement made has been more rapid than could be reasonably expected, and those who have labored here may feel like thanking God and taking courage."

COLORED SCHOOLS OF NASHVILLE.

Let us now in order to better illustrate the advances made by the Colored people, introduce sketches of the prominent Colored schools—the colleges of Nashville, Tennessee—a city that has justly earned title as the "Athens of the South." But before doing so it may not be inappropriate to speak briefly of the situation of Nashville and its admirable adaptability as a great educational centre. These advantages have been recognized by many prominent educators for many long years. The learned Dr. Philip Lindsley—founder of the University of Nashville, in his baccalaureate address delivered on the first commencement of the University in 1826, spoke the words of a prophet, while endeavoring to further the magnificent educational scheme which he had projected, and the splendid results of to-day seem so like fulfillment of his bright anticipations, we are constrained to quote his words:

"A more eligible or healthful site, for such an establishment, cannot be found in the Western country. *Here* is the place, and *now* is the time, for generous enterprise. Here let us erect a university so decidedly and confessedly superior in every department that a rival or competitor need not be feared. Let us make ample provision for every species of instruction—

scientific, literary, professional—which our country demands.   Let education be extended to the physical and moral, as well as to the mental faculties.   Let agriculture, horticulture, civil and military engineering, gymnas-
tics, the liberal and mechanical arts—whatever may tend to impart vigor,
dignity, grace, activity, health to the body—whatever may tend to purify the
heart, improve the morals and manners, discipline the intellect, and to furnish it with copious stores of useful, elementary knowledge—obtain their
appropriate place and rank, and receive merited attention, in our seminary;
so that parents may, with confidence, commit their sons to our care, assured
that they will be in safe and skillful hands—under a government equitable,
paternal, mild, firm, vigilant and faithful—where their every interest will be
consulted, their every faculty be duly cultivated, and where every effort will
be made to render them intelligent, virtuous, accomplished scholars."

What a remarkable prophecy, and yet how true in its fore-
casting wisdom.   If Nashville presented then, the most
eligible and healthful site in the West for the establishment
of a great university, what may be said of it to-day with its
central position, its great railroad system, its metropolitan
advantages, and its widespread reputation and multiformed
advantages as a seat of learning?   Time brings many wonderful changes.   Fifty years after Dr. Lindsley's prophecy the
"far off hills" that now skirt the city's suburbs in the memorable and awful days of the "Sixties" bristled with cannon
and gleamed with the bayonets of the contending hosts;—the
valleys were vast encampments—the hills frowning fortresses.
But sixty years after, we see that the deep furrows that time
and war had plowed through the face of nature have been oblit-
erated by the *cosmetiques* of the age—progress and improvement.   The city is stretching its capable and wide arms to
the country, and wooing it to fond embrace.   The cordon of
forts has become a cordon of universities.   Here is the great
Vanderbilt University—with its departments of Literature,
Law, Theology, Medicine and Dentistry.   Here is the Nashville Medical College—the State Normal School, Ward's
Seminary, the Montgomery Bell Academy, and here, too, the
proud hills that hold these splendid universities—like a central glory, do not look with envy, but "as iron sharpeneth
iron," stand proximate to the Colored schools—The Baptist
Normal and Theological Institute—Central Tennessee College
—Fisk University—and Meharry Medical College—noble
institutions, which to-day stand out the climax of the civilization and Christianization of the Americo-African.

These schools, it must be remembered, are the result of
only a few years work.   The pioneers, the laborers in this
educational field began here under the most discouraging

circumstances, but they have builded wisely and well. In 1874, Elder Daniel Wadkins, a prominent and well educated Colored man, who had long been identified with advanced movements in behalf of his race, published a sketch of the origin and progress of colored education in Nashville before emancipation, and to read his account is to impress one with feelings of shame and mortification that our Colored citizens were so long and so systematically kept under the ban.

However, let us speak now only of the present, and introducing the following sketches make due acknowledgements to the several gentlemen who have kindly aided us.

NASHVILLE NORMAL AND THEOLOGICAL INSTITUTE.

BY REV. D. W. PHILLIPS, D. D.

This school was established and is still supported by the American Baptist Home Missionary Society. There are at present eight other schools of a similar character supported by the Baptists in the following places: Washington, D. C., Richmond, Va., Raleigh, N. C., Columbia, S. C., Atlanta, Ga., Selma, Ala., Natchez, Miss., and New Orleans. An agent of the above named society was commissioned to this State in the summer of 1864. After surveying the field he commenced teaching a class of Colored young men in the basement of the First Colored Baptist Church. Soon a lot of land was purchased near Fort Gillem, and a wooden building erected 120x 40 feet, two stories high, and a basement under a part of it. In that, much hard work was done under many difficulties, but with very encouraging results. The design of the Institute was to prepare young men to preach the gospel, and both men and women to teach schools. Our object, at the first, was not understood nor appreciated. That a man called by God to preach his gospel needed any other qualification than strong lungs and throat was a new idea among the Colored people. There was no demand for educated ministers. Since then a very great change has come over the better endowed of the young. people. Now this class see very clearly that the preaching needed is not bawling and retailing pretended visions, but a rational expounding of the word of God and enforcing the precepts of Christianity. Considering their antecedents and the little they still have to encourage them they make very commendable efforts for their own education. During the last scholastic year—1878-'79—the students of this Institute paid toward their own expenses not far from $6000.

The location of the Institute was not good—though the best that could be had at the time; the building was rough, uncomfortable and inconvenient. After some years it became too small. A new site was purchased on the Hillsboro Turnpike, about one mile outside of the city, consisting of thirty acres of land, with a mansion house and outbuildings. The location is very beautiful, high, and commanding a grand and wide prospect. The buildings consist of the mansion house—48 by 80 feet—four stories high, furnishing apartments for the teachers, and dormitories for the young women ; and Centennial Hall—49 by 185 feet, four stories high, with ample basement, furnishing accommodations for the boarding department; the main story is devoted to public rooms ; and the three stories above furnish dormitories for

NASHVILLE BAPTIST NORMAL AND THEOLOGICAL INSTITUTE.

COLORED SCHOOLS OF NASHVILLE.   143

about one hundred and forty young men.   For this building the Institute is indebted most of all to the benefactions of Hon. Nathan Bishop and wife, of New York city.

The Institute was removed to its present location three years ago last October.   Ever since then it has been enlarging in all directions.   The number of students has about doubled—the course of studies has been raised.

Its leading object, as at the beginning, is to advance Biblical knowledge and practical Christianity, believing that the word and Spirit of God are the only power that can raise any people. All the scholars have a lesson in the Bible every day.   All the branches of education commonly taught in schools of this class, whether called by some humble name or some high sounding title, receive ample attention in this Institute. The plan is to afford to the Colored people all the advantages for education that they need.

The students at the Institute are carefully watched over.   It affords me great satisfaction to be able to say that from the beginning till now no serious breach of morality has occurred.

During the vacation—and considerably in term time—the greater part of the students are engaged in teaching; and generally they bring with them testimonials of good success.

CENTRAL TENNESSEE COLLEGE.

BY J. BRADEN, D. D.

During the latter years of the civil war, the city of Nashville was thronged with Colored people, who were endeavoring to escape from places where their newly-acquired rights of freedom were hardly recognized.   In doing this, they found the larger cities, where the Federal soldiers were stationed in considerable numbers, the only places of refuge from a class of outrages, that were of too frequent occurrence, and that continued after the close of the war, and against which, the civil law was scarcely the shadow of a protection.   These people were poor beyond description.   They had nothing. They were homeless, moneyless, and almost naked, and ignorant of all provident manner of living.   The Government did much to relieve their physical wants, but left much of this, and most all of their intellectual and moral culture, to the philanthropist and the Christian.   This work was cheerfully undertaken by the Freedman's Aid Societies, in which the various Christian churches united.   The Methodist Episcopal Church was a large contributor of both workers and means, and aided in establishing schools for the freedman, and in supporting the teachers.   In 1865, after the formation of the Freedman's Aid Societies by some of the leading denominations, the active members of the Western Branch of the Freedman's Aid Society, who were connected with the Methodist Episcopal Church in Cincinnati, organized a society, the object of which was to aid in the elevation, intellectually and morally, of the Freedman of the South.   This society has had a vigorous existence, and has raised and expended in this work over $750,000, and has, in addition to this, property in school buildings and land, to the value of $275,000.   In 1865, the Methodist Episcopal Church began its denominational work in Nashville.   A school was organized under the direction of Bishop Clark, by Rev. A. A. Gee, who employed such teachers as were available.   The building used was the church formerly belonging to the Methodist Episcopal Church, South, and known as Andrew Chapel, which was purchased by the Methodist Episcopal Church, and since known as Clark Chapel.   This mission school grew rapidly in numbers, the scholars crowding the rooms provided for them.   In 1866, Rev.

10

John Seys, D.D., for many years missonary to Africa, was appointed pastor of Clark Chapel, and Principal of the mission school. The school becoming too large for the building, it became necessary in the spring of this year to secure more commodious accommodations. The large brick building known as the Gun Factory, on South College street, which was in the possession of the Federal Government as abandoned property, was turned over to the proper persons, for the use of the school. The building was fitted up for school purposes, excepting the school furniture, by the Freedman's Bureau.

In the fall of 1866, at the first session of the Tennessee Conference of the Methodist Episcopal Church, Rev. W. B. Crichlow was appointed pastor of Clark Chapel, and Principal of the school. A large corps of teachers were employed, and the school numbered in the aggregate attendance during the year nearly eight hundred scholars.

During the month of July of this year a Board of Trustees was organized, and a college charter obtained from the Legislature. Up to this time, no tuition or incidental fee had been charged, in view of the poverty of the people, and the fact that there was no provision made for their education by the State. But in the autumn of 1867, the city of Nashville opened free schools for the Colored people. In view of this fact, and that the object of the school being to prepare Colored teachers to become the educators of their own people, and to prepare young men for the ministry, and not wishing to do work that others would do, and do well, a tuition fee was charged of one dollar per month. Rev. J. Braden was appointed pastor of Clark Chapel and Principal of the College school. The Trustees had received from the Missionary Society of the Methodist Episcopal Church, ten thousand dollars, to aid in securing a site and erecting suitable buildings for the school. They succeeded in purchasing an eligible lot in South Nashville, not far from the Medical College, and proposed to erect buildings at once, and move the school into them, as the Gun Factory was only temporarily in the possession of the Government. But such was the opposition to having a school for the Colored people erected there, that a decree was procured from the Chancery Court annulling the sale, and the money was refunded.

The school opened in the Gun Factory for the second year on the 15tn of September, 1867, and during the year numbered, notwithstanding the city free schools, and the tuition fee of one dollar per month, charged at the College, over two hundred. Of the teachers this year, Rev. J. Braden was elected President by the Board of Trustees, Miss Emily Preston, Miss Julia Evans, Mrs. S. L. Larned, and Mrs. Mary Murphy assistants. During the year efforts were made to secure a place for a building, and attempts were made to purchase property in Franklin and Murfreesboro, but the opposition to the education of the Colored people prevented any purchases. Threats were intimated that it would not be safe to start "Nigger Schools" in either of these places. The feeling that a school for the Colored people, established by the Methodist Episcopal Church, in any of the smaller towns in Middle Tennessee, would be insecure to person and property, led to the abandonment of the idea of leaving Nashville, and also of seeking property outside of the corporation. Property was purchased on Maple street, known as the Nance property. The only building on it being a large brick family residence; and as the Gun Factory had been returned to the creditors of the company who built it, and rented for the city schools, the school was moved to this building, and the school year opened late in the autumn of

CENTRAL TENNESSEE COLLEGE, NASHVILLE, TENNESSEE.

(145)

1868, under the supervision of Rev. G. H. Hartupee, who had been placed in charge of the school by the Trustees, Rev. J. Braden having resigned his position at the close of the previous year.

During the winter and spring of 1869, with the aid of the Freedman's Bureau, which contributed about $18,000, there were erected two brick buildings, furnishing a large and commodious chapel, with dormitories above it in one building, and school-rooms and dormitories in the other, capable of accommodating about two hundred students. At the close of the school year 1869, Rev. G. H. Hartupee resigned, and Rev. J. Braden was re-elected President. The first Catalogue was published this year, and indicated an enrollment of 192 students in all departments. The primary class was thrown out of the course of study, and none admitted who could not read in the Second Reader.

The Catalogue for 1870-'71 showed an enrollment of 226. The departments organized were the Intermediate, Academic and Normal, Preparatory and Theological. Many of the students in the Academic and Normal Departments were engaged in teaching; and although but partially prepared, yet such was the ignorance of the Colored people in the country places, that students who had not advanced beyond the Third Reader and simple Addition, found employment as teachers, and did a good work in imparting a knowledge of letters and reading to their people.

For 1871-'72 the total number of students was 241. The students were more punctual, and attended school for a longer period than before, and seemed to have clearer ideas of acquiring knowledge of the higher branches. Classes in Algebra, Geometry, Latin, Greek, Natural Science, Biblical studies were taught, and passed such examinations as gave great satisfaction to the numerous visitors and examiners who were present, at the close of the year.

The number of students for 1872-'73 was 270. Over one-fourth of the entire number engaged in teaching during the year.

In 1874 the number of students was about the same as the previous year. Raising the standard of admission from the Second to the Third Reader cut off a number who made application to enter the school. The number of students from a distance boarding in the Institution was largely in excess of any former year. Many who had been out teaching returned, earnestly desiring to improve themselves for more efficient work in this department.

In 1875, there were enrolled 240. Of these one was in the College class, 29 in the Preparatory, 25 in the Theological and 56 in the Academic and Normal, and 152 were in the common English studies. In 1876, the enrollment was 210. In 1877, it was 227. In 1878, it was 295, and in 1879, it was 287. The prospect for the present school year, 1879-80, is that the attendance will be larger than any previous year. The advancement in the studies pursued may be seen in the fact, that in 1867, not a student was advanced beyond the common English branches, and the majority of them were in such primary studies, as spelling, reading, in the First, Second and Third Readers, Elements of Arithmetic and writing. In the Catalogue for 1879, the conditions of admission are that the candidate must read in the Fourth Reader, and have some knowledge of Arithmetic. Such a condition ten years ago would have kept out five-sixths of the students. In addition to the common English studies there have been classes completing the study of Algebra, Geometry, Trigonometry, Analytical Geometry, Astronomy, Mechanics and Calculus in Mathematics, and have read the usual authors of the College course in Latin and Greek successfully, as well as having creditably

MEHARRY MEDICAL DEPARTMENT,
CENTRAL TENNESSEE COLLEGE, NASHVILLE, TENN.

completed a course in Natural Science and Belle Lettres, and the usual degree
of Bachelor of Arts, has been conferred. That which seemed incredible a
few years ago, in the intellectual capacity of the Negro, has actually been
accomplished. Young men and women who were born slaves, have finished
some of the higher courses of study in the College, and are taking high rank
among the educated of our land. In the School-room hundreds of the students of this College have proved themselves most successful teachers. They
have been commended by Boards of Examination and county Superintend-
ents for their proficiency in the studies on which they have been examined.
Others have made commendable progress in Biblical studies, and now occupy some of the most important positions in the churches to which they belong, honoring their positions by clear and earnest presentations of truth, and
intelligent Christian lives.

MEHARRY MEDICAL DEPARTMENT.

In 1874, the nucleus of the Medical Department was formed and has
gradually developed into a thoroughly organized school. The Brothers
Hugh, Samuel and Rev. Alexander Meharry, D. D., furnished means to
carry forward this department, and three classes, aggregating twelve, have
graduated and have met with a very cordial reception from the members of
the profession, where ever they have settled. Two of them have had practice in yellow fever, Dr J. S. Bass, in Chattanooga, in 1878, and Dr. L. D.
Key, near Memphis. Both acquitted themselves creditably in their positions of danger. All graduates have passed a thorough examination on the
full course in medicine, and have demonstrated their ability to deal with the
Science of Medicine successfully.

THE LAW DEPARTMENT

Has a small beginning, but will no doubt grow as have the other departments.
It is the aim of the Trustees to furnish the means, as far as practicable, for
qualifying the students for any profession in life, which may be open to
them. The great demand for workers in Africa, is not forgotten, and it is
confidently expected, that some who are, or have been students in this
school, will find their life work, in that rapidly opening Continent. The
men who most impress the world are those who wrestle with the problems
of every-day life, hence the education of those who are to battle with these
problems should be practical. The education which this school proposes to
give is of this kind, fitting its students for the farm, the workshop, the store
as well as for the school-room, the office or the pulpit.

THE RESULTS

Of the thirteen years of the existence of this school, may be summed up
as follows : The course of study has advanced from the primary English, to
the full College course, which has been successfully completed by some of
the race who have been held as incapable of mastering any but the com-
monest studies. The conditions of admission are such as would have been
impossible for any considerable number of the Colored people to comply
with when the school was opened, in 1866. Hundreds of young men and
women have been fitted for successful work as teachers of their people, in
the school-room, in the home and in the church. The labors of these students
compare favorably with the same kind of labor of white teachers. The
same may be said of the Theological and Medical students. The positions
which the former occupy in the church, and the reception which the latter

receive from the Medical profession, is clear evidence of the ability of these educated students to discharge acceptably and successfully, some of the gravest duties of life.

COLLEGE BUILDINGS.

The buildings of the College are five in number, plain, substantial brick, admirably adapted to school purposes, and costing over sixty thousand dollars. Most of this sum was contributed by the Methodist Episcopal Church, and the results of the past work of the school is seen, in the hundreds of schools taught by thoroughly competent teachers educated in this institution, in a multitude of Sunday-schools that have been organized and conducted by these teachers, in connection with their day schools, in the increasing intelligence of the colored people where these schools have been taught, in the higher estimate of the social virtues, a better idea of home and its sanctity, clearer views of the relation of husband and wife, parents and children, a better comprehension of ownership, a more intelligent view of freedom and the duties and responsibilities of citizenship, more intelligent work in the Sunday-school and church, and a more elevated view of Christian life and duty. The expense of the school, outside of the current expenses, has been paid by the contributions of the Christian people of the North through the Freedman's Aid Society of the M. E. Church. The students mostly paying their own personal expenses as tuition, board, etc., which have been placed so low that all the energetic and industrious may be able to meet these requirements.

While the school is under the patronage of the Methodist Episcopal Church, and the doctrines of the Bible are interpreted in harmony with the standards of this branch of the Church of God, yet no efforts are made to influence those who belong to denominations viewing Biblical doctrine from other standpoints, to change their views or church relations. With the growing influence of the Church among the colored people in the South, there seems to be nothing in the way of the future increasing usefulness of this school. With the Divine Blessing resting upon it, in the future as in the past, many of the students each year having been converted while attending the College, the gradually increasing attendance of students, the school will send forth, each year, an increasing number of those who are favored with a Christian education, to bless their people and to aid in the work of their real elevation.

FISK UNIVERSITY.

BY PROF. H. S. BENNETT.

Fisk School, from which Fisk University grew was formally opened Jan. 9, 1866, in Government buildings, west of the Chattanooga Depot; known as the Railroad Hospital, under the auspices of the American Missionary Association of New York and the Western Freedmen's Aid Commission of Cincinnati.

The land on which the buildings were located was purchased. Rev. E. P. Smith, Field Secretary of the Association, Rev. E. M. Cravath, Secretary of the Middle West Department, and Prof. John Ogden, representing the Western Freedmen's Aid Commission, becoming personally responsible for the payment of the notes. These notes were afterwards assumed by the American Missionary Association.

Gen. Clinton B. Fisk was at that time in command of the Freedmen's

Bureau, and entered heartily into the work of opening the enterprise. The school took its name in honor of him.

Under the efficient management of Prof. John Ogden, a normal instructor of national reputation, the school at once became very flourishing. During the first two years upwards of 1200 pupils were in attendance.

In August, 1867, the school was incorporated as Fisk University. This step was rendered advisable by the fact that the city schools were opened about that time to the Colored children of Nashville. About that time, also, Gen. O. O. Howard, of the Freedmen's Bureau, donated from Bureau funds $7000 to the school for educational purposes. It was then decided to incorporate the Institution for the higher education of youth of both sexes. It was accordingly chartered August 22, 1867, with a board of nine Trustees, three of whom were to be chosen each year, and were empowered "to fill vacancies, prescribe courses of study, and confer all such degrees and honors as are conferred by universities in the United States.'

EDUCATIONAL WORK.

The School and University were under the management of Prof. John Ogden, from the opening till 1870. From 1870 till the summer of 1875, Prof. A. K. Spence was Principal. In 1875, Rev. E. M. Cravath was elected President, which position he now holds.

The idea of training teachers for the common schools of Tennessee was early developed. Prof. Ogden's ability as a normal instructor secured marked results in this direction. Teachers for the Colored schools began to go out as early as 1868. From that time onward from 30 to 150 pupils of the Institution have engaged in the work of teaching annually, and the pupils educated in Fisk University are now teaching annually more than 25,000 pupils in day and Sabbath-schools.

The University also furnishes the means of higher culture. The college curriculum has been marked out, and college classes are now in operation, pursuing the classical, mathematical and scientific studies usually taught in American colleges. Departments of medicine and law are to be added as soon as the University feels able.

The Commencement Exercises, in May, 1875, were marked by the graduation of the first class from the College Department. This class consisted of Messrs. Jas. D. Burrus and John H. Burrus, and Misses America W. Robinson and Virginia E. Walker, upon all of whom the degree of Bachelor of Arts was conferred. In 1877, Miss Laura S. Cary was made Bachelor of Arts, and Mr. Young A. Wallace, Bachelor of Science. In 1878, Messrs. Henry S. Merry and Albert P. Miller were graduated as Bachelors of Arts. In 1879, Bachelor of Arts was conferred on Messrs. Preston R. Burrus and Austin R. Merry, and Misses Jennie Hobbs and Lulu Parker.

Perhaps it will be of interest to know how these graduates have succeeded in meeting the practical duties of life. The following statement will show: Mr. Jas. D. Burrus is now instructor in Mathematics at Fisk University; Mr. John H. Burrus is studying law, and will locate in Nashville; Miss Virginia Walker, now holds an important position as teacher in the colored public schools of Memphis; Miss America Robinson was one of the Jubilee Singers, spent three years traveling with that troupe in Europe, afterwards studied one year at Strasburg, Germany, and has just entered upon teaching at Meridian, Miss.; Miss Cary held a position as assistant instructor in Greek at Fisk University until her death in the summer of 1879; Young A.

JUBILEE HALL, FISK UNIVERSITY, NASHVILLE, TENN.

Wallace is in charge of the Colored schools at Florence, Ala.; Henry S. Merry is Principal of one of the Colored schools at Clarksville, Tenn.; Albert Miller is in charge of the Mendi Mission in Sierra Lone, on the West Coast of Africa; Preston R. Burrus has charge of a Colored school in Kansas; Austin Merry is Principal of the Colored schools of Jackson, Tenn.; Jennie Hobbs is a resident graduate at Fisk; and Lulu Parker, on account of ill health is the only one not actively engaged.

RELIGIOUS WORK

The importance of preparing young men for the ministry has ever been recognized in this Institution. Rev. H. S. Bennett began the work of theological instruction as early as 1869, and has kept it up ever since. The classes have ranged from three to fourteen each year. Many young men have thus been taught for the important work of preaching the Gospel to the people.

Early in the spring of 1868, a church was organized upon the most liberal basis, for the benefit of teachers and pupils. Regular preaching has been held from the beginning, and every year has witnessed the conversion of many of the students. The moral influence of the school upon the hearts and lives of the students has been very powerful.

THE JUBILEE SINGERS.

Any complete history of Fisk University must give some recognition of the remarkable career of the Jubilee Singers, through whose instrumentality the permanency of the University was assured.

Geo. L. White became music teacher in the Institution during the first months of its existence. His untiring energy and rare skill in training voices produced marked results in the musical department. Several concerts during successive years were given, which attracted much public attention. As Mr. White progressed, he culled out the best voices, and organized them into the choir of the University.

About the year 1870, it was felt that the University must secure a new location and erect new buildings, or be sadly crippled in its work. After much deliberation it was concluded that the only feasible plan to raise funds was to send Mr. White to the North with his company of singers to give concerts for the purpose named. Mr. White had such an interest in the success of the University, and so much enthusiasm in the work, that he took the entire pecuniary responsibility of the movement upon himself, and started October, 1871. After several months of almost crushing difficulty the tide turned in the favor of the little troupe, and by May, 1872, they had netted $20,000. They were received with the greatest enthusiasm by the most highly cultivated audiences, and under the power and pathos of their quaint "slave songs" tears flowed like rain.

Another campaign, over the same territory, resulted in like success, and $20,000 rewarded their labors. In the spring of 1874 they went to England and remained one year. There their success was even more remarkable than in this country. They were received with the greatest consideration by the Queen, and the Premier—Mr. Gladstone, by the Earl of Shaftesbury, by Rev. C. H. Spurgeon, and other dignitaries of Great Britain. While in England they cleared $50,000. In addition to the $90,000 they had thus secured above all expenses, they received in donations of books, apparatus, furniture, etc., $10,000 more, thus raising the net product of their labors to $100,000. Since their entrance upon the campaign they have been about eight years in the field, made several trips to Europe, and have so far netted about $155,000.

Among other trophies of their success abroad they were presented elegant life-size portraits of Wilberforce, the Earl of Shaftesbury and David Livingstone, which now grace the walls of the drawing-rooms at Fisk University.

Mr. J. B. T. Marsh, writes as follows to the *New York Evangelist:* "Rev. Dr. Thompson, in his letters from Berlin, bore testimony two years ago to the fine impression they made upon the lovers of music in the German capital —a success as great, under the most different conditions, as when the roof of the Boston Coliseum echoed with deafening applause over their spirited rendering of 'The Battle Hymn of the Republic,' in the Peace Jubilee of 1872.

"I shall never forget the rapt expression of Mr. Gladstone's fine face as he listened, four years ago, in his drawing-room at Hawarden Castle, to one after another of their slave songs; nor the wonderful spell which held the great audience in the Haymarket Theatre, London, as they sang 'Steal away to Jesus,' after one of Mr. Moody's powerful sermons; nor the sublime eloquence of Dr. Sommerville in a speech inspired by their thrilling song, 'I've been Redeemed,' in the Crystal Palace at Glasgow."

UNIVERSITY BUILDINGS.

With the funds thus earned by the Jubilee Singers, twenty-five acres of land have been purchased on, and contiguous to the site of Fort Gillem, one mile Northwest of the Capitol of Nashville, Tennessee, one mile Northwest of the Vanderbilt University, and very accessible to the city and the railroads. The site is, with the exception of the "Capitol Hill" the most commanding and beautiful around Nashville. The view is unobstructed in every direction, and presents to the eye the most pleasing variety of hill and valley, forest and city.

The following description of the building we clip from the *American* ot January 2, 1875, in an account of the dedication :

"The building is in the form of an 'L,' and has an east front of 145 feet, and a south front of 128 feet. Including basement and cellar it is six stories high, and is supplied with all the modern conveniences of water, steam and gas. It is heated throughout by steam, and each room has a radiator. There are 375 gas burners in the house. The entire building contains 120 rooms. Jubilee Hall is to be the dormitory department of Fisk University, but until suitable college buildings can be erected, will be made to answer all purposes. The building is drained by a twelve-inch sewer pipe, which runs 1,500 feet to a natural aqueduct, which connects with the river. The building is made of the best pressed brick, with stone trimmings. The style is a modern English. The main entrance is on the South front, (illustrated by our handsome cut), and is composed of a stone stairway, with pillars supporting a small stone balcony, which is to be adorned with a bust of Lincoln. Over this is placed, in gilded letters, "Jubilee Hall." The iron door facing has the same upon it. The front door is composed of black walnut of massive proportions, and having complete bronze trimmings. The side light and transom are furnished with richly colored glass. On the right of the hall are the reception rooms and parlor, one 16 by 32 feet, the other 20 by 32 feet, connected by large folding doors. On the other side of the hall is the office, and beyond the assembly room, about 20 by 32 feet proportions. Opposite this on the cross hall is the library, adjoining it the music room, and further on smaller rooms that are to be used as dressing rooms for visitors and transient guests," etc., etc.

The ground was broken January 1, 1873, the corner stone was laid October 1, 1873, and the exercises of dedication took place January 1, 1876.

THE DEDICATION.

The dedication of Jubilee Hall was a marked event. The audience was composed of people of both races, some of the most prominent citizens of Nashville being present. It was a delightful day, and a vast throng assembled. Over the door leading to the platform from the hall, were the flags of America and England, looped up with magnolia leaves.

On the speaker's stand were seated Revs. T. O. Summers, D. D., J. C. Granberry, D. D., and N. T. Lupton, LL. D., Professors in Vanderbilt University; Rev. J. Braden, D. D., of Central Tennessee College, Rev. D. W. Phillips, D. D., of the Nashville Institute; Rev. J. B. McFerrin, D. D., Corresponding Secretary, and Rev. D. C. Kelly, D. D., Assistant Secretary of the Missionary Society of the Methodist Episcopal Church, South; Rev. J. B. Lindsley, Dr. W. P. Jones, Ex-Senator Fowler, Judge Alexander Campbell; Prof. J. W. Coyner, Prof. Cole, Joseph Carels, G. W. Hubbard, J. J. Carey; Gen. Clinton B. Fisk, Rev. W. E. Strieby, D. D., Corresponding Secretary of the American Missionary Association, Hon. E. P. Smith, Rev. G. D. Pike, Rev. W. S. Alexander, Edgar Ketchum, Esq., Samuel Holmes, H. W. Hubbard; Prof. A. K. Spence, Prof. F. A. Chase, Rev. H. S. Bennett and the lady teachers of the Institution.

A noticeable feature in the audience was the large number of white citizens present. The Sixteenth Infantry Band was in attendance, and while the multitude was assembling, played the National airs, closing with "Dixie" and "Yankee Doodle" amid loud and long continued applause.

Gen. Clinton B. Fisk, President of the Board of Trustees, took the chair and invited the vast audience to unite in singing,

"Praise God from whom all blessings flow."

The audience remained standing while Rev. D. W. Phillips, D. D., invoked the Divine Blessing, The University choir sung,

"Steal away to Jesus."

Selections of Scripture were read by Rev. J. Braden, from an elegant Bible which had been presented to the Jubilee Singers, by the Presbyterian Church in New York City, of which the Rev. Dr. Burchard is pastor.

Addresses were then delivered by Gen. Fisk, Rev. Dr. McFerrin, Rev. Dr. Strieby, Rev. G. D. Pike, Rev. E. P. Smith, and others. Without exception the addresses were elegant, chaste, and appropriate. We would like to republish them entire, did space permit. The Rev. Dr. McFerrin was greeted with much enthusiasm, and spoke with great earnestness. Inasmuch, then, as Dr. McFerrin is a prominent Southern clergyman, it will not appear invidious to quote the following extract from his speech:

"I am here this morning contrary to my expectation. I have an appointment forty or fifty miles south of this place to-morrow, and must depart in a moment to meet that engagement. One of the greatest things in a Methodist preacher, is punctuality, but when I knew you (addressing Gen. Fisk), were here, I could not forego the pleasure of meeting you, of greeting you, and of giving countenance, little as my influence is, to this great occasion. (Applause). I was very glad to hear you say here to day that the first considerable sum of money placed in your hands, to be used in pro- moting educational facilities for the Freedmen, was contributed by a Southern Methodist preacher.[1] (Applause). I hope it may never be said hereafter anywhere, that we of the South are opposed to the education and elevation of the Colored people. Then, sir, you made another remark that touched me deeply. There's not recorded such an instance in history, that a few men and women, like the Jubilee Singers, have, within the space of a very few years, raised $100,000 for the education of their race. But the beautiful point in it is this, that I had some hand in that. (Applause). Now, you ask me, ' how do you account for that,' and I tell you that it is owing entirely to camp-meeting songs. I helped to teach the Colored people the camp-meeting songs which lie at the foundation of Jubilee Hall. I have heard these songs sung during my ministry of fifty years. I thank God that after delivering hundreds and hundreds of discourses to Colored people, I have lingered around to hear these beautiful songs, which were sung until the break of day. If the teachers here will teach them to send up songs and shouts of praise to Jesus, I simply say AMEN. (Loud applause). I want you, Gen. Fisk, and all others to understand, that the Southern people, as far as my information extends—that is, the intelligent, patriotic, and Christian people of the South, with perhaps a few exceptions—rejoice in the education and elevation of the Colored people, and fully appreciate the grand work you are doing for them. (Loud applause). I stand on my native soil, and bear this testimony. It meets the hearty co-operation and sincere approbation of all Christian people."

CONGRATULATORY DISPATCHES.

Gen. Fisk remarked that a large company of friends in Great Britain were that day celebrating with the Jubilee Singers, this glad occasion, and had just sent the following dispatch from Leeds, where they then were:

CABLE TELEGRAM FROM ENGLAND.

" British friends and Jubilee Singers send greeting. Hitherto hath the Lord helped us. May Fisk University be inspiration to struggling humanity in America, and light to Africa's millions. May Great Britain and America ever thus unite to extend Christ's Kingdom.

LEEDS, 9, A. M.   E. M. CRAVATH.

RESPONSE FROM NASHVILLE.

" Fisk University responds with thankful greetings. To the Jubilee Singers, to their friends at home and in the land of Wilberforce and Sharp, we owe what God hath wrought. May the two flags floating to-day from Jubilee Hall ever symbolize the united purpose of both lands to fit the struggling Freedmen of America to carry light to Africa."

LETTERS

Were then read by Gen. Fisk, from a number of prominent gentlemen, ex- pressing their interest in the cause to which Fisk University is devoted, and regret that they were not able to attend. The letters were from Mr. D. L.

The gentleman to whom Gen. Fisk referred, was the Rev. Dr. A. L. P. Green, of the Southern Methodist Church, to whose " beautiful and blameless life," Gen. Fisk, paid high and eloquent tribute.

Moody, the Evangelist, Gen. Garfield, M. C., Hon. L. Q. C. Lamar, Hon. W. E. Dodge, Bishop Payne, Hon. Geo. H. Stuart, and Hon. John Eaton, U. S. Commissioner of Education.   All in all, it was an auspicious event in Nashville.

APPARATUS.

There are other features about the University that may prove of interest. Let us speak first of our apparatus :

This includes a few of the common instruments for the illustration of Physics, such as air-pump, condenser, electrical machine, galvanic battery of ten Bunsen cells, Ruhmkorf coil, Geisler tubes, spectroscope of two prisms, and barometer.   In Astronomy there are a planetarium, orreries, and an astronomical telescope of $3\frac{1}{2}$ inches aperture; and in chemistry, apparatus for illustrating the principles of the science in the class-room, and a small laboratory for those wishing to become practically acquainted with the processes of Chemical Analysis, both qualitative and quantitative.   This is furnished with a good balance.   There is a magic lantern for lecture use, as also a fine microscope made by Beck, of London, with five objectives, ranging from three inches to one-fifth of an inch.   In Applied Mathematics there are a theodolite, a compass, and a plane table.   There is an urgent need of the common pieces of apparatus for demonstration in the various departments of Physics, especially mechanics, hydrostatics, acoustics, heat, optics, and electricity; also, in the Laboratory, of a good lathe and set of lathe tools.

MUSEUM.

In Natural History, Geology, Mineralogy and Ethnology, there is a collection of over three thousand specimens.   The most of these are well arranged and labeled, the whole covering 650 square feet of shelf room, besides several hundred duplicates, reserved for exchange.

LIBRARY.

This now numbers seventeen hundred volumes, including many valuable works of reference adapted to the wants of the different departments of the University.   Additions are made annually from the interest of the Dickerson Library Fund, a fund contributed by Sabbath-schools in Great Britain, and from other sources.

In connection with the Library is a Reading-Room, in which the students have access to various newspapers and periodicals.

LITERARY SOCIETY.

The Union Literary Society is managed by the students, subject to the general authority of the Institution, for their improvement in public speaking, writing, and parliamentary usage.   It has a valuable library to which additions are made as the funds of the Society permit.

LECTURES.

A course of lectures, two each month, forms an important part of the educational privileges of the Institution.   During the past year, lectures have been delivered by Dr. G. W. Hubbard, of the Central Tennessee College, Rev. W. G. E. Cunnyngham, D. D., Editor of the Sabbath-school papers of the M. E. Church South, and Rev. M. B. DeWitt, Editor of the Sabbath-school papers of the C. P. Church, Charles Edwin Robert, Esq., and Rev. Dr. C. D. Elliott; also by Professors H. S. Bennett, F. A. Chase, C. C. Painter, President E. M. Cravath, Mr. J. H. Burrus, Prof. A. K.

Spence, and Mrs. A. K. Spence, of the University. Lectures are expected the present term from Rev. Dr. Fitzgerald, Rev. Dr. W. E. Ward, Dr. J. B. Lindsley, and Morton B. Howell, Esq.

TESTIMONIALS RESPECTING FISK UNIVERSITY.

The inquiry is often raised by friends in the North relating to the sentiment and feeling of the whites of Tennessee toward Fisk University and its work. The answer may be found in the highly complimentary testimonials by the highest official authorities. The University Catalogue for 1879 contains a letter from ex-Governor James D. Porter, written near the close of his four years' administration, and one from Hon. Leon Trousdale, after four years experience and observation as State Superintendent of Public Instruction. Also, joint resolutions of the Tennessee General Assembly, passed after the visit of the members in a body to the University, on the occasion of the regular quarterly public rhetorical exercises in March, 1879. The sentiments expressed by these official representatives of Tennessee can be safely accepted as the prevailing sentiment of the State.

LIVINGSTONE MISSIONARY HALL.

The great pressing necessity of Fisk University is a second building to correspond with Jubilee Hall. While in England the movement was undertaken by the Jubilee Singers to build Livingstone Hall, a monument to the memory of the great African explorer, and also to be an expression of the great work of the University in training men and women for the evangelization of Africa. Already Fisk University has five pupils at work in Africa —which is but a foretaste of what these Institutions are to do in that direction.

Owing though, to the commercial depression in England and on the Continent the efforts of the Jubilee Singers were but partially successful. The speedy erection of the building has been, however, since secured by the pledge upon the part of Mrs. Daniel P. Stone, of Malden, Mass., of $60,-000 to carry on the work. Ground has already been broken in Netherland Square, and Livingstone Hall, a handsome building, as will be seen by the illustration, will soon be built.

Other donations have been received, chiefly that of $20,000 from the executors of the estate of Mr. R. R. Graves, of Morristown, New Jersey, but the Institution is still fostered and helped by the American Missionary Association from its treasury.

Quite appropriate here, mention should be made of the bill recently introduced in Congress by United States Senator Bailey, of Tennessee, to aid the education of the Colored race. It is not our province to discuss the merits of the bill, but to mention the fact that Senator Bailey is a Democrat, represents a Democratic State, and his movement having been heartily endorsed by such leading Democratic journals as the New Orleans *Times*, Atlanta *Constitution*, Nashville *American* and Vicksburg *Herald*, is sure indication of friendly feeling on the part of Southerners toward the Colored race. Senator Bailey's bill in the preamble recites:

"That $510,000 have recently been covered back into the United States Treasury from the appropriations for the pay of bounties of Colored soldiers, which remain unclaimed after seven years, owing to the impossibility of discovering the claimants, and asserts that under the circumstances the Colored people should have the benefit of said money for their educational improvement and elevation.   The bill, therefore, directs the Secretary of the Treasury to invest $510,000 in United States registered 4 per cent. bonds, to be apportioned in equal parts to the following institutions for the education of Colored people: The Howard University, Washington, D. C.; the Hampton, Virginia, Normal and Agricultural Institute; the Fisk University, of Nashville; the Atlanta, Georgia, University, and the Straight University of New Orleans.   The trustees of these institutions are to be entitled to use the interest or bonds in such a manner as in their judgment will best promote the ends for which they are chartered, but the principal of the bonds is to be inalienable."

As an addition to this part of our work, we also give the following from the Nashville *American*, of November 13, 1879, relating to the American Missionary Association:

"The annual meeting of the American Missionary Association was held in Chicago, a days few ago, and was the most successful and enthusiastic one ever known in the history of that body.   This Association is the almoner of the funds contributed by the Congregational churches of the country for the support of missions among the Negroes of the South and Africa, the Chinese in the United States, and the Indians.

"The following facts relating to the work of the Association among the Negroes of the South will be of interest to our readers:

"'The receipts from collections, etc., during the past year amounted to $215,431.17; receipts for special institutions, $99,019.50, making a total of $314,450.67.   Of this large sum $122,965.19 has been spent in the South, mostly in the work of educating Colored youth.   Under the care of the Association are eight chartered institutions in as many different States, as Fisk University in Tennessee, and Atlanta University in Georgia; 12 graded or normal schools; 24 other schools—44 in all.   The number of teachers, 190; number of pupils, 7207.   Among these 80 study theology, 28 are in law, 64 in medicine, 63 in the college department, and 169 in the college preparatory.   The total number of pupils taught during the year by those who have been in the schools of the Association is estimated at 150,000.'

"The Association also fosters 57 Congregational churches, with a membership of 4600.

"It is through the influence of this body that $150,900 has been secured for the erection of buildings for school purposes in various parts of the South. This large fund is donated by Mrs. Stone, of New England, and will be available during the coming year.   One of the buildings will be Livingstone Hall, of Fisk University, which will cost $50,000—$15,000 of which was secured through the instrumentality of the Jubilee Singers while in England.

"The appropriation made by the Association to Fisk University for the current year is $10,000, that amount being required above the receipts from tuition, boarding and other sources to meet the annual expenses.

"During the past three years the Association has paid off a debt of $100,-000, and at the same time maintained its work up to the highest point of efficiency.   Of this debt $36,380,79 was paid during the past year.

LIVINGSTONE HALL. FISK UNIVERSITY, NASHVILLE, TENN.

11

(159)

"The statement of this fact at the annual meeting furnished the occasion of hearty congratulations, and of devout thankfulness to God.

"In view of the fact that the Association is now out of debt, and that the country is just entering upon a career of unexampled prosperity, it is expected that the Association will be enabled to carry on its work with enlarged results."

RELIGIOUS ADVANCEMENT OF THE RACE.

No one will deny that there are vicious and degraded men and women among the Colored people.   It is not our purpose, nor will it ever be, to shield from scorn and contempt the ungodly, the low, the mean, the vulgar.   We acknowledge that the Colored people have their full share of evil-doers. But the man who attempts to place the whole race among "criminal classes" and refers to the blacks as this distinct element of society in this country, perverts the truth and slanders the people.   Criminals are developed from every rank of society, from every shade of complexion, from every grade of life, and spring from good families, the wealthy and educated as well as from ignorant and vicious parents and associations.

Recognizing these facts, we dare assert that whatever else may be said derogatory of and detrimental to the Americo-Africans as a race, we have yet to hear of the first infidel or atheist among them.   As a rule, those who profess Christianity, are God-fearing and God-worshipping people.   Admitting that much of their religion is yet crude and superstitious, there is, on the other hand, much that is pure and unwavering in faith, and deep-felt and unswerving in influence.   As to the charge of superstition, let us quote from two eminent authors—first Quatrefagas who says: "If it be said that the Negroes are superstitious, tell fortunes, and protect themselves against *witchcraft* and the evil eye, it may also be said, the amulets of the French peasants are identical with the *grisgris* of the Negroes"[1]   And then Raynal, who says: "Slavery was one of the causes of religious superstition. The slave without country, family or liberty, without one single earthly possession, without a single moment of time except granted by his master—what horrible pictures of hell came to his benighted soul?   What wonder that his religion was a religion of superstition, of hypocrisy, of fear, of servility?

[1] The Human Species, p. 496.

and never of love! How absurd it seemed to us fellow
Christians, that God would condescend to love a Negro!"[1]

But thank God education and culture will bring this people
out of this benighted state, and it is already doing it in a most
wonderful manner. Still this brings us back to the original
assertion, and we are forced to confront a most unpleasant
fact. Unfortunately we find that it is among the Caucasians,
the sons of Japheth that modern infidelity, of the kinds we have
to deal with, has its origin and prevails, and this notwithstanding the sublime principles of Christian morality that
have been preached to them since the coming of the Master,
notwithstanding the blessings of liberty that have been their
birthright, notwithstanding the advantages of literature and
the numerous masterpieces of art and the progress of true
science, it is a lamentable truth, that Christian education—
though it is ever advancing, has succeeded less than the
friends of humanity wish for. Indeed, if we examine its influence on the improvement of mankind who can abstain from
saying, "The harvest truly is plenteous, but the laborers are
few." For, who has not seen children of the most pious and
exemplary parents indulge in scepticism, and plunge themselves into profanity and vice? Who has not observed that
licentiousness often prevails in the most enlightened and refined classes of society? But if we search for the propa-
gators and disseminators of open and avowed enmity to the
Christian's God, it can be found in the transcendentalism of
Germany, in the fleshly atheism of France, in the sophistical
materialism of England and in the blasphemous Ingersollism
of America, but at the door of the Americo-African not one
grievous sin of this sort can be laid. Some objector may
say it is because the Negro is not well enough educated to
entertain such advanced religious views. To this we reply,
thank God. But he *is* far enough educated to avoid them,
and let us thank God for that also.

It must not be understood that the Colored people were
without religious instruction and religious privileges during
ante-bellum times. We would not be guilty of a statement so
reckless. Every privilege was granted them possible under
a slave regime. Colored churches were numbered by thousands, and nearly every plantation had its chapel. We have
not full statistics on this point, but we have before us an

---

[1] History of West Indies, vol. iii, p. 273.

"address to Christians throughout the world, by the clergy of the Confederate States," in which is stated that the "total number of communicants, (*i. e.*, of regular marked down attendants at specific places of worship) in the Christian Churches, in the Confederate States, was about two millions and fifty thousand, of whom the blacks came in for five hundred thousand, or one-fourth of the 'adult population of Negroes." We have also a copy of the proceedings of the General Convention of the Protestant Episcopal Church, held at Richmond in 1862, giving the following points: In Alabama, "increasing attention is given to the religious instruction of the blacks." In Mississippi, "on every hand is observed the increasing desire on the part of masters to give unto their servants the blessings of the Gospel and the Church." In North Carolina, "religious instruction of the slaves has been followed up, it is hoped, with increased diligence and success." But in South Carolina, "about fifty chapels for the benefit of Negroes on plantations, were in use for the worship of God and the religious instruction of slaves." One parish had "thirteen chapels for Negroes, supplied with regular services." In Charleston, there was "a mission chiefly for the benefit of slaves; and among the 1942 confirmed during trienniad, 1211 were colored; of the 4775 baptized, 3557 colored; of the 667 married, 374 colored; and of the 5672 communicants, 2819 colored."

It is impossible to estimate the increased membership in the Colored Churches of the South. We recently saw the statement that the Colored Baptists of the South would number six hundred thousand, but whether the other denominations have gained as rapidly we cannot say. This, however, may be taken as indicative of great gains in all quarters.

Vast improvement is noticeable also, in the architectural character of Colored Churches in the South. Some of the newly erected church buildings are models of elegance, and architectural triumphs worthy the pride of the Freedmen. In one Southern city, we have in mind, no less than four superb church edifices have been erected since the war, each one costing not less than $20,000. Inside, they are fitted up with all the modern improvements — gas, heating apparatus, stained windows, carpeting; regular salaried pastors have their lecture rooms, their studies, and all of the necessary conveniences to a properly conducted church. Some of the churches have splendid organs, and we may say nearly all the smaller are supplied with melodeons and choirs with trained voices. The following extract by a correspondent of the Macon, Ga., *Journal and Messenger*, gives the idea quite succinctly:

'One Sabbath, this 1879, I preached for the Second African Church, of Savannah. No other white person was present. I think the law still stands, as in 1860, requiring white men to be present. Freedom repealed it *de facto*. There was a quartette and a noble organ. A thousand people were said to be before me, and the church was large. I was invited to sit with the business meeting that followed. My last meeting was with Calvary, New York. I might have shut my eyes, and save for an error in some church phrase, and the deep tones, have thought myself there. A noble church, an intelligent people—and, while I am still deeply Southern, I am getting proud of our Colored citizens. They do improve."

Prominent among the many Colored Churches of Nashville, particular mention should be made of the First Baptist Church, of which Rev. Nelson G. Merry is pastor. Mr. Merry is a man of ability and of widespread popularity, and has, perhaps, more personal influence than any one man in Nashville. St. Paul's Church—Methodist—Rev. Mr. Green, pastor; Mt. Zion Baptist Church, Rev. Jordan Bransford, pastor; Howard Chapel—Congregational—Rev. Geo. Moore, pastor; Clark's Chapel, Rev. D. W. Hayes, pastor; Mulberry Street Baptist Church, Rev. W. P. T. Jones, pastor; Wilson Spring Church, Rev. A. Buchanan, pastor; St. John's A. M. E. Church, Rev. William Shaffer, pastor; Caper's Chapel— Methodist — Rev. N. B. Smith, pastor; Bethel Chapel, Rev. C. O. H. Thomas, pastor; Thompson's Chapel, Rev. John Pickett, pastor.

COLORED NEWSPAPERS.

Another indication of the rapid advancement of the Colored people is the fact that there are already not less than twenty-five newspapers in the South edited and published by Colored men in the interests of their race.

Progress may be noted, too, in the numerous benevolent and literary organizations established in the towns of the South.

SOCIAL ADVANCEMENT.

Some one has drawn for us the following picture of "The Olden Times," so sweet, so tender, so truthful, it will touch the heart of every true Southerner:

"What nights were the nights on the old plantation! The mellow light of the harvest moon crept through the rustling leaves of the talls oaks, fell softly upon the open space beyond, and bathed the brown old barn in a flood of golden glory, while the songs of the Negroes at the corn pile—lusty chorus and plaintive refrain—shook the silence until it broke upon the air in far reaching waves of melody. The moon pursues her pathway as serenely as of old, but she no longer looks down upon the scenes that were familiar to your youth. The old homestead and the barn are given up to decay, and the songs of the Negroes have been hushed into silence by the necessities of a new dispensation. The old plantation itself is gone. It has passed away, but the hand of time, inexorable and yet tender, has woven about it the sweet suggestions of poetry and romance—memorials that neither death nor decay can destroy."

And yet, O tender-hearted writer is there not cause for joy when we see the shackles of bondage and the errors of superstitition give place to the higher culture—the broader sweep of soul—the beneficence that a good God has conferred upon His late unhappy children? There was "Black mammy," and "Aunt Susan," and "Uncle Ben," good old souls, they have gone to their reward, they have "laid down the shovel and the hoe"—they sleep, they rest—but their children are free. The cabin has been exchanged in many instances for the cottage. The influence of home is having its effects on the race. For, with the blessings of freedom and the benefits of education, we find delicacy of sentiment and refined manners steadily growing among the Colored people. "Plantation manners" are being supplanted by proper courtesy. The rude, boorish ways of the farm, odd motions, ungainly attitudes, awkward gestures, are giving place to dignity of demeanor that follows mental and moral culture as morning follows night. Two or three generations hence the delineator of "burnt cork drolleries" will have to rely on the fertility of his imagination for support, because faithfulness to nature will demand a higher view of the Colored man. In the Negro, it is true that the fountains of pathos and of humor are situated close by each other. Sharp showmen have seen this, and when they wished to express a funny idea, or to say a smart thing, they have resorted to Negro delineations. More than this, the black man has given to America its only distinctive song music. Not only in their quaint camp-meeting hymns, but in the tender and touching ballads, such as "Way Down on Sewanee River," "Massa's in the cold, cold Ground," and even that soul-stirring patriotic air that found an echo in every Southern heart—that nerved the Southern arm to deeds of daring, when the wild yell rising from the trampling charge tore through the ragged rifts of battle-smoke and drowned the thunder of artillery, as the bands of the Confederacy struck up the strain of "Dixie."

But to-day we find the Colored man at home. If he invites you to enter, you may expect to find not barren walls and carpetless floors, but rooms neatly furnished, prints, chromos, engravings gracing the walls, and a stand of books—modern and ancient history—the novelists, Scott, Thackeray, Dickens, some of the poets, Longfellow, Moore and Shakespeare. This may not be universal, we do not mean to say it is, but there are numerous instances to prove the truth of our view.

We may note also, improvement of the race in modes of dress. The Negro is the dandy of the human family, and while it is not intended to utter one word in extenuation of idleness or shiftlessness or reckless and extravagant habits, we do say if they can dress better and live better, and obtain these things honestly, who has the right to complain?

MATERIAL ADVANCEMENT.

If it be asked what are the material proofs of the Negro's improvement? we answer, that already we see springing into growth intelligent young laborers competent to do their share toward enriching the world with necessary products; industrious citizens contributing their proportion to aid on the advancing civilization of the country; self-providing artisans, vindicating their people from the never-ceasing charge of fitness only for servile positions; agriculturists, who are taking a more intelligent view of farming; merchants, business men, who are adding something to the commerce of the Union, while they lay by for themselves snug and comfortable sums; professional men, lawyers, physicians, teachers, ministers, who are furnishing numerous examples of the intellectual and moral capabilities of the race, and while advancing themselves are advancing their people, and advancing our country to its ultimate standing in the fore-front of the most illustrious of nations.

It is to be regretted that more figures could not be obtained to prove this, but the following from the Atlanta, Ga., *Constitution*, will prove of interest:

"Some days ago the *Constitution* published the returns to the Controller-General's office, giving the total of property held subject to tax in the State. It will be remembered that the total of taxable values had fallen off about

$1,000,000 in the State. We now have a showing to make that is the reverse of that. The Negroes of the State, instead of seeing their property decrease, have snugly added to it, and their total goes up to $5,182,398 this year, against $5,124,875 last year, giving a net increase of $57,523. This does not represent the actual increase of Negro property, but much less than that. The bulk of Negro property has decreased in value at least 10 per cent., so that merely to hold their own, they would have had to add about $60,000. They have not only done this, but have gone $57,523 over their old figures. In the one item of land alone, the Negroes have added 39,309 acres to their possessions during the last year, making a total of 341,199 acres owned by Negroes in Georgia. This record is a good one, and shows that whatever may be said elsewhere, we have the best of proof at home that the Negroes are prospering. There are only four Negroes in the State worth over $19,-000—so that the property of $5,182,398 is divided in small lots among the Negroes of all classes and all sections."

Another prominent Southern journal—name not now remembered, recently said:

"The South has passed through a political and industrial revolution. Very naturally, reconstruction was accompanied by disorders, but local remedies appear as soon as the presence of the Federal Government is removed, and these are the only effective remedies. Throughout nearly the whole South the recently-enfranchised freedmen exercise, unmolested, all the duties of citizenship. Twice as many of them vote in Mississippi or South Carolina as could vote in Massachusetts, for, in that State, as a condition of voting, a man must know how to read and write. The white votes are divided, and are bidding for the Colored voters. It is not essential that the National Government should be Republican, but it is essential that all men should be equal under the law. The Negroes are also improving their material condition. A large and steadily-increasing number own real estate. In the city of Atlanta they are assessed for $3,000,000. In Kemper county, Miss., one in five own lands. In Vicksburg, one out of ten adults own their own homes—a better average than will be found in Boston. Yazoo county, Miss., has a dozen Negro planters worth $10,000 each. These are evidences of a rate of progress absolutely marvelous, when we consider the revolution through which the South has passed, the bitterness of defeat in a great war, and the prejudices of race and color."

Appropriate to this subject, we also quote from an article in the *New York Tribune*, by Mr. Edward Atkinson, a very shrewd writer on commercial topics. He says:

"The crop of cotton of 1876 and 1879 was the largest ever raised. The ten crops of 1852 to 1861, inclusive, being the last crops raised by slave labor, numbered 34,995.440 bales. The ten crops of 1870 to 1879, inclusive, being the ten last crops raised by free labor, numbered 41,454,743 bales. The excess of the ten years of free labor amounts to 6,459,303 bales. The value of the ten last crops, of which about two-thirds have been exported, has been not less than $2,500,000,000, and has probably amounted to $3,000,000,000. The increase is progressive, the excess of the five last crops over the five crops immediately preceding the war has been 3,932,415 bales.

"It was formerly alleged and currently believed that the free Negro would not and that white men could not work in the cotton field. Who, then, raised these last crops? If it is the Negro who has done the most of this work, then is he not the financial power of this land by whom specie payment has been restored? The Negro population of the South, which may have diminished or kept stationary in point of numbers during the first few years of freedom, in which they were adjusting themselves to the care of their own families, is now rapidly increasing. The improved methods of cultivation, and the use of various kinds of manure have caused the crop of cotton of the more northern States to mature about one month earlier, have made it more capable of withstanding drought and worms, and have greatly improved its quality."

And also the following from the Hopkinsville *New Era,* one of the most intelligent journals in Kentucky:

"There are not a few persons in this community who are accustomed to say that the emancipation of the slaves impoverished Christian county, and that our people can never recover from the loss inflicted by that act. While those who utter such sentiments are constitutional growlers, their talk has more or less weight with that large class of people who never think or investigate for themselves. We have recently had occasion to examine some statistics touching the production of Christian county before and since the war, and we have concluded to give the public the benefit of the facts at hand. In 1850, a year of more than average agricultural prosperity under the slave regime, Christian produced 45,678 bushels of wheat, 1,235,290 bushels of corn, and 6,312,076 pounds of tobacco. In 1878, Christian produced, with free labor, 971,920 bushels of wheat, 2,335,599 bushels of corn, and 7,846,928 pounds of tobacco. Does that look as if the agricultural interests of this section had been seriously crippled by the liberation of the slaves? We dare say every thrifty, enterprising section in the South can show a similar increase of agricultural products."

THE "EXODUS."

Although it is likely to prove a question only of the moment, we feel compelled to say something about the much-talked of exodus of Colored people from the South. It is not our business to look into the cause of this movement, we have only to deal with the fact that it exists. Senator Ben Hill, of Georgia, discussing this subject in the United States Senate, December 18, 1879, said he thought "this emigration question would settle itself. The Negro was no longer a ward. He was free to go where he pleased. He had been of those who doubted the capacity of the black man to become a good citizen, but he was glad to put himself on record as admitting that the black man had done better than he was expected to." Gov. Hampton, of South Carolina, recently said in a speech at Abbeville, that the whites "ought to respect the rights of the Negroes, pay them good wages, make them feel independent, let them vote as they please, and try to add to their happiness in every possible way, so as to endear them to the State." And lastly, the Vicksburg *Herald* thinks that "the fellow in Congress who wants to investigate the exodus is wasting his time. A good price for Southern products, patience, kindness and justice will soon settle the exodus."

Yet the exodus continues, and the question arises, Is there no remedy? no hope? Yes. There is a solution, and we believe only one correct solution of the problem. We are not overwise on the subject. It is patent to all who think, to all who use their eyes. Make the Colored man a permanent fixture in the South—induce him to become a settled citizen. It is easy enough. Let the Southern planters who now own large farms, and find taxes such a grievous burden—the laws of labor unsettled, and unreliable, and they themselves "land poor" though "the lords of manors"—let them divide up their immense tracts into small farms—twenty—forty—sixty —and one hundred acre homesteads. Sell to the Colored man on reasonable terms—exorbitant prices are never fair, induce him to settle and improve, induce him to become a tax payer, get him interested in the control of affairs, and we will soon cease to hear of carpet baggery and scallawagery. As it is to-day they are but nomads—a race of four or five millions, many without "local habitation." What wonder they form a dangerous element of society? We have complained much of white tramps. Their marauding depredations and high-hand deviltry. Scarcely a newspaper is printed that does not contain some account of their outlawry. But the Negro, although he is not permitted to claim any spot of earth as his own, although he is the target of all the envomed shafts that prejudice and hatred may let fly— to-day he presents a better record for morality and obedience to the laws than the grand army of "turnpike sailors" who roam the land.

Then why should the Colored man be forced to leave the South? why should he wish to leave? This is the home of his youth—here all his associations have been formed, here all of his memories cluster, and here lie the bones of his kindred. There is work enough for all who are here, and for many more who will come. There are rich lands to cultivate, mines to work, towns to build, roads to make, streams to navigate, a thousand hills, valleys and plains to set in grass. They are born-agriculturists, and to a large extent will continue so. Happy for them that this is the fact. No condition in life can surpass, if equal, that of the intelligent, independent farmer. Here then is a genial climate, a fruitful soil. Here are the elements of prosperity and enrichment. Agriculture and Commerce are twin brothers. Like the Siamese twins they cannot be divided. Their interests are identical. The future of the South is òne of diversified manufacturing industry. The white man may turn the throttle-valve or unlock the shaft, but he cannot long labor under the burning rays of our sun. Yet he must have the raw material. Who then is to supply this material—who will supply it if the Negroes go?

There should then be no conflict of peoples—no clashing of interests. Amiable relations should prevail. The law of humanity is reciprocity. Mutual interests bind nation. to nation and race to race. Indeed, this is the law of nature as plainly written as nature herself. The sun would be but half a sun amid the spinning planets if it did not clothe them all with its own brightness and make them helpers, giving as they receive. There should then, and there soon will be an end of strife. This country does not want any more bloody revolutions, or low-lived contention. It must be peaceful, amiable, literate, learned, artistic and moral.

Above all what we want first is, a reformation of the courts, modification of laws. Or, to express it as Senator Ingalls lately said, after conversing with a colored emigrant from Georgia, we need a reformation of all such systems as "the convict system in Georgia, amounting to practical slavery, and under which the Negro who stole a biscuit was imprisoned ten years, and the white man who killed a Negro sentenced for only two years."

POLITICAL RIGHTS.

So far we have steered clear of this question, but if it be asked what benefits have resulted to the Colored man from political enfranchisement, we may be pardoned for introducing the following extract from the sketch of Thomas Jefferson, written by Judge Baldwin, of Mississippi, relative to Mr. Jefferson's views of the liberty of the people, and the popular system of suffrage :

" *It elevates the masses.*—By making a man independent of external control, he becomes his own master. He relies on himself. He gets that individuality of will, which is the distinctive attribute of freedom and of manhood. With it comes self-respect. With these and the political power with which he is clothed, comes the respect of others. He feels his importance in the

State, in his family, in his neighborhood. He becomes informed, more or less, as to those things with which he has concern. He associates with men with whom he can profitably converse and exchange views; he attends public discussions. The currents of intelligence, which circulate over the country, come to his mind. His port and bearing are those of a freeman. He educates his children. He sees them rise up to posts of honor and distinction. He strives to accumulate property, that their position in the world may be better than his own. He is thus a contented citizen. There is no cause of discontent. He cannot resist the government, because it is his own, and he has no cause of quarrel with it. He cannot rebel against the administration of the law. The functionaries, chosen mediately or immediately by the people, are but executing the laws the people have made and can repeal. *Privilege is the preservative of caste.*—Superior wealth, talent, information, or social position, wi h superior political privileges, would keep a chilling distance forever between the higher and lower classes. But a community of privileges and rights, and the dependence of the higher upon the lower classes for political elevation, repress pride, bring equality into fashion, and prevent the heart-burnings and jealousies which would otherwise prevail. It makes the population in a good degree homogeneous." And this and much more, Judge Baldwin assures us, "We can trace as germ principles of popular rights to Jefferson. He planted the seed in the mind and heart of the nation, and it produced its fruit in due season. No man's influence has been so great as his in this country. Jackson's, though stronger, probably, at first had more of will, and less of principle for its base, and therefore, will not be so lasting." [1]

SOCIAL EQUALITY.

There is no need of alarm on this score. It is useless and absurd to talk of *caste* or equality in a country where there are no *castes*, and no nobility ; where in a single city, one man shall own ten millions of money, and a hundred thousand men not a cent ; where the millionaire of to-day may be the pauper of to-morrow, or the beggar of this week the capitalist of the next; where every man is the chooser of his associates, and makes for himself his own society. The absurdity of this thing was shown when the Civil Rights Bill fell a dead letter on the land. It will appear more so as the Colored people advance in education, for no right-minded, high-toned, cultivated Colored man or woman would think of *forcing* their society any sooner than a refined white person would. And yet even in this direction there are true Southern people advancing most liberal opinions. The following from the Nashville *Banner,* of December 31, 1879, is about the most pronounced thing on the subject we have lately seen :

"The truly refined gentleman, whether white, copper-colored, or black, never attempts to throw himself into company where his presence is un-

[1] Party Leaders—By Jo. G. Baldwin, author of The Flush Times of Alabama and Mississippi. N. Y., D. Appleton & Co., pp. 83–86.

pleasant. The disposition of some colored people to demand every position accorded by the law, only tends to excite opposition and retard the advance. The more it is persisted in, the longer will the contest continue. The very fact that some of them have made such advances in education and refinement, that only race antagonism excludes them from social intercourse, proves conclusively that it can be done by all with the proper care, study and attention. And our word for it, in time, all distinctions, of whatever character, will gradually disappear. The great iceberg that now rears its frozen head between the two races will, under the warming influence of education and morality, melt away, leaving nothing whatever to interpose between them. Then all those things so eagerly desired by them will seem as small and as undesirable as they now appear unattainable. Let alone juries and churches and all those chimeras that now appear so alluring; they will only retard the advance of the African, and he ought to know that by arrogantly demanding rights that only belong to the worthy, whether of the blacks or the whites, he thereby renders his position harder to bear, and lowers himself in the consideration of the only people whose good opinions are worth having. Amend this fault, live uprightly, educate yourselves, acquire independence, adopt energetic habits guarded by frugality, be moral without ostentation and offensive affectation, and time will do all the balance. You, of the present generation, may not live to see it, but the time will come, and soonest in the South, when no distinctions will exist on account of race or color. We say in the South; because the South is the true friend of the Negro. The South does not affect a consideration for political purposes they do not feel, but the sons and daughters of the South cannot and will never forget the faithful nurses who attended their toddling footsteps, nor the patient cooks who fed them from their own scanty stores, and therefore dare tell them the truth, that they may profit and amend by it."

In conclusion, we say to the Americo-Africans, lift up your hearts. If true to God, true to your country, and true to yourselves, you have nothing to fear. Fidelity in this threefold character will bring blessings brighter than our pen can picture. Go on in the glorious work of education, practice morality, be just, be industrious, be moderate and economical.

What a glorious future is before these people! What a splendid history they should make for themselves—a history which it will be the agreeable task of some of their cultured scholars to write. The darkness of the past will be utterly dissipated by the effulgent glory of the future. The time for trepidation is over. The solid foundation of future happiness is laid for the Colored man.

So passes on the swift procession of the years. The year 1860, was destined to witness the overthrow of slavery. The year 1880, dawns on the better days of freedom. The year 1900, we dare believe, we dare affirm, will open upon the earth with not a slave under the pavilion of God. No more despots in Europe—no more chains for Africa—in Asia, advancing millions—in America, a happy, prosperous, God-loving people, moving steadily and full of rejoicing, onward and upward toward,

> "That God which ever lives and loves,
> One God, one law, one element,
> And one far-off divine event,
> To which the whole creation moves."

THE END.